The Master of Everything

A Story of Mankind and the World of Illusion We Call Life

James Nussbaumer

For permission, serialization, condensation, adaptions, or for our catalog of other publications, write to Ozark Mountain Publishing, Inc., P.O. box 754, Huntsville, AR 72740, ATTN: Permissions Department.

Library of Congress Cataloging-in-Publication Data

Nussbaumer, James. – 1957

The Master of Everything by James Nussbaumer

His in-depth study of the lessons contained in the book "A Course in Miracles", combined with frank descriptions of his prison life, guide the reader to a supreme freedom of their own, through the deepest levels of forgiveness and a profound experience of the Oneness of the "Christ-Mind".

1. Metaphysical 2. Manifestation 3. Co-Creation 4. Power of Thought

I. Nussbaumer, James 1957 II. Metaphysical III. Title

Library of Congress Catalog Card Number: 2015938187

ISBN: 9781940265087

Cover Design: noir33.com

Book set in: Calibri Light

Book Design: Tab Pillar

Published by:

PO Box 754

Huntsville, AR 72740

800-935-0045 or 479-738-2348 fax: 479-738-2448

WWW.OZARKMT.COM

Printed in the United States of America

*There is that in me—I do not know what it is—
but I know it is in me ...*

*I do not know it—it is without name—it is a
word unsaid,*

It is not in any dictionary, utterance, symbol ...

Do you see O my brothers and sisters?

*It is not chaos or death—it is form, union,
plan—it is eternal life—it is...*

Happiness.

—Walt Whitman

Acknowledgments

I owe a deep thank you to Carol, my editor—a white dove who seemed to sit on my shoulder through her devoted correspondence from Florida to me in an Ohio prison while I was writing this book. Your help was like a gentle whispering in my ear. I thank you for your constant clarity and structure in your voice, telling me things like: "Your reader wants to see your heart. Go there, Jim, and explain this section deeper," and always urging, "Make your thoughts alive and real." You have shown me how to release the dreamer in me from dreams of fear. I am grateful for this higher calling.

To my publisher, Ozark Mountain Publishing, I thank you for your confidence in me and for pulling me in an ascending direction by offering me a home for this work. I feel I've gained a calm assurance of Heaven with you.

To those authors, poets, publishers, musicians, and other professionals whose names were unavailable for me on material I'd come across during my years in prison, which helped inspire me with the information contained in this book, my grateful thanks. Your living in the light while I was writing in the shadows is proof of your extension. You know who you are and this is my best effort in acknowledging you.

To my family, I am forever grateful to you for remembering who I truly am.

Table of Contents

Part VI: The Light That Will Give You Certainty

Part VII: Grandeur or Grandiosity?

Part VIII: Peace Is in Who You Are

Part IX: Knowing the Whole

Part X: Truly Giving and Receiving

Part XI: You'll Find It Once You Know It

Part XII: Being on Your Way

Introduction

There is not a single doubt in my mind it was divinely intended that my life's journey be greeted by the publication that would open my mind and set me free: *A Course in Miracles*. These teachings of inner peace have answered my lifelong questions to the mystery of all that exists, while proving to me the truth about forgiveness.

A Course in Miracles asks us to hear this single question: "Who is the Light of the real world except God's son?" Surely this is a question for us to absorb, but more so, it is merely a statement of the truth about ourselves. For we are the Light of the world. *You* are the Light of the world, and the light emanates from your Source, which is the Creator of all that is real. This is the opposite of a statement of pride, or arrogance, or self-deception. It simply states the truth about who you are.

I am in prison as I write these words, by hand into a composition journal—the old-fashioned kind, with a black-and-white mottled cover and lined pages. I look back to when I was first shoved, hard, into a six-by-nine-foot cell, clothed in rags. As I stumbled to the floor, the overbearing guard growled, "Welcome to the State." I sat there on the floor in the corner of that cell, pretty much the same individual as I am today. However, today I see that truth has moved to the front of my mind. I believe this change, both drastic and subtle, had much to do with my survival, since I'd been stripped of my world, or maybe my dignity. Dignity seems like something we need in order to survive as who we think we are. Well, at least we were taught this. As I write these words now, I have nothing in this world other than who I am. I often wonder, *Does this mean I do have my dignity, after all?*

I describe in this book some of my experiences of prison life, but many of them I'll never mention to anyone, only because they really don't matter. I will describe what I have experienced as an "undoing" of old patterns of thinking, which has been a transformation initiated, and then guided by, a part of me that eternally lives. The process necessarily required this stripping away in order to bring on the new patterns, which are truly of who I am. I began an inward journey that tells me it will continue, because it's taking me where I must go. It's a journey about not only "who" I am, but also "what" I am. I can tell you it is peaceful, blissful, and exciting. And I can tell you the same process is available to you, regardless of your circumstances.

I remember sitting there in that stinking cell, moving quickly to the depths of my mind, without realizing how deep I was going. The experience was definitely more than just what I'd been cautioned it might be; many would say shock. I heard one guard telling another guard that I must be in shock when I wouldn't answer any of their questions.

Something was directing me to go deep, where a feeling or sensation welcomed me. I almost felt like a child again. It was that feeling of being cradled and told everything would be okay. I also know that I had no choice but to accept the embrace. I realized in the weeks and months ahead inside these block walls and steel bars that what had embraced me was my own true strength. It was as if I were being waved on inside of me to join in, but I still had to go deeper where something was waiting to greet me. The sensation was mysterious and encouraging, as though whatever was waiting had been hidden away for all those years of my life. Physically I was very weak, and this inner place that had been obscured for so long was really my long-lost home.

Much of the world lives by a thought system that teaches us that our body should be regarded as our temple. This is true; however, it applies only to the surface of who we express ourselves to be, where gaining and winning are important. But for the most part, honoring the body is only a minor step in answering that one question much of the world struggles with. That is, "Who really am I?"

Our temple is not a structure at all, such as a building or our body. Every temple has its altar where holiness abides; otherwise, it wouldn't be a temple. But rather than viewing our body as the temple, let's consider the structure of our temple as our "true essence" or "being." Deep within that structure of life is where our altar sits, and it is at this altar where we see our life's purpose. This is "what" emanates the light, or is the true essence of who we are. This is our "being," if you will.

I wrote this book entirely in longhand from behind bars in an overcrowded, overbearing, and obnoxiously overloud prison environment, where inmates live in one another's faces all day and all night long. The atmosphere is violent and volatile. Often I believe this is what brought these words from my mind through the pen and onto the paper. I sit here and wait to be released by a judge who says he used me as an example. The waiting is extremely difficult, but I know it is temporary.

This project has saved me in more ways than one, and it grew as I did. I wrote the book solely by myself, with helpful suggestions from a Oneness of which we all are a part. The Oneness I call God. Writing this book has kept me busy each day, and at times I would lose sleep at night, anxiously waiting to pick up where I left off the day before. It has consumed me.

Each day I received as a gift words that I could not seem to find the previous day. I would often wake up in the middle of the night, and think, *That's it*: A sentence that was needed to complete a paragraph or a metaphor to help explain an idea. Something to assist in an area I seemed to be stuck would appear in my mind.

When the final chapter was nearing its completion, a blissful feeling continued to flow through me. I knew I was going to miss this project. I was sad, too, because I could not get it to mature beyond the handwritten stage, due to the rule stating no computer usage whatsoever in this backwoods prison system. My only other resource was not really a resource at all, but was available if I wished to stand in line to use the ancient, poor-quality prison typewriter. Need I say, not nearly up to a publisher's standards. This was a feeling like not being able to send your cherished kid to college—a kid who desperately desired to change the world.

But regardless, my words did mature into book form, handwritten into a growing pile of journals. This would be fine for the time being. "Help will be on its way in due time," a voice inside me continued to assure me. As the journals sat in the bottom of my footlocker, that same voice encouraged me to keep writing.

This book surely is a child to me, and in many respects it has been like the experience of watching my daughters grow to adulthood. I remember asking them in a joking and affectionate manner, on their birthdays when they were little, to promise me not to grow any older. I would say that I wished they could remain cute little girls forever. But inevitably they did grow up, and today they are beautiful women, doing what they must to make the world a better place.

Just like my little girls, this book is ready for its next phase. Sooner or later the words will be in your hands, and hopefully helping those who are lost or confused in their own way, as I once was. Or perhaps those who are searching, but not certain what it is they actually want to discover, will find their true free will as I have.

Of course, by the time you are reading this, my task of writing this particular book will have been completed. But from where I stand now, I'm wondering how I will find a publisher who sees it as part of its purpose to get involved. Other individuals whom I have not yet met will have to arrive on the scene to help move the process along. I see this as a natural progression, just as the many other adults who arrived to play a role in the maturing of my daughters.

I can honestly and openly tell you that I have been advised by the "One Who Knows" that I should relax while I proceed with the suggested promotion of this book. I've been advised also to trust that the right people will show up at the right times to assist me with the various procedures. Events are being arranged at this very moment while I continue with my work.

In fact, events are being arranged right now that will give you a reason to seek out this book, or come across it, or have it given to you as a gift. I have already been instructed to turn over everything to my Teacher and Guide. He guarantees this project will arrive in time as a published book for those who are ready to calmly listen, see, and learn, as I have.

By the time you are reading this, I will have already been traveling extensively throughout the country, and who knows where else I may land? It is important that I talk to individuals everywhere about what I have learned and witnessed along my own spiritual journey.

For those who are already ready, and for those who can glimpse readiness, if you can remember that forgiveness is the key to unlocking the door to your own inner depths, then you will live a life that encompasses your own true free will. You will know this to be your *Home*.

Part I

Looking Beyond and Letting Go

Chapter 1

Forgiveness Does Grant Freedom

I was nervously treading water, watching my boat sinking fast, and without a life preserver. I could no longer swim against the current. My world was going down like the *Titanic*, due to my own seemingly deadly errors. I was turning fifty, and felt anchored to the bottom of the lake, lost for air.

For many years a transformation had been urging a shift in me, but out of fear I resisted. I chose to remain in thick fog, thinking I was safer there. I felt as though I couldn't find my peace, so I tried on the weird belief that I could make something of myself that I was not meant to be. That was until the summer of 2007, when this overdue transformation seemed to take charge by forcing its way through the obscurity I had spent so much energy maintaining. The jolt, to say the least, gained my attention.

As I see it now, this was the beginning of an "undoing" process that would eventually set me free. This undoing entailed the gradual, ongoing obliteration of a manmade thought system I had been buying into for most of my adult life. Later I would learn that the parts I believed were dying in me had never really existed at all. I would learn my beliefs were nothing but an illusion, and that what is unreal surely does not live. But at the time, I felt myself drowning in a sea of disbelief, confusion, and terror.

An indictment had been issued by the grand jury of the State of Ohio, and I was soon to be arrested for a selfish mistake I made through my business practice as a financial advisor. After twenty-five years in business one might think I would have known better. My actions were not a part of a Ponzi scheme, but more a brash mishandling of the money of three clients totaling approximately 100,000 dollars. You read that right. Yes, it was one hundred thousand dollars, not millions, or even hundreds of thousands of dollars. However, the funds were my responsibility and tough times had left my bottom line near empty, so I did not have the ability to repay the money—at least not right away. This angered the "example setter" judge and prosecutor. I would be sent to prison. To this day it still seems like a dream. Or should I say a nightmare?

Going to prison is not an easy ordeal to live with, and I surely never wish it on anyone. The authorities seized all of my material possessions, or what was left of them, and I was left penniless. All that was left of me is what seemed to be a vacant mind. I use the word "vacant" because the material world that had consumed me for my entire life had just vanished in an instant.

I had received terrible legal advice from a lawyer who was ill equipped to be honest enough about my case and was no match for the well-polished prosecutor and a judge who wanted to be known as tough. He set an example, all right, by dishing me out a ten-year prison sentence. After I was given my sentence, a lump rose in my throat as a guard snapped handcuffs onto my wrists. My lawyer gave me a wink and a nod and then whispered into my ear that he "should" be able to get me an early release— but the money needed to be right. He added in his best salesman voice that my daughters should sell my house on the lake quickly. He said a realtor would not be necessary, as he had an associate who would handle everything. He figured there might be some equity left before the seizure and garnishments were ordered.

His words did not come close to rescuing me from the nausea that the fall of the gavel had produced in me. Reality slammed down hard. But my lawyer was right in that I would be eligible for an early release, and this was a tiny bit of something to hang on to. Only it got worse. I later found out that I would not be eligible until I completed five years and six months in prison. And worse again, as from prison six months later, I read the front-page news about my lawyer's death due to a drug overdose. It seems he was found face down in the winter's snow of his backyard, loaded with cocaine. Searching for a new lawyer from prison would not be an easy task unless I could get some outside help. But I had time and plenty of it.

Of the people in my life, only a few had stuck with me, and those few continue to encourage me with their support. The others have chosen not to, and for those, I don't even try to understand or make sense of it. In prison it is often said, "Once you are sent here, you will find out quickly who your true family and friends are." Many once-loved ones shy away when someone goes to prison. They all have their reasons, but it's sad and it hurts. I don't mean this as an attack or accusation toward anyone; it is merely a fact of life for a group of individuals who become destitute by being imprisoned. We are always extremely thankful for a shoulder to lean on, or cry on, or to hug; for a good-spirited mind who may write a letter and ask, "Is there anything I can do to help you?" For those who have remained behind me, and for their support, I am eternally grateful.

The words you hold in your hands are about prison and life; but also about the life of the imprisonment much of the "outer" world lives in, with the world itself as our jailor. If the world doesn't jail us, then often we do it to ourselves. It seems we have preferred bondage over freedom. But more important, this book is about forgiveness, so we can release ourselves from the prison we made that binds us. Forgiveness does indeed grant freedom. I'm not talking about the brave fronts we often put on, when we run around telling people that we forgive them and how much we love them. The forgiveness I'm talking about is not toward any certain individual or groups of people we may feel have harmed us. I'm talking about forgiving *yourself*, first by overlooking the illusions you and much of the world live by. Looking beyond these illusions or untruths is the answer to peace, and that is where real love exists.

5

The bondage I just mentioned can only be our unforgiving mind. For myself, it has always been a mind full of fear and unanswered questions. A continuous state of turmoil and misery always seemed to be just around the corner. Sure, I was trying to hide my fear, and hide from it in fear. But was I really hiding? It seemed as though danger was always lurking nearby, ready to grab me.

The unforgiving world, which helped us make the mind that we think is who we are, sees no mistakes or errors, but only sees sins. It has eyes that see through dark glasses and wants to live, yet wishes it were dead. It wants forgiveness, and yet it sees no hope. It doesn't know how to escape and can't figure out that this prison cell we live in is not locked. The door slides open with our own true free will. I will devote this book to explaining to you how to slide open that door and walk through—free.

Chapter 2

Starting Over on a New and Narrow Lane

My lawyer had called and left a message on my answering machine to inform me a warrant had been issued for my arrest. He suggested I show cooperation and turn myself in at the county jail. *But what does he know?* was my first thought. I was angry about the whole mess and didn't understand why he hadn't by now worked out some sort of a deal with authorities for repaying the money. I just could not fathom why felony charges were necessary, but my own hopelessness told me I was finished.

I could have easily turned myself in, but I needed a few days alone to gather myself, take care of unfinished business around the house, and more. After all, bail had not yet been set, and it was unlikely I would be able to come up with the necessary funds. I was just about flat broke and envisioned my immediate future: housed in the county jail, awaiting a trial. I was preparing my mind for the inevitable. I stayed away from the house as much as possible, never knowing when a police car would show up to take me away.

One evening as I was driving through the country, as I often did, taking in dusk over farmlands, going nowhere, I decided to check in on God. I headed to my hometown, Massillon, to stop in at Saint Barbara's Catholic Church. I wanted to just sit for a while where I could find memories of my childhood school days. The church and school had been there for years, even before my time. In fact, my father went to the same school.

I found that the church was locked up for the night. While not disappointed, I made a bit of humor of it by telling myself that "God must have closed up shop for the day." I got back in the Toyota Camry, pushed in the Billy Joel *Innocent Man* CD, and headed back onto more country roads. *The scenic route,* I thought to myself as I sang along to the song "Keeping the Faith." I decided to pick up a pizza and a bottle of good wine and head for home, regardless of any warrant for my arrest. *After all, why am I hiding?*

Unable to sleep that night, tossing and turning while the obvious was flooding my mind, I looked over to the bedside table to see the red, lighted numbers on the clock: 2 AM. I got out of bed, wandered to the French doors that went out onto the deck, and glanced down the slope in the backyard to the quiet lake. The full moon glistened and glowed over the calm, glasslike water. A moon like this always sent peace through me. The serene view was enough to keep my eyes on the water, as an incessant ringing in my head alerted me to thoughts of the police, who would soon be pounding on the door. There was no escaping it. *What's the point of continuing to go on any longer with this charade of a life?* These dangerous types of thoughts ran through me.

Still gazing down at the lake, I continued to punish myself with guilt. Suddenly, out of nowhere, I noticed a circle of ducks in the water near the boat dock, looking up the slight incline toward the house. It was odd at this time of night for ducks to be on the lake, but even odder, it appeared those mallards were looking directly at me. They seemed to swan back and forth as they paddled near the dock while keeping a circle formed, watching me as I watched them. It seemed as though they were aware of my presence and maybe even my mood.

The starry night was warm and beautiful, so I put on my housecoat and slippers to walk out into the yard and down the slope near the dock at the lake. Sure enough, these six ducks were staring right at me. Certainly it was strange, but of a peaceful nature as I considered these creatures of God, simply stopping by to say hello. I picked up a twig and gently tossed it into the water, and they paddled away. But even as they slowly streamed away, the ducks seemed to be looking back at me until they faded into the darkness.

I sat on the dew-soaked grass and continued to stare out over the lake, which was my friend. For years I had known this lake, and I'd caught many fish here. In fact, when I was a kid a section of my property had been a fishing lot owned by my parents. Before that an uncle and aunt had owned the property. And many years earlier, back to the 1940s, my grandparents had owned property adjacent, where my mother had spent much of her childhood on the lake, fishing, swimming, and boating. The property had passed out of the family for several years until I recently purchased it, along with a new house built by the previous owner. Many would say what a coincidence this was. Or was it?

Thoughts like these and my memories of the lake were overshadowing my immediate pressures, and I decided to lie down and gaze out into the starry moonlit sky until I dozed off. A catnap I would allow myself, I thought. … Then I entered into a dream that had only two characters, which were two different reflections of myself—each with a different shape and size, as though seen through a carnival mirror. One of me, which was the real me, had a tall, lean shape with a narrow neck and head, with an animated face. The other me was short and fat, with a round face and head that resembled that of a sumo wrestler.

The real me was thrown into a dungeon and sentenced to remain there for the rest of my life. The dungeon was dark and musty, and the only time I saw anyone was once a day, when the other me, a massive unpleasant guard, opened the heavy steel door and placed a plate of food on the floor. He then would shut the door and go away.

I began to rot in the dungeon for years and thought I was going mad. Finally I made a decision. I would rather die trying to escape than spend another day in that dungeon. My plan was to wait behind the solid steel door for the guard to bring me food.

When the guard opened the door I would attack him. Because the other guard-me was so strong, I, the prisoner, was sure he would overtake me and kill me. But I was fine with that. I was better off dead than being trapped forever in misery and darkness.

I positioned myself behind the door. I reached over and braced myself against the door handle. When I touched the door handle, something strange happened. It began to turn. The weight of my grip made the handle move, and the door cracked open. It wasn't locked!

I didn't know what to do. I stepped forward and opened the door a little further. It made a loud crack. I looked into the hallway and saw the guard looking directly at me. This was strange, since the guard was the other me, and frightening. The guard had a firm look on his face but stepped aside, as I, the prisoner, walked through the door and right out of the dark dungeon into the light. That was it. There was nothing to it; that simply I was free.

I woke up in a chilled sweat and breathing rather heavily as the sun came up over the lake. Also the ducks were back, in the same circle by the dock, looking at me once again. My eyes were teary as I sat up and thought about my dream, trying to make sense of it. After sitting there a while, watching the sun reflect on the water, I realized that I had been my own prisoner. The dungeon was my own body, with a false or illusive self that was guarding over everything that constitutes who I am. It was as though I had believed all along I was sentenced to my body, as if it were a prison cell. Yet the only thing that had bound me was my belief that the prison door was locked, and that a frightening guard was stationed there, making sure I didn't wise up and leave—and that I must remain this way until I died.

I thought to myself, *Man, all I need to do is change my belief in these things, and the door swings open. I have never really been under guard and bound at all.* I couldn't believe that all my life

I'd been allowing my body to be a self-imposed limitation that kept me from who I am truly meant to be—more so, who I *need* to be.

I got up off the ground and headed back up the yard to the house while still in awe of the morning sun over the lake. Before I opened the door to go inside the house, I looked back over my shoulder for another glance at the beautiful lake. I noticed the ducks frolicking and splashing, and their quacking sounded like the laughter of small children playing. My former frenzy left me, replaced by a mood of peace and calmness. Without any thinking, the softness and gentleness of that scene in my mind sent a message to me that everything was going to be okay. It was a feeling that told me to just "let go," and I knew I needed to trust that I was merely starting over on a new path. Things and events were going to happen that simply had to be, but I would be fine.

I went into the house, put on some clothes, made a pot of coffee, and sat for a while before deciding to take a walk around the lake. I filled up my large thermal coffee mug, walked out the front door, climbed the outdoor flight of fourteen steps to the driveway that led upward to the street, and headed down the narrow lane that winds itself around the lake. As I sipped my coffee I enjoyed the awe of nature. A wood hen hammered away in the background, and it seemed like a day fish would be biting. I had a fresh clean feeling, without any other thoughts as I strolled around the lake in an uninterrupted state of bliss.

As I was approaching back toward the house, three deer darted out several feet in front of me, and I could see the look in their eyes. Meanwhile, the wood hen echoed again in the background. I admired the gracefulness of the deer as they leaped into the wooded acreage adjacent to the lake. I found this to be an excitement on that particular morning, I guess because of my lifelong fondness for these creations of God.

Now about forty or fifty yards or so from my house, I noticed a county sheriff squad car sitting at the end of my driveway. I knew why they were there. Without any anxiety or nervousness, I walked up to the driver's side window and identified myself to the deputy. I was ready. He gently and politely handcuffed me, guided me into the back seat, and escorted me away. This was the last time I would ever see my home on the lake.

Chapter 3

The Window

I resided in the county jail for two months, due to my inability to find bail money. This is where I would remain until being bussed off to prison. I had already been escorted on at least a dozen round trips to the courthouse for various hearings—not a very lovely trip at all, being bound by shackles, a belly chain, and handcuffs, along with a van full of others. You would think they were holding me for murder or some other type of severe offense. But this is the norm for all felony cases, regardless of their nature. A prisoner is a prisoner.

This particular trip seemed to be a much shorter van ride, compared with my other court appearances. My guess is that I no longer felt any use for time. Nor would I have to live any longer with the person I'd so desperately been trying to be for so many years. I didn't know who I was now, but I didn't care, either. To the public I was just another convicted felon.

"My career is finished, as well as my life," I would repeatedly mumble to myself while chained to the inside of the van on the rides back and forth to the jail.

On this day before Christmas Eve I had not yet been sentenced, but, taking my lawyer's advice, I pled guilty to charges of forgery and theft that would send me to prison. I thought it was odd that there was no plea bargain. My attorney insisted I trust him.

Once back at the jail, I noticed the young female deputy who unlocked the leg irons from my swollen ankles was about the same age as my twenty-one-year-old daughter Megan. While the young deputy escorted me down a long corridor leading to my cell, I briefly recalled my own headstrong twenties. But I'd never gotten into the kind of trouble I was in now.

13

The deputy apologized and was pleasant as she gestured for me to enter the tiny cell where I would remain for at least another thirty days. I still was to be sentenced, which would mean one more round trip to the courthouse and back, and I was told that due to prison overcrowding I would have to wait for a prison bed. During that time a pre-sentence investigation would be performed, which would weigh heavily on the judge's decision as to how much prison time I would receive. I was also told that my sentence could be determined by my ability to pay fines— just like in the old western cowboy movies, when a judge would say, "That'll be thirty days or thirty dollars, it's up to you." In my case I was broke, and if this scenario were true, I was in hot water.

The jail cell was only six feet wide, with a concrete bench about a foot from the floor that held a torn, thin foam mattress, or what was left of one. The steel bars and concrete surrounded me securely, and being dressed in the rags they called an orange jumpsuit, I was not going anywhere. A small window was positioned near the top of the high block walls within inches of the ceiling. That window reminded me of the window in the fruit cellar of the basement in my grandparents' old house.

I found that by lying on the floor and positioning my body against the wall of that cell, I could look up and through the window to see the sky. My hopes were to try anything, however slight, to strap onto some sort of sanity. But my depression told me there was nothing to see out that window anyway, and the numbness I felt only added to the confused void that held me.

The jail cell was cold, and darkness was the view through the window, just as my depressed thinking said it would be. But I did notice a hint of the glow from a nearby moon. The noise around me, and up and down the long corridor of cells, was horrendous, louder than a crowd in a sold-out arena. But my numbness almost managed to block it out as I half-heartedly thought of ways to end my life.

A recurring thought that haunted me was, *how can I live with myself?* Then suddenly I became aware of what an odd thought that really was. *Am I one being or two? If I can't live with myself, then there must be two of me. There must be the "I" and the "self" that "I" cannot live with. Maybe only one of them is real. But how do I know which one?*

My supper of beans and rice on a plastic tray was slid into the cell through a slot in the bars at floor level. I left it untouched on the floor until lights out, when I awoke from a brief nap to clammy darkness. The guard came by to nab the food tray—well, at least I thought she did. The moon had changed positions and was now squarely framed in the tiny window, which my eyes grabbed onto.

I now had a companion, the moon, and it remained in the window for what seemed to be a few hours. Even after it moved its position, its glow was still apparent, with a backsplash of stars filling the sky. I remember the calming, peaceful sight as I lay on the floor against the wall to gain the only available view. With my body still numb, that sky seemed very friendly.

My mind would vacillate between "thinking" and "no-thinking," or the "I" and "self." My "no-thinking" was merely a fixed gaze through the window and into the sky, nothing more. The "thinking" part of me continued its questions on "how to live with myself." This side of me was getting weaker and more frightened as I began to recognize that there was nowhere as a body that I could go or hide. The more I remained on the no-thinking side, the less fear I felt.

Then I remembered a thought, or a willingness, I had: to never feel the need to hide anything. It said to "let go" of whatever held me to the habitual thinking that had consumed me for so long. I began having more thoughts, telling me that, although I was heading off to prison now, there was nothing to be afraid of. But still there were sustaining fears and self-pity I could not get a grip on, such as, *Why is this happening to me?* and *What is going to become of me?*

As I continued to focus through the window, an additional, brand-new thought came clearly through my mind: "Nothing you see from this jail cell means anything." It was my thought, my own, for sure; but I "heard" it as though it was talking to me. Or maybe I can say it was thinking for me. This one thought persistently hounded me through my numbness.

My eyes opened widely as I suddenly realized the window was gone. It had simply vanished, along with the cell, the bars, the concrete floor, walls, and bench. The entire building was gone. There was nothing, only me, now sitting up in an Indian-style position with arms crossed over my legs. I was still staring at the moon and stars and even noticed how calm I was, and yet amazed.

Next, the darkness of the sky faded quickly away. No sky, but oddly all its glory, remained and had merged together, and I felt held by it. The stars had gathered into dense groups and attached themselves to the outer edges of the moon. Now the moon was centered in an endless array of sparkling clusters, lighting up my view of the magnificent sight that welcomed me.

I looked down at my feet and legs, and they were gone too. I raised my hands and arms, and they were gone. Since I had no hands to feel my face, I was convinced it no longer existed either. My entire body was gone. But I was still there; I existed, feeling a sensation all around me as the most peaceful I've ever experienced.

I thought to myself, *How can I feel and see all this beauty and the light without having eyes to see with?*

Another sensation or thought entered my mind that said, "It's okay, relax, you are already being taken care of. Plans are made. Things and events are being arranged at this moment, getting things ready for you. You're going to do well."

Next came a thought that told me all my errors were not real, so not to worry—that at that very moment from many places, forgiveness was shining on me. It also said to "let go." The emptiness and numbness were gone, along with everything else that had faded away. I've heard and read about people who have said they hear voices talking to them; for example, people who say, "God spoke to me." However, with me, here, this was not the case. This was pure thought, rather than a voice. So pure a thought that there was no doubting or questioning it whatsoever. So real that it is unexplainable, but is certain. A thought with "no-thinking."

I said to myself, "So this is what everything is all about. I am real, regardless of my body." I went on to consider that this is what the Bible really means by "There is no death," and why Jesus demonstrated "There really is no death." I had always felt deep down that I was fooling myself or allowing the world to fool me. Now I was able to see how I had deprived myself by allowing my mind to buy into this "fire in hell" concept, and the devil below. There is no such thing.

Next, all of a sudden, the moon and stars grew so bright with light that my eyes blurred, watery with tears. As I raised my hands to wipe them, I realized everything had reappeared as if nothing had ever happened. I was sitting there, cross-legged, with all my body parts, and inside the jail cell.

What I experienced was not a dream and was real, however so brief—maybe an instant. Time seemed to have suspended itself, so it didn't matter how long the experience lasted. I looked up to see the tray of food was still there. The guard had not yet picked it up.

You, as well as others, have had similar type experiences, perhaps only to quickly dismiss them as a daydream or your imagination running away. Who knows how real your own experiences might have been? One thing for sure that we do know, though, is that the world is always at our side, vigilant and ready to quickly dismiss them as fantasy or delusion.

Chapter 4

Looking Beyond by Letting Go, as You See through the Window

The thoughts I would consistently have of *two of me*, or *two masters*, or the *good and bad sides in me*, I would come to realize were what forced me to choose between my body and the real me. Or, we can say *reality*, the true reality. There is no doubt about the Light that touches me—all of us—and now I know that my body goes along with me for the ride, at least for a while yet.

Thanks to the window, and later what I would learn from *A Course in Miracles*, I'm able to see that I am drawn to the abundant light and realize it has always been with me; now my will is to extend it. I'm able to perceive and acknowledge that I have everything I need within me. I'm realizing that I must usually "perceive" before "knowing." My mind projects my bodily image, and my guilt and fear make it seem real—but it's not.

For the time being, guilt and fear remain with this world as separate illusions. When I say "for the time being," it's because time is all that we see. All of our physical perceptions are based on time. But we can progressively subdue time, the realm where our "thinking" side identifies with a body and its boundaries— who and what we think we are. We can learn this is the unreal or unnatural self we have made. This is all that Jesus wanted us to understand when he said, "Forgive them for they know not what they do." We don't know our real self, and to forgive will allow us to "let go," so what we did make of ourselves can be undone.

I found that when I am afraid of something, I am acknowledging its power to hurt me. We all believe in what we value. If I am fearful, then I must be placing value in fear; therefore I must be valuing wrongly. This fearful habit of mind is destroying our chances for peace, and we must have peace within us before we can extend it. Recognizing this, we can more clearly understand the Bible where it says, "The peace of God passeth understanding." The statement means that peace cannot be valued wrongly, nor can it be shaken at all by errors of any kind.

When we no longer feel vulnerable to attack, separated or rejected, we can then lengthen the instants of pure thought, or "no-thinking," where we reinterpret for our mind what it is we truly want. The bottom line is that we all want peace, but are in fear of how to achieve it. Even the murderer wants peace, but his own fears are so deeply rooted, and his real self so shallow, that he cannot begin to see forgiveness in the world he is a part of. Forgiveness means to *overlook*, or *let go*, and then *look beyond* the errors to the realm where the Will of God exists. In other words, when you have overlooked someone's errors by looking beyond their body that made the error, then you have forgiven them. This is also how you must forgive yourself.

You can start forgiving yourself right now as you read this book, by acknowledging the belief you truly value and want to live by, without guilt and fear. In other words, begin right now to start *looking beyond* your guilt and fears by *overlooking* them.

The initial step is to reinterpret how your mind sees the world, which you have made by following a pattern that others have set for you. Then you can turn around these habits of mind by living your own free will, which requires forgiveness, or "looking beyond" the world's workings and the "you" that you made. Look beyond it all and find out what "you" see—your vision, if you will.

Without forgiveness you will remain in the dark, guilty and fearful, and will naturally see death. But the Light that is within you has a willingness to extend itself. This is the realm where there is no death. You may be asking, "How, then, can I escape darkness and enter the real world?" It's simple: by "letting go" of all that chains you and using your real vision to look through the window. "What is real vision?" you might ask. My goal is to help you find out.

Chapter 5

A Meaningless World

It seems that each generation looks back to previous generations to learn from their mistakes, as well as their successes, in order to improve their progress into the future. These passed-along lessons serve in all generations that follow as the rationale for making a better world—except that we're unaware of what we see.

We've all heard it before, that "the problem with history is it keeps repeating itself." Or should we say that *we* keep repeating ourselves, and are afraid of true change? This is the reason we don't understand what we see, which leads us to get upset and fear something that really isn't there.

A dictator fears that a group of non-Christians are a threat to the power he strives to achieve, for example. In turn, he makes a decision to eliminate them from the face of the earth, resulting in massive numbers of Jewish people being exterminated.

Nations continue to engineer the most sophisticated killing devices, and with a tap on a keyboard we can annihilate much of the earth's population. Additionally, the United States of American, which prides itself as "the land of the free" and is supposedly the most sophisticated and civil country in the world, executes its own natural-born citizens. Rather than focusing resources more on methods of rehabilitation—especially for crimes resulting from problems of addictions or poverty or mental illness—we spend millions of dollars to put individuals to death in the name of creating a better world. Would this be the "Home of the Brave?" No, this is the Home of the Fearful. Is this insane or what?

This book is not intended to be political, nor is it intended to pick on or label groups of people, but it is intended to send you a message about your own fears of change. This is what will make a better world. It's hard to teach an old dog new tricks, and similarly, our old ideas about time are difficult to change. Everything most of us believe is rooted in our concept of time, and the mind-habits that make us miserable and lead us to err depend on our unwillingness to learn new ideas about it. This is precisely why we need new ideas about time.

The first time-related idea I'll discuss, about "seeing the past," is not really as strange as it may sound. What if *before* making a judgment about everything we might look at, we acknowledged to ourselves that the only thing we are seeing is the past? Please bear with me as I explain.

Let's consider when we sip on a cup of morning coffee. Do you actually see a coffee cup, or are you merely looking at your past experiences of picking up a cup, inhaling its aroma, anticipating the jolt of caffeine, and taking a drink from it? Out of your past you are remembering the feeling of the rim of the cup against your lips while having breakfast. How else could you have known whether or not the coffee is hot, and that the cup can break if you drop it? What do you really know about the cup, except what you have learned from the past? Your past learning has taught you the *idea* of this cup.

Our minds are always preoccupied with past thoughts and impressions, and this, of course, is why we see only the past. No one really sees anything. We are all seeing our past images projected onto the movie screen of our lives.

Our preoccupation with the past is the cause of the misconception about time in which our seeing suffers. The mind seems to not want to grasp the present, which is really the only time there is. The present does not tick forward, and each present moment is always only that one moment, and then it is gone. A new moment rushes right in. Each moment of each day is always a brand-new moment, unrelated to any past or future moments. As you read this now, that moment is gone and you are in a new moment, and so on. This is why your moments *cannot* understand time and *cannot*, in fact, understand anything—and thus we perceive messages of a meaningless world, which upsets us. A present moment is not your past, nor your future, but it is where you live.

One thought we can be sure of about the past or the future is that it is not here. To think about it at all is to think about illusions. An illusion is not something, but rather nothing— something that is "not here." Very few have realized what is actually entailed in picturing the past, or in anticipating the future.

Let's be sure not to confuse the mind with the brain. The brain is your body. Your mind is of you—but it is not you, not the true self. The mind is actually blank when it does its picturing or imaging of past and future. This is so because when your mind thinks it is acting separately and on its own, and anything it thinks about is an illusion, or nothing—"no-thing." It can be said that these illusory ideas that preoccupy our mind are blocking out truth. The only constructive idea we can have at this point is to recognize that our mind has been merely blank, rather than believing it is filled with ideas. This acknowledgment is the first step in using your real vision, thus giving you a glimpse of spirit, or who you are.

It is not necessary to understand, at this point, that you can see nothing as it is now. But it's a huge step toward undoing your false ideas to be honest with yourself and to acknowledge the fact that you do not understand. In the beginning it may be difficult for you to believe that what your mind seems to picture is really not there. This idea can be quite disturbing and may meet active resistance in many forms, which we will be discussing all the way through this book. But once again, acknowledging any type of disbelief or discomfort with this idea is a great starting point. Why? Because you are actually holding a vision of truth. This may be your first experience of real vision. The truth is vision.

A good question to ask yourself is: How many meaningless thoughts do you have that show you a meaningless world? It seems our perception of the world is determined by the world. But please do not confuse perception with knowledge; we will be discussing the difference later on.

Have you ever tried to use only your present-moment thoughts to determine the world you live in? Each new moment then becomes a new world, or a new birth. This type of vision will take some practice, but also can become automatic, and a new way to live in this world. It is your release from the world you learned from and is the key to where forgiveness lies. Could you dare to consider living each moment of each day, automatically overlooking errors and automatically looking beyond them to where God's Will exists, which is your true free will? You would always be living a life of automatic forgiveness. Forgiveness would be your life. Being taken advantage of just would not exist, because you would always be looking beyond the errors of this world and would be at one with God's Will. You could say, this condition would have you being God's Will. Now, at this present moment, can you see who you truly are?

Chapter 6

We Are His Extended Thought

"How can you actually go about forgiving?" you might be asking. When you are upset for whatever reason, even with, say, a "meaningless world," it is necessary to correct a major perceptual distortion most of us have. You believe that what upsets you is a frightening world, or a sad world, or a violent and insane world. But if you're being honest with yourself, you can acknowledge that these attributes were given to the world by you, caused by how you "think" of the world.

The thought of a meaningless world engenders fear; but meaninglessness is impossible, because nothing can exist without meaning. This would be an illusion. If you believe the world is meaningless, then your fears of the world do not exist either, and are another illusion brought on by illusion. Now we're seeing insanity!

It may seem that you would not perceive something that has no meaning. On the contrary, you will be particularly likely to think you do perceive it. Why? Because it reinforces your belief that your own illusions of the past are real. But remember, you assign meaning to the past to fill a void, a black area in your mind. Your own "thinking" body believes it is lacking and feels empty, so it works diligently to make its own ideas of the truth. This "thinking" is separate from God, but therefore you have also observed His extension to you, which is the real you. Yes, each one of us is *His Extended Thought.*

As you recognize the meaningless and the false as being merely what they are, your confused and empty body becomes doubtful, fearful, and guilty, because it senses a separation from its *Source.* Anything that separates from its source naturally experiences panic. When our loved one suddenly dies or leaves us, we experience loss and pain and fear due to the separation. For now, there is no reason for your confused self to try to understand everything I am writing, but there is every reason to "let go" and make room for what you do understand.

Look at it this way: The sun, known as the source and the center of the physical solar system, extends itself with its rays, though it can often be obscured by cloud cover, depending on where you are positioned here on Earth. Nevertheless, the sun remains forever, as its rays continue to extend, and the clouds eventually dissipate without affecting the sun or its rays. Just as the rays of the sun extend, regardless of cloud cover, so are you the extended Thought of God, regardless of the clouded thinking your mind *dreams* up.

To recognize reality, or to know the Light, is to be enlightened. Jesus, one of many enlightened individuals to ever walk the earth, and the one whom much of humanity has been drawn to, was aware of the dreaming mind. As a man, he had the knowledge from within, and was aware of the extended Thought of God as who we all are. His many messages told us simply to uncover our eyes and see the Light that is already there. There's no reason to wait for some future event. It's with us now. He also expressed this message more deeply, essentially saying (my interpretation): "You believe you are a body; however, you can choose between loveless or miraculous channels of expression. You can make of yourself an empty shell, but it can only express 'nothing.' You can destroy your body, your medium of communication, but not your potential. You did not create yourself."

Part II

Searching for the Hand of Destiny

Chapter 7

Growing Pains

A Zen master speaks to his students about a great warrior of ancient Japan who once marched out to meet the enemy with an army one-tenth the number of the opposition. This general's name was Nobunaga, and he said to himself, "I will win. I am sure." But his men had doubt.

En route to the field of battle, Nobunaga paused to offer prayers at a wayside shrine. Then he told his soldiers: "Destiny holds us in her hand." From his pocket he took out a coin. "I will toss it. If heads comes up, we will win. If it be tails, then we must prepare for our death." He flung the coin skyward. It flashed in the sun's light and then fell heads up. A roar of courage shook the inspired soldiers. Eager to fight, Nobunaga's men won their battle easily.

"No one can change the hand of destiny with the toss of a coin," the victorious warrior's aide told Nobunaga after the fighting was over.

"Indeed, one cannot," Nobunaga replied. Smiling, he held up the coin he had tossed, which was double-headed.

Each of us has a destiny that is chartered beyond our own thinking. But the world we live in sends us in a multitude of directions, so the courses we pursue in life are not always of our own choosing and we often work to achieve goals that do not reflect what we truly want. The individual who believes he is complete master of his own destiny exists solely in the eyes of his own ego.

I began to idolize the Beatles at age seven, when I first saw them perform on the *Ed Sullivan Show*. Later, as a determined young boy, to be all that I could be, I wanted to know more about "Lucy in the Sky" and I fantasized about being on the cover of the Beatles' *Sgt. Pepper's Lonely Hearts Club Band* album. I yearned to be a part of the "revolution" and the "evolution" they sang about. Their free spirit and free will struck me, and I wanted it too.

Growing up in 1960s Ohio, I was the oldest of six children in a low-income Catholic family. My father worked as a welder at a local factory and my mother was a registered nurse at a local hospital. My dream beyond rock-n-roll was to be a football hero at Notre Dame, but this was also the dream of all the other boys I played parochial league ball with. My desire felt to me that it was bigger than the others, so the dream continued for a while.

I did pretty well and scored many touchdowns as a small halfback, and I was told that the other teams keyed on me each game. By the time I was a freshman at Central Catholic High School, though, my size had not yet caught up with my desire. At the team's official weigh-in, I came up with the idea of placing a few weights into my pockets to portray a heavier me on the roster. The scale teetered at 96 pounds. I was very concerned about my weight and height, if I were to earn a scholarship to play football for the Fighting Irish of Notre Dame.

I tried all the proven stretching gimmicks and sprinkled loads of wheat germ over every meal, but I just could not seem to grow. After the freshman season I was forced by lack of pounds and inches to awaken from the dream of tearing up the turf at Notre Dame. I finished high school in a few more years with slightly above-average grades, only because I did not ever prepare for tests, and my physical form finally had matured.

My parents had always been, and still are, devoted Catholics, and they expected the same from their four daughters and two sons. My grandparents, too, occupied the same third-row seat every Sunday at 11:30 AM at Saint Barbara's. It was an old parish with generations of "good Catholic" families, with a cemetery behind the church for the members who had passed along to a "better place."

At Sunday mass I would sit in confusion, bored with the sermons and readings, and impatient with the kneeling, standing, and sitting. I was an altar boy and was often seen fidgeting and daydreaming of girls, football, music, and anything else other than my duties on the altar. Occasionally I would get a nasty look with a signal from Father Daum when I was late ringing the concentration bell at the most boring part of the mass. Of course, at that age I didn't understand it.

What I wanted to know about the most was the secret conversations Jesus had with the apostles. I figured there had to be parts left out of the fragments recorded in the Gospels, which I also suspected had to have been touched up a bit after all these years. I wondered what they really talked about while out for the day on Peter's fishing boat. How did they hang out together? What jokes did they tell one another? How did they talk about the local women? I always believed that Mary Magdalene was Jesus' wife, and I still do. I wanted to know more than the people who wrote the history books were willing to tell us.

I guess it was during my high school days when I admitted to myself that God was not this old man with a white beard wearing a white robe, sitting on a golden throne somewhere past the sun, who handed out favors to those who prayed the most. The theology classes seemed to not want to go into that sort of thing. The study was more about making sense of the New and Old Testaments. The Exodus and the travels of Paul following Jesus' death did interest me, but I always wanted more. My doubts were not about God ever, but I doubted the experts who interpreted all these teachings. Why was I supposed to trust someone else's view of things? The only answer I could ever get was, "Because the Bible says so." Everyone seemed afraid to put their own interpretation into the "Holy Word."

Don't get me wrong; my upbringing did give me a strong foundation, for which I am grateful, and there were many teachers, nuns, and priests whom I admired. It was also nice to find out that Father Kaylor—fresh out of the seminary when I was a high school senior, sporting shoulder-length hair—was a Beatles fan. He felt that even Jesus would have been listening to "Let It Be" and "Hey Jude." I now hear it is a plus for the school that he is today the school principal—although I also heard he is minus the hair.

But I still wanted answers that they just couldn't seem to commit to. Now, as I look back, I believe they must have had the same questions and also would have liked answers.

I started college at Kent State, not knowing at all where I was heading, other than to parties. Quickly I realized I wanted to put the books down for a while and get into the real world. As uncertain as I was, and impatient for answers and growth, I knew one thing for sure, and that was I needed to earn money. The answers I was getting at the beer parties sounded good while listening to Bob Dylan and Joni Mitchell, but they weren't good enough for me. I needed to move on. So this was when I started looking at the sky, and I flew right to it.

By 1975 I was the property of the United States Air Force. My girlfriend Lori, who months later became my wife, got to tag along, compliments of the Air Force. "How cool is this?" is what I proudly felt.

I found some answers, and the truth about Viet Nam fairly quickly. Many of my new airmen friends were recently back from tours of duty in Viet Nam, and the war was now over. I got to hear the war stories firsthand over beers at the NCO (noncommissioned officers) club. They were training me as though I might be sent there, but fortunately for me no additional troops were being sent.

The 1970s were pretty wild but safe for me, even as an airman. The Air Force did take good care of me, and in 1978 Erin was born. As a young father with inspiration extending through me and into my gorgeous daughter, my responsibilities kept a lid on the wilder times. I needed to be serious and help make a clear path for Erin's future. Plus, the oath I had taken to die for my country if necessary held strong in my heart. I guess you could say I was the "gung ho" type, and this excited me.

I remember one night on a training exercise, a few of us under the stars until sunrise. About a dozen of us were all gazing at the starry sky while we maintained our position at our C141 aircraft. The exercise called for the arrival and departure of several aircraft throughout the night. This intensified our discussion about the cosmos and the mystery behind the universe. I've always had a keen connection and a curiosity regarding all that is visible and beyond in the sky. One of the guys said to me that it appeared as though I knew something they didn't, as we all spoke and gazed in awe of the beauty of that particular night. I cannot say that I knew something, but I have always felt connected somehow.

By the mid-1980s the Air Force was behind me, and so was my marriage to Lori. We would both say later, it had outgrown itself. Now I was a new rookie in the financial services industry, training hard and making it as a broker. It was the "yuppie years," which meant hippies were joining the business world, and rather than bell bottoms and tie-dyed shirts, the wave was three-piece suits with suspenders. I was making financial decisions and designing investment strategies for others, as well as myself. This was now my place in the world, and I had a house and a fast car to keep me honest at working long hours. It was the thing to do, at least for me.

A business professional: that is who I would be to the world. The answers I discovered were called "money, and more money." Money was to solve all problems. I was living fast, having fun and success. However, one thing was wrong. It really did not feel right to me. Something was missing, but I bought some advice from a veteran in the industry who told me, "Something will always seem to be missing." I worked harder, stayed with it, and was making a life for myself. My questionable Catholic faith remained with me in the form of all the "Hail Marys" that seemed to be embedded into my prayer system.

Then my bachelorhood was interrupted, by the beautiful auburn-haired Lori, who knocked me off my barstool one evening and onto the dance floor. Yes, another Lori. In fact, she became "Lori number two," as I was so often teased in a fun-loving manner by friends and family, who wholly supported my loving relationship with her. It wasn't long before the "new Lori" became my wife, and about ten months later the lovely auburn-haired Megan Rose was born into the world.

I now felt I had the task to make a future for the two half-sisters, Erin and Megan. One thing for certain in my mind was that these two girls would be given the opportunity to share a life together as sisters of one family, regardless of their having different mothers. I was firm on this, and I needed to convince my ex-wife, Lori number one, Erin's mother, to cooperate. It all worked out well, though like any other family we ran into a few minor complications and hassles along the way. But something always seemed to accommodate both sides of the split family.

To this day, Erin and Megan are as close as any two sisters could possibly be with their seven-year age difference. In fact, their resemblance to each other is simply lovely, even though both complain occasionally about the cowlick in their hairline—the same cowlick that I have lived with, passed on to me by my mother. As I write this, Erin is a schoolteacher with her own family, and Megan pursues law school.

I remember one cold clear winter night that the two girls, Lori number two, and I spent on ice skates at a neighborhood lake. A star-filled moonlit sky was the only witness to a conversation

Lori and I had about God, life, the cosmos, and our future together. I can still see the moon glistening into Lori's deep-brown beautiful eyes as we pondered our mortality, the future of the girls, and more.

She looked lovingly into my eyes as we stood across from each other on our skates, with a cold steam showing proof of our breath. But the loving look she gave me was that of a friend more than a lover. In a light tone she said to me, "I don't know what you are, Jim. I feel as though I can see through your eyes and directly into you. It's scary. What are you, honey?" She hugged me and skated off, giggling like a child being mischievous. Lori passed away only a few years later, following a fight with cancer. She was only thirty-five.

The twenty-first century dawned before I knew it, and by this time I was pretty much established as a financial advisor. More and more of my client base was made up of the affluent. I was spending a lot of time in Clearwater, Florida, organizing and expanding my business practice into a branch office while enjoying warm winters, and my travel was extensive.

I began rubbing elbows with the country's top advisors, learning their secrets and their ways of living the good life. They welcomed me and were always helpful. I noticed there was one common theme among these individuals, and it was that they all seemed to truly have a passion for their business, before the money. It seemed to be their life, or who they were. This was something I could not feel, and I struggled with a lost feeling of not belonging. I was playing a game of pretending to be something I was not. I felt like an actor—as if I were a piece of the puzzle, but of some other puzzle, that didn't fit. Or a game piece that was in the wrong box of a board game. Although my efforts did pay off financially, so I was able to taste the "good life," I was fooling myself. I knew it was really not *my* "good life" I was tasting. It was the good life that the world painted a picture of. I felt no true rewards.

By now I was seriously involved with Dania, who I literally bumped into in an elevator while in Florida. Before long we married, bringing another daughter into the world. Kacy Mae sports the same cowlick as her two beautiful half-sisters, father, and grandmother. Kacy is extremely precious and loving, but requires special care due to her learning disabilities and the fact that she cannot speak. Despite her special needs, Kacy Mae seems to have an inner joy and a peace within herself that attracts many people. It's as though she has something we all want. Now a lovely young lady, she continues with various therapy programs, and her amazing progress sparks a light of hope in all of us who love her dearly.

I began to get nervous about the economy and stock markets bouncing around and crumbling. My marriage began crumbling as well, and Dania and I separated, placing more pressure on me, which I was not handling well. I began losing clients right and left, and my small self-built destiny was in the gutter. I was openly admitting how much I hated the business and myself for allowing it to consume so many years of my life. All for the money—the house on the lake, the operation in Florida, and the other things money can buy. And now, back in divorce court squabbling over who gets what, I was lost, with no money to bail me out. However, this thinking told me to dig in harder than I ever had before, so I worked diligently to make things happen and regain financial security.

I began straining my mind for endless hours, trying to devise some kind of new strategy to drum up business. But I had to hurry because I was running out of money fast, and this "drumming-up" plan was also costing money. I was making promises I wasn't sure I could keep. *Maybe, just maybe, if I do some of "this" and a little of "that," I can make something kick in*, went my thought process twenty-four hours a day. I was exhausted and beat up.

This was not good for my emotional condition, and I knew help was needed as I began to mortgage the house and take out loans that I had no confidence I'd be able to repay. I was looking for answers, and I wanted them fast. I read all the motivational books recommended by the high achievers in my industry and listened to the many recordings of the masters themselves. I went to seminars on change, optimism, healing, you name it, and nothing was able to save me. Something kept pushing me to search further and not give up hope. My boat was sinking fast, and I needed rescue.

While browsing the self-help section in a bookstore in Port Richey, Florida, I stumbled upon a book by Dr. Wayne W. Dyer called *Your Erroneous Zones*. I connected immediately as I stood there in the store paging through it. *His message was for me*, I told myself. In the weeks and months ahead, I eventually purchased every one of his many books and absorbed every word as though it was intended specifically for me. Over time I became a huge fan of Dr. Dyer, and I appreciated the fact that at one point in his own life, he had experienced a similar confusion, and he was able to discover the answer.

Not only did I read and study all of his material, but also that of others Dr. Dyer had recommended. I was hearing them all loud and clear, but I still could not seem to budge. They were proving to me that the light was in the window, but I just could not get the window shade up that was obscuring my light. I was afraid, and began more and more to force things and push everything, including my thinking.

As I read Wayne Dyer, and many of the other writers I respected, I often noticed that on occasion they referenced a publication called *A Course in Miracles*. "What is this Course in Miracles?" I would often ask myself, and let it twirl in the back of my mind. I would, of course, tell myself that I needed to check it out. "One of these days," I would say. It was totally unlike me to procrastinate on researching and seeking out this publication.

But this is what happened. I had put the *Course in Miracles* on the back burner, so to speak. Again and again I would hear mention of this publication, and I did nothing.

By this time my mind was so flooded with panic and turmoil that frustration was all I was about each minute of every day. In an effort to create capital to keep my business alive, I acted alone in crossing an illegal line within the financial services industry. I borrowed money from my clients' accounts, with the full intention of paying it back before anyone was the wiser. My thought system saw a way to "fix everything" through various investments that had failed once before, but now were on the rise. *A sure thing*, I told myself.

You know the rest. The plan failed, and I hit rock bottom. I was so busy searching for the hand of my own destiny, where all along all I had to do was lift up the window shade and let the light in.

Chapter 8

Being Ready

At age fifty I became a prisoner of the State of Ohio, and anything that could go wrong or go against me, did. But I was willing to put up with it, because something inside me was telling me that "this has to be, for a while, anyway." Besides, I had no choice in the matter. As much pain as I was going through, the Voice kept telling me that I was going somewhere and to simply hang on.

On that cold morning of February 1, 2008, I was transported in chains to Lorain Correctional Institution. I felt as exhausted and uncertain as ever before, but hadn't lost the sense of the promising thoughts and expansive vision that had jolted me during my stay in the county jail. Lorain Prison would hold me for reception and intake processing for a period of three to nine months, while I was assigned a security level and waited for a spot in the overcrowded prison system. In that year alone, the state had brought in around 30,000 new prisoners. For the time being I would remain in maximum security, though I'd never been violent and posed no escape risk. This meant being locked in a cell 24/7, other than to shower twice a week and to march to the dining (chow) hall three times a day.

After a buzz haircut and an issue of prison clothing, I was taken to Prison House 4, where I would spend the next few to several months. As I watched the guard slide a huge key into the heavy steel door to House 4, my thoughts of what prison must be like raced through me, as I said to myself, *Well, this is it*. The guard forewarned me to follow him directly to my cell without looking at the other inmates waiting to harass me.

As he slowly swung open the vault-type door, blasts of insanely loud noise surged directly through me. I stepped into the prison house, which held 260 prisoners, all double-bunked into single cells. I immediately noticed the high ceilings, which reminded me of an arena. The circular design featured two tiers, called ranges, that resembled a balcony and ran all around the outer walls. A two-bar railing separated the pit from the cells lined up one after another.

This was certainly a lions' den, and I could see immediately that in order to survive I would have to decide what kind of lion I was going to have to be. This surely was not the place where the "lion and the lamb would lie together."

After sixty days I was notified I was being transferred to a medium-security prison, Richland, which would only be an hour's drive for my girls to visit their locked-up father. But a few weeks later, on the morning of the transfer, the state changed their plans for me. Without notice I was loaded onto an old rickety bus with about fifty other prisoners, handcuffed, shackled, and chained with interlocking arms. We were driven to Belmont Prison, over three hours away in the opposite direction. Belmont had a nasty reputation for gang activity and carried the nickname "Gladiator School." I tried to contain my anger, helplessness, and dread.

When I arrived at Belmont it was not what I expected, but what is? Belmont certainly lived up to its reputation with "gangs" and "gladiators." On my first day there I counted eight fights, resulting in each inmate being taken to "the hole." Unlike Lorain, there were no cells in the regular holding quarters, but rather rows of double-bunked beds thirty inches apart, warehousing 272 prisoners to each house, squeezed tightly into five rows. Belmont has eight of these prefabricated houses with tin roofs, totaling approximately 2,400 prisoners, and all of them had one thing in mind: survival. Being a medium security level prison, for approximately seven hours most days prisoners are permitted to roam the prison yard, gymnasium, and library. These hours of the day, with all of the eight houses intermingled, are a relentless test for one's survival.

Following an eleven-day confinement that I spent in segregation, known as the "hole," I was lying on my bunk trying to recover when a fire drill was enacted. The yard was open, so to avoid the fire drill proceedings, I quickly left the scene and found my way into the prison library, which was not a part of the fire drill. I needed something, anything, to lift the fog in my mind. The library has limited material, mostly old and used. Books and well-thumbed magazines are donated by local libraries that must unload their outdated material. A good find requires a tough search, and I continued to browse until I noticed Dr. Wayne Dyer's book *Real Magic*. I had owned this book prior to prison, and it was one of my favorites. This was like an old friend out of the blue paying me a much-needed visit. I immediately checked the book out of the library for two weeks and held on closely to every word, thankful for the boost.

Upon returning *Real Magic*, I decided to search a section of philosophical type books, which had all been published years ago, according to their copyright. An unusual old-looking, battered, blue-covered book with faded gold lettering popped out at me. I casually pulled it off the shelf, and it fell to the floor and landed on my foot, partially opened to some torn and raggedy pages. As I bent over to pick it up, I noticed the gold lettering said, to my surprise, *A Course in Miracles*. I quickly made a double take to make sure what I'd just read was correct, and immediately all those years and circumstances where I had heard mention of this Godsend flashed before me. I said to myself, with a warm, glowing feeling inside, and also to the book as if it had been looking for me, "So this is what you are? I am so glad to finally meet you, and of all places. How did you get here?" Both elated and nervous, my hands shook as I hugged this book in my arms.

I knew right then that whatever was contained within these pages was written for me. As it turned out, this copy was the condensed version, with all three volumes included in one publication. Please keep in mind this is not a publication you would ordinarily find in a prison, as you would a Bible, which is available everywhere. Nevertheless, as I stood there in the library at the bookshelf where I met my new *friend*, I went to the copyright page to see it was dated 1975. This was the year my search for answers truly began, as I saw it. I quickly skimmed through it to catch glimpses of some of its wording, and found it to be extremely deep and difficult to understand, like a foreign language. *At least for now*, I thought, resolving to learn this new language as best I could.

As I flipped through the book, feeling eager and rushed, I was stopped at a section in smaller than normal print, which grabbed my attention. I stood there with tears in my eyes as I read the following, which seemed as though it were speaking to me:

> This course is a beginning, not an end ... No more specific lessons assigned, for there is no need of them. Henceforth, hear but the Voice For God ... He will direct your efforts, telling you exactly what to do, how to direct your mind, and when to come to Him in silence, asking for His sure direction and His certain Word.

This message then directed me to go to the workbook page 487, and I did what it said. All I can say to you now is that the message I found there did tell me what to do.

I examined the inside of the ragged and marked-up cover to notice that the book had been received by the prison library two years prior and had not once been checked out by another inmate. A name and phone number was written inside the front cover by a woman in Sedona, Arizona, with her handwritten message: "My will is that *this* finds *Its* way to you."

I figured the book had once belonged to her, and for some reason she had donated it to a charity. The writing seemed to be years old, and made me think it might have ended up in an estate sale or a charitable sale for some social club, or what have you. In any event, it somehow found its way across the country until it landed on my foot, and at the very time I was in critical need for it to be with me.

The condensed version of *A Course in Miracles* contains the 669-page text, the 488-page workbook for students, and the 92-page manual for teachers. I immediately checked it out of the library and began to read each word of its deep content. At first I found much of it difficult to understand; nothing seemed to make sense. However, I felt the words connecting in a peculiar way I cannot describe. I felt I was being pulled toward something, but also welcomed. What I was beginning to experience was both exciting and inexplicable. I knew to the core of me that for some strange reason this publication was destined to show up in my life. Later, and still now, I have a sensation that it was written for me.

Among my many questions was: "Why didn't I find this sooner?" Since then, I have found the simple answer to that question, which I easily accept. I was not ready. The *Course* was destined to show up in my life when I *was* ready, when the time was right. I immediately began to realize answers I'd been looking for, and felt I was being pointed in the right direction with all I would encounter during my days in prison. Since this book was the library's only copy and not my own, I decided at first to quickly read it cover to cover without missing a word, regardless of what I did not understand. After all, I was in prison and had plenty of time to do just that. But I knew I would need to have my own personal copy eventually, because I had already accepted it as my life—a commitment I wanted. I was not even aware if the book was still in print or available in stores. I needed to find out, and as a prisoner we have zero computer access and limited telephone use.

I initially thought of writing my longtime friend Ron, who had stuck by me by coming forward after I was sent to prison to offer his help in any fashion. I thought that maybe Ron could find me a copy of *A Course in Miracles*. But there was one snag. As a prisoner, and due to drug smuggling into prison, I was only permitted to receive brand-new books, shipped to me directly from an approved vendor. I decided to hold off for now on notifying Ron, and in fact, I never did mention it to him at all. I didn't want him to think I had gone overboard with my emotions and fallen for some "save the day" self-help book. The timing wasn't right, and something was urging me to see it this way.

Most people do not realize the importance to prisoners of an outside support system, such as Ron, and I continually thank him for all his efforts in helping me. He writes me consistently each week as a matter of fact, and our relationship as friends has grown strong. He visits me as often as he can, even though he lives in Florida. He tells me it gives him an excuse to check in on his eighty-two-year-old mother, who lives in Ohio. One day I will repay Ron in a special way.

* * *

After about three months of renewing the *Course* from the library, I was feeling a oneness with these words. I asked the librarian, who had worked as a state employee in this same library since the prison opened in 1995, if she had ever heard of *A Course in Miracles*. In a very abrupt and authoritative fashion, she answered, "A course in *what*?" She had never heard of it. I asked around among a few other inmates who I thought might be likely, and all of them answered "No." To this day I have not run into a single individual in the prison system who has ever heard about *A Course in Miracles*. I had to do something—at least try to get a copy of the *Course*, and even thought about asking the librarian if she would work with me somehow. But somehow I waited and remained patient for a little longer.

While at my bunk one morning, reading and studying the age-yellowed, dirty, and faded pages of the library's copy of the *Course*, I was called to go see the house sergeant. My request a few months prior for a bed move had finally come through. I was being moved to a much quieter section of the prison house, to an area earmarked for what they called "senior housing." A senior was a prisoner age thirty-five and older! At least now I would get a break from my bunkmate and the neighbors, who called me "Pops."

Upon arriving with my belongings at the new bunk location, A-96, I plopped my property onto the mattress and steel springs of the bunk and greeted my new bunkie. Next to our double bunk was a rusty old wall locker, decorated with initials and dates back to the 1960s scratched into the metal. I would share this cabinet with my bunkie; each of us would possess one side. The top of my half of the locker cabinet was terribly dusty, and I began to wipe it down. I noticed what appeared to be a thick book underneath a torn and dirty rag that was part of an old towel. As I removed the cloth, I was shocked to find a very clean and minimally tarnished copy of *A Course in Miracles*.

Is this some kind of a joke? I thought. "But how could it be a joke?" I asked under my breath, my voice shaking with utter confusion. Right away I asked my new bunkie, whom I did not yet know, if he was aware of the book's rightful owner. He simply shrugged and shook his head. All he could tell me was that it had been sitting there for ages, and the previous occupant used it as a sort of shelf where he placed his girlfriend's picture. The book was not used for reading material at all. It had simply been sitting untouched for God knows how long.

I circled the bunk, asking all around while holding it up high, whether anyone had misplaced it. Nobody would claim it. My new bunkie finally said, "Dude, give it up. I tell you, dude, it has been sitting there for a long time. Just keep it, it's yours." I cannot describe how I felt that day. I was shaking with anxiety ... and wonder. I had already been a student of the *Course* for about three months, and now this book suddenly appeared to end up becoming my own private, personal copy.

How did it get into this prison and into my wall locker? As I mentioned earlier, the Bible is everywhere in this place of despair, hopelessness, and loneliness, and is widely used. But no one I have ever met while in prison has ever heard of *A Course in Miracles*. Was this a miracle in itself, this publication showing up like it did, and with the events that put me there? I'll let you decide the answer to that question as you read on.

For me the *Course* is not just another "how-to" or inspirational self-help book to lead one to gain a positive outlook. It has become my personal teacher for life. It doesn't replace the Bible, but it does add *new thought*, and has shown me how to open the window shade without forcing it and allow the light to shine through. I am being taught to relax, calm down, and understand myself, while knowing why I am here in this body. It took me by surprise, the "hard way." But as I said earlier, it took till then for me to be ready.

Many people have made comments that the *Course* is an attempt to form a cult. These individuals are totally misinformed. *A Course in Miracles* states right up front that it is *not* a cult, for a cult needs an idol—a leader or a guru. *A Course in Miracles* has no rules about dress or diet; it doesn't require you to leave your family or give it all your money, as you might expect from a cult. No; its curriculum focuses on truth and our *sinless* identity. It leads us to freedom from guilt and to a place where we can see fear as merely an illusion. It teaches that the opposite of fear is love, and both cannot coexist. It opens our true vision to our Source, which can only be God, and helps us to know that we all have a unique purpose while we are here. It gives us the *Guidance* to understand how to proceed with that purpose.

My lifelong commitment to studying and teaching the *Course* has opened a new door for me, unleashing a flow of universal intellect seeding itself into my true essence.

A gift has been given to me in my friend Ron, who comes to visit me here in prison, supporting me, helping me, giving me updates as he works with attorneys to do the tasks necessary to set me free, hopefully soon. But if I must endure the duration of my ten-year prison term, I am prepared. I am very fortunate that I will, for sure, one day walk out of these prison gates. I live with many others who are serving life sentences and will never take their kids or grandkids out for ice cream. I offer them a shoulder at times, and my ear to vent some steam, as my heart remains open to them. For now, this is my purpose. My stop here is temporary. Ron has said he sees a glow about me. He has asked me about this change, but I have not yet told him about the *Course*. He is not ready, but will be one day, and most likely will be when I can live outside these prison walls.

The book you are holding right now is about you and me. It's about Truth, the main roots of the oak tree; Strength, producing the acorn; and Love, the Thought helping the seed to sprout. Its outer expression is the tree, and the process is Life, otherwise known as God.

This book has a purpose: to make you aware of the Thought of God, which will awaken you so you can sprout. Not everyone is ready for the message I give here, but many are. I hope to make your life better, only by continuing to show you what I have learned, and not by preaching to you. I have discovered "Truth to be unalterable, eternal, and unambiguous," as the *Course* tells us. It applies to everyone and everything God created, and only what He created is real.

The world offers a flood of false images we have been trained to believe suit us. I want you to open your mind to who you and I truly are. I hope this book will help you to face the world with truth and strength, free of guilt, so you will be able to say, "Without your help, world, I am able to see my world the way I know it to be."

I hope that what you have read thus far has given you some momentum to proceed with an open mind, to see that you are more than what you have been giving yourself credit for. Let's move forward together, at Godspeed, and increase this momentum in order that you find your true free will: Your purpose for being who you are.

Part III

Awakening to Your Destiny

Chapter 9

Losing Ourselves in the World

"Life's a bitch then we die."

These were the words I overheard in a debate between two sixty-something inmates as I was sitting on a bench adjacent to these two men. We all three gazed out beyond the barbed wire, into a wooded area miles into country and farmland. It was just after sunrise; otherwise, I would most likely not have been able to find a seat anywhere in the yard, due to the overcrowded conditions. I was hoping to catch a glimpse of wildlife and was not a part of their conversation, so I continued to daydream as my eyes panned for a vision of naturalness.

Mesmerized by a flock of Canada geese flying overhead, I couldn't help but respond inside my head to a question one of these gray-haired guys brought up: "When is this world going to wake up?" Their concerned conversation had been circling around the observation that we live in a fearful world, faced with crisis every day. One of them remarked how the old ways of interacting with one another weren't working anymore.

With the quacking geese fading into the horizon, I pondered man's survival being threatened by ever-growing, seemingly insurmountable problems. Our species faces extinction unless we are able to rise above the limitations of our condition through an overdue evolutionary leap. A significant portion of the world's population is recognizing that humanity is now faced with the decision to either evolve or die, and many are already striving toward this change.

What is this condition we must save ourselves from, and what is the corresponding evolutionary leap?

Some years ago I was fortunate enough to view a thirteenth-century work of art that hangs in a gallery in Florence, Italy, by an artist whose name was lost centuries ago. The artwork—a tapestry showing Adam and Eve's expulsion from the garden—got me thinking. Its meaning was clear: the couple are being driven from the Garden of Eden for their disobedience of God's commands.

In the foreground of the scene are Adam and Eve. A wise old owl sits in a tree looking on, while a monkey with his tail in the air seems to be jabbering, "I told you so." Above them, in a gold-patterned robe with a hood wafting over His head in the breeze, is the figure of God. One hand seems to be firmly pushing the rebellious pair from the garden paradise, while the other hand points to a winged angel with a flaming sword, guarding the Tree of Knowledge.

The Bible relates that the Lord clothed Adam and Eve in animal skins, which the tapestry depicts. Because they violated the law for residence in the spiritual realm, God sent them forth to till the ground from which they were supposedly formed, so the story goes. Through the ages, it has been insisted upon that God guaranteed long suffering for the first humans and their unborn descendants, and we have all along been taught to believe this. Many to this day have misunderstood the nature of humanity's long-suffering by viewing it as pain and toil, rather than the mind of creation choosing to be separate from the Thought of its Creator, causing confusion about their own identity.

The story goes that Adam blamed Eve for giving him the forbidden fruit (a new identity), which they both ate (chose to separate from the Mind of God), and likewise, Eve blamed the serpent, who had a reputation for being crafty. Placing blame on someone or something is as old as the Garden of Eden. Thus the separated world began to build "outside" and continues today.

The wise old owl makes a point by raising a question that has burdened man ever since the separation. How could the two defend themselves unless they felt threatened and believed that their own defense could save them? Their guilt for making a separate identity became their reality, and they feared their new identity, which they had taken upon themselves. They didn't know what to expect. This layered fear upon fear, which caused chaos and panic.

A Course in Miracles goes deeper into the meaning of the creation story to teach us that in the creation, God extended Himself, forming our mind out of His and giving us the same loving Will to create as one with Him. No child of God can lose this ability to be creative. We are perfect and creative with our mind as part of His, where there is no emptiness or lacking. But instead we have learned to make projections—thoughts of our choosing, which are based in the fear of or belief in separation— rather than using our creativity to extend ourselves. We project an image of our body and other bodies, for example; but a projection is not an extension.

The inappropriate projection of images occurs when we believe that emptiness or lack exists in us, and that we can fill it with our own ideas instead of truth. You might think of it in this way: a projection is sent forth and is separate from us; an extension is a part of us, remains one with us.

You may view the projected image of the "Big Bang" or the violation of the "Tree of Knowledge" as the symbol for the separation, which occurred millions of years ago, but in reality was only an instant ago. Regardless, the following beliefs reflect how the mind of humanity came to separate from God's and to form projections to make up for a perceived lack. We continue these steps today, due to our fear of lacking, which maintains our illusion that we are a separate identity from that of our all-loving Creator.

- First, we believe that what God created can be changed by our own mind.
- Second, we believe that what is perfect can be rendered imperfect or lacking.
- Third, we believe that we can distort the creations of God, including ourselves.
- Fourth, we believe that we can create ourselves, and that the direction of our creation is up to us.

These related distortions represent a picture of what actually occurred in the separation, or we could call it the "detour into fear."

In the *pre-separation* nothing was needed, due to the "oneness" of all of creation. As portrayed in the tapestry, the monkey goes on to criticize Adam and Eve while following them out of the garden paradise. He sarcastically scolds them for ever considering planning for the future or organizing the present to be any better, when they already had everything they needed. The prosperity of the pre-separated mind was within and not located "out there."

Ever since, the same journey continues, as the world operates from a belief system that teaches we must protect ourselves from what surrounds us. We feel the world is threatening—that there is danger lurking, which has the power to call on us to retaliate. Consider the battle over nuclear power as proof enough of the furthering of our defense structures due to our thoughts, fears, and doubts that preclude our true essence.

What is our true essence, you may ask? We'll be discussing this at greater length later on throughout this book. But for now, let's try to understand that the first part of the mind to separate was formed as what is now called "consciousness." Our "true essence" is the part of consciousness that is aware of this split and strives to learn how to find the path back Home. Our true essence doesn't care or worry about the repercussions of the split mind, such as the many legalities and penalties, along with various moral systems and leaders who try to teach us how to live—all of which merely serves to reinforce and increase our sense of threat. Our true essence is not fearful, and therefore doesn't need or seek defense. Our true essence doesn't seek safety because it perceives its existence beyond our body. This true essence of who you are is what the *Course* calls your "right-mind" or "right-mindedness." In this state you are perceiving yourself correctly about your true reality. Any thinking you may have that is based on this "right" perception, we can call "right-minded thinking" or simply "right-mindedness." Right-minded perceptions can feed and strengthen right-minded thoughts, and vice versa.

But hold on. There's another section of the split mind that is quite the opposite, called "wrong-mindedness." Wrong-minded thinking causes continued splitting and fragmentation. Wrong-mindedness includes avoiding the unknown and feeling guilty. It makes us feel fearful and frightened because we believe in a body that is failing us; therefore, we believe in death.

The wrong-minded attempts to recover what we believe to be lacking form the illusory thought system we can call *ego*. The ego was fabricated by the conscious mind, and that is where it abides. The ego's awareness of its own fabrication is why the ego fears God. The fear of God is nonsense, because our all-loving Creator does not want to be feared, but thanks to the ego, humankind continues to suffer from this belief to this day. This will continue for millions more years to come until we reach *Atonement*. Full "at-one-ment" will mark the end of all time; we will be talking about this more a bit later.

The Garden of Eden represents a state of mind in which there was no past or future, and where nothing was needed. Time did not exist, nor did space, because nothing was physical. Adam was dreaming when he listened to the lies of the snake. But keep in mind, the conversations between Adam and the serpent occurred during the pre-separation. The Bible says that Adam fell into a deep sleep, but nowhere is there any reference to his waking up. The world as a whole continues to dream and has not yet reawakened. The separation is a dream, a fantasy of making a better identity. Awakening is impossible while we dream up our own truths, based on an idol we have called ego, which is nothing more than illusory thoughts. It's not real.

In the pre-separation, or in the part of our mind that never separated at all, is the real world where idols do not exist and therefore are not real. Yes, it's all a dream, and only an instant will have gone by when we awaken. But we must awaken slowly as long as we dream of time. This slow, nurturing awakening is the process of Atonement, the ultimate goal. This slow awakening can be compared to the experience of having a nightmare while sleeping in the dark, and a light is suddenly turned on. Initially you may think the light is part of the dream, unless you naturally slowly awaken to find out the light is real and never was of the dream.

I'm able now to see how my fears of the unknown sent me in directions where I undertook certain measures to make my own truths. I disregarded what I considered to be incompatible with the beliefs and values I had chosen, in order to achieve a reality my ego wanted. What I didn't accept is that everything happens—all events, past, present, and future—for the purpose and good of the whole One Mind. The purpose is the real world, and the events are the scripts being played out in the dream. What is the "Whole" again? The One real mind of all of creation that never really split at all. It is the Whole that does not dream, and this is what your "right mind" is able to perceive.

The whole mind, which never thought of separation, does not recognize the split.

Okay, pause to take a deep breath. Please be patient; as we move along, this will come to you in time as a revelation, which is personal and cannot be fully explained, but it can be known. Try to see that this is what time is being used for, and that the Holy Spirit uses time to get you to the path where your destination is the Atonement. You will be introduced to the Holy Spirit, or your personal Guide, in detail in a section just ahead. So for now, try to keep your thinking in a neutral mode.

Consciousness, or ego, does believe in whole, but only individual wholes—like people, nations, or races. Believe me, the ego has as many wholes as it can possibly make out of the dreaming split mind. What has been happening is that we continue to choose broken or split-off pieces of the whole to construct our defenses, putting them together to our liking to stand against other pieces of the whole, without regard to all true relationships within the universe. This insane process is the very essence of the unknown, causing chaos and distrust, and harming or killing others for their own safety. This is the destructive insanity of a split and fragmented mind that projects images of danger.

For example, take the death penalty in the United States. Many in this country believe it deters people from committing murder. This thought pattern of the ego seems to be bigger than that of the murderers themselves. So who are the real killers?

Careful studies of the deterrent effects of the death penalty were made by comparing homicide rates of two similar states with opposing laws. There was no supporting evidence of an effective deterrent. In fact, many believe that the death penalty actually increased the homicide rate, permitting some people to feel they have a right to punish others in the same way that the state does, by killing them. The studies also showed that more than 85 percent of all murders were committed in fits of rage induced by drugs and alcohol—although not one execution ever healed a drug or alcohol addiction. Nonetheless, we continue to spend endlessly on perpetuating the death penalty and little on rehabilitating addicts and alcoholics.

I have spoken to survivors of death row; some have been my friends in prison who were originally sentenced to death by electrocution. Before their execution date, the State of Ohio pulled the plug on "Old Sparky" (the electric chair), reverting to the more humane lethal injection. With "Old Sparky" outdated, legally these lives were spared now that the state no longer had an electric device to do the job. You might think these prisoners would feel relieved, but this is not the case. They all have a similar attitude. They want to be executed. They want to project their guilt onto the state.

If the death penalty doesn't work, why do voters insist on keeping it? For most, they seek the satisfaction of revenge. But "an eye for an eye and a tooth for a tooth" is not a sentiment that nice folks like to acknowledge, so they conjure up their own rationales. With this we take the sides of our leaders who will rage against drugs and crime, just to mention a few. What we fight we simply get more of.

For instance, we continue to build prisons, and the United States prison population has increased 400 percent since 1980. We declared a "War on Drugs," and more illegal drugs are being abused today than ever before in history. Millions of abortions have been performed because we decided to make it lawful to kill unborn babies. This kind of logic enormously satisfies the ego and strengthens the separation between wholeness and fragmentation of our real selves. Wholeness is obscured by the cloud cover of a false identity.

For centuries humanity has been trying to awaken, only to see killings when opinions diverged from church doctrine and its versions of truth. In reality these doctrines are all bundles of doubt, creating more ego. We have made ourselves heir to the laws that govern this world we think we so desperately need. If we continue to see ourselves as pieces of these splitting wholes, or egos, the laws of scarcity, fear, and death will rule us. But if we can see ourselves as the Thought of God and our real Home resting in an awareness beyond this world, only then can we begin to live by the universal laws that created who we truly are, which is perfect love.

We do have a choice. All of us, individually in our right-mindedness, can resolve to live each day in a new way, being spontaneous and alive with trust, trusting in who and what we are. Or we can continue to say, "Life's a bitch then we die."

What if we stopped asking for things outside of us to change, but rather for something within us to change? But first we need to understand what *within* really means. Our greatest resource for changing the world can be our capacity to change our mind about the world. Do we project images, or do we extend inspiration with love? This won't happen overnight, and for sure will take at least a few generations or so to sink in. Our true world leaders will be the ones who take us in this direction, where politics will be a thing of the past and seen as illusion.

The awakened mind is one that knows and trusts itself and its Source. We must awaken to truth, and you, who now have begun reading this book to this point, can start that evolutionary leap, along with others, by asking yourself one question: Can I sense my true essence, or am I losing myself in the world?

Chapter 10

The Ego Has Its Own Interpretation about Your Life

At times in our lives, many of us lose ourselves in the world, and we may feel as though the loss is beyond all control. But I am convinced that personal tragedy is a time for unexpected or learning, along with continued growth. It's instilled in every one of us to transform our negative or bad experiences into positive outcomes. This is our natural *right-mindedness* at work.

We have been conditioned to believe that the kinds of losses we bring on ourselves label us as failures—forever. I have seen this type of wrong-mindedness firsthand in the prison system, when in the name of rehabilitation, it teaches prisoners that they will only be suitable for certain types of jobs on the low end of the pay scale when they are released. It seems as though their own training in how to improve prisoners' ability to function in the outside world has focused on helping them get used to being treated like subhuman beings. Not only the prison system buys into this oppressive approach, but so does the general public. It's total nonsense, of course. Prisoners are not all uneducated pack animals, and you would understand this if you were one of the many who have made a mistake and went to prison yourself. But you don't have to be sent to prison to feel as though you have lost yourself and gotten onto the wrong track. Whether your loss is due to your own negligence, or Mother Nature, or politics, or anger—no matter what, it's okay. You can relax. In fact, relax is exactly what I've been doing, and I hope to help you to do the same.

Much of my own losses, including the actions that sent me to prison, were due to my making wrong-minded decisions— driven, ironically, by my belief that I knew how to make things better for myself in family, business, and personal matters. My independence, I thought, was my real strength. There seemed to be a voice of fear in my head—fear I wasn't successful enough, happy enough, important enough—that I was certain I could drown out with proclaimed positive thinking. But in fact, I was merely thinking like a separated mind from God.

I figured if I strived for a positive attitude, God would be behind me. After all, wasn't I taught that I could always count on God? I thought all I had to do was give it my best shot, backed up with some prayers, and if I made an error or an uncontrollable circumstance occurred, then God would be there to bail me out. And it seemed there were times when He indeed did bail me out, whereas other times He abandoned me. I always prayed long and hard from my heart, at least I thought so, sending out my requests to God wherever it is He resides. When there were no answers or results I'd pray even harder or make some sort of sacrifice. With the determination I inherited, the words "giving up" were not in my vocabulary.

When my prayers were not answered I would feel guilty, and fearful, insecure thoughts would fester. "What have I done wrong? God, please show me," I would ask again and again through more prayer. In my business I would call this type of repetition "beating a dead horse."

A motivational book, cassette tape, or CD would temporarily set me into a mode of positive outlook, and I'd start to see a brighter future. But really I was only ensuring that the future would be just like the past.

These cycles would repeat throughout the years, becoming a vicious circle with ever-mounting frustration. I went from negative to positive, and positive back to negative. Each time I'd work hard to find a more permanent positive strength. Around and around, like a merry-go-round, I went, only to become dizzy and exhausted and even more frustrated and frightened. However, since then I have discovered how to learn to get from "no-where" to "now-here."

From now-here, it's time to discuss what I have been learning about the promises of the ego that never seem to come true. We will look at where the ego abides and how it survives. The ego is not the devil, because there is no devil and there is no hell. The ego is nothing but illusion, and so is the evil it tries to scare us with. If having nothing or being nothing sounds exciting to you, then you are trusting in the thought system that will lead you to the land of false hope. For in this nothing or "no-thing" thought system, the ego's judgments promise you will have everything you think you want.

You will discover that the Holy Spirit reverses any judgments made by the ego. This is so, much as a higher court has the power to reverse a lower court's decision. I will discuss this without being religious. *God's Holy Spirit* is what I call my personal advisor or guide, and He is of the Mind of God, just as we are also of this One Mind. The Holy Spirit is installed into all our minds much like a helpful antivirus device in your computer. You can call your inner guide Oscar, or Alice, or whatever you'd like. Because of my upbringing I know what's appropriate for me, and I feel comfortable using the name "Holy Spirit." But keep in mind that religions hold no special copyright or exclusive rights to this terminology.

Later on we will discuss in depth how and why the Holy Spirit is our Protector, Comforter, and Healer. But for now, I will tell you that the Holy Spirit will do anything for you, and will undo any problems caused by the ego, which also appears to be in you. The ego's distorted thinking believes that to "undo" means to destroy. This is not the case, and you will be seeing the difference.

Nothing we perceive through the ego is interpreted correctly. Our ego-driven decisions are always wrong, because they are based on errors that we will fight to defend. The ego works diligently to maintain our guilt and fear, now and for generations to follow. Why? Because, lacking awareness, our fear guarantees our allegiance to the ego.

I could give many examples of how the ego's interpretations are misleading, intended to keep us in a fearful mode, which offers us the illusion of control. For those raised in a Christian tradition, not only does the ego cite the Bible for its own benefit—for example, making and keeping you fearful and guilty—but it even interprets Scripture as a witness for its pursuit of its superiority. Here are just a few examples I'll share with you, and also how the Holy Spirit *reinterprets* these passages in His Own Light, which is your true Light:

> "I will visit the sins of the fathers unto the third and fourth generation" (Exodus 34:7). The ego's way of interpreting this passage is particularly vicious—a clear attempt to guarantee the ego's survival for generations to come. However, to the Holy Spirit this statement of Scripture means that in later generations He can still reinterpret what former generations misunderstood, and thus release the thoughts from our ability to produce fear. Let me ask you, doesn't the Holy Spirit's interpretation make you feel more *comfortable*?

> "Vengeance is mine, sayeth the Lord" (Romans 12:19). Here's another scare tactic the ego uses in its interpretation of Scripture in an attempt to keep us feeling guilty and fearful. The ego implies God will punish us or will punish our enemies. But God does not seek vengeance against His own beloved Creation. That would be like God seeking vengeance against Himself. Remember the beginning of this verse reads: "Dearly beloved, avenge not yourselves; but rather give place unto wrath." The Holy Spirit in you knows this passage to mean that you must give up the vengeance you feel to the Holy Spirit, who will undo it in you, because it does not belong in your mind, which is part

of God. Now I ask you, doesn't this interpretation give you a sense of being *healed*?

Gradually over time, the ego's interpretations have instilled themselves in us, making us feel fearful toward our Creator. However, the Holy Spirit is always the part of you that will cause you to feel truly *protected*. Before we move on, please try to answer this question honestly with yourself: If you were able to have no fear of death, what do you think you might see?

Chapter 11

The Ego's Use of Guilt to Make You Fearful

Earlier we discussed the ways the ego ensures that history repeats itself. This includes our ongoing "fear of God," as well as the concept of the return of Christ. Of all the different teachings of the "second coming of Christ," many wish to believe that a human being called Christ will appear with a sword in a suit of armor, brandishing a sword, slashing the bad, and taking the righteous into His arms. Whoever decided what being righteous really entails? What is it we must do to be considered righteous?

I'm sure you have questions about this. But sometimes the very process of questioning can leave us feeling a bit guilty for not buying into the ego's tricks to keep us fearful. After all, we were taught what is "good and righteous" by our elders and clergy, who presumably want a peaceful world. Were they tricked as well? If you do feel guilty for going against the grain of what generations have passed down to us, don't think about it too much, but do accept that it is there. Acknowledge this guilt much as you would an ingrown toenail, by just being aware of it, and move on. Moving on doesn't mean the guilt will not follow you, because it surely will. So simply accept that too. We're going to talk later about these illusions that cause us to harbor guilt.

Allow me to take you back to my years as a financial advisor, when I would often host lectures and workshops for groups of people who were seeking investment strategies for their retirement. This was an ideal way for me to drum up new business, and I would invite existing clients, asking them to bring a few guests. A nice dinner was always provided. Often I would be asked questions, and I would welcome comments from the group about their money worries or their investment successes.

I would usually start off by asking if anyone had a story they would like to share about their money.

One evening a man about age seventy, who always insisted I call him "Pops," raised his hand to speak. Pops was already a client of mine and feared he would outlive his nest egg, as did most who attended this particular lecture. I thought that Pops's flamboyant style—white haired, well manicured, always nattily dressed with a bow tie—would send some humor into the air and loosen things up a bit, so I told him to continue.

Pops began to tell us all about his love for gambling and that this passion was funding his nest egg without any risk. He wanted to share his methods for always beating the slot machines. This intrigued me, as well as the audience, since as the "expert," I was advising people on how to manage a profitable, but safe, investment portfolio.

Pops went on to tell us that he and his wife, Velda, had just returned from Lake Tahoe on one of their scheduled quarterly trips, which were always to somewhere exotic. He explained the "system" he had developed for winning on the slot machines. Through his careful observation of them over the course of many years, he had learned how many unsuccessful pulls it would take on average to get a successful pull of the lever. This calculation would depend on the type of machine and other varying factors.

Pops would observe a frustrated gambler who was ready to quit—sometimes many at once in the area of the casino he was studying—and calculated where a machine would be on his scale of likelihood for a money-making pull. When the timing was right, Pops would take over the machine, and within a few pulls the bells would be ringing. By his acute perception of the frustration in the minds of other gamblers, Pops was able to prevail. What intrigued me the most was his adamant claim that his success was due to his observing the frustrated mind, rather than the individuals themselves.

Additionally, Pops had a system with his winnings. He would immediately put one-third aside and made arrangements to send it home in the form of a cashier's check. He would have several checks waiting in his mailbox when he and Velda returned from their trips. While still away, Pops would use the balance to reinvest into his business at hand: ruling over the slots. His story pleased me, because now I could see how his portfolio, which I handled, was being nourished. He said he always made sure there was enough left over for him and Velda to fly first class and stay at first-class hotels. Pops, in more ways than this, is a first-class friend of mine.

Velda always accompanied her husband of fifty years on these trips, but she did not gamble at all. In fact, she would not ever set foot into a casino because of her beliefs, passed down to her, that gambling was "not of the Lord." This was fine with Pops, and he respected his wife's decision not to be involved. Velda enjoyed herself at the pool and spa, or she found a quiet place to read and simply soak up the beauty of the hotel. She always seemed to make a new friend and found plenty to do while Pops was hard at work. After Pops concluded his business for the day, the couple would enjoy a nice dinner, maybe some dancing, and simply enjoy their time together. Pops said it was always a good trip for both of them.

During the questioning at the lecture, Velda revealed that the real reason she would not step into a casino, even just to watch her husband in action, was that she feared God would see her in a house of sin. Her family had preached against it for generations, and I'm sure for their own good reasons. After all, Velda is a lovely woman. But she added that she also worried that if it were time for Christ to return, she could not bear the thought that he may find her in a casino. This was Velda's way of being ready.

Fear, brought on by guilt, has been imbued in us for generations. *A Course in Miracles* does not try to replace our religious beliefs, nor does it promote (or condemn) gambling. The goal of the *Course* is merely to help us in a psychological way to develop inner peace through forgiveness. This is why the *Course*, as well as my book, wants you to understand how the ego in all of us works. The illusory ego is a part of our split mind, as long as we remain in this dream of time and bodies and a separated mind. We will talk more later about the dream and healing the split mind.

Chapter 12

Undoing Your Sense of Separation

The ego works hard to reinforce your fear, because only the fearful can be egotistical. The ego's logic is amazing. It knows that our mind has the means to end the dream by healing the split mind, ending the separation that by definition ends the ego. We are conditioned to believe that our only way to gaining peace is through the ego, and the ego understands this. Self-reinforcing, it encourages us to maintain our beliefs. It is terribly afraid of change, because it thinks change threatens peace.

The ego tells us that here, on Earth, we can find a way to stop our losses and end unhappiness and loneliness, that without the ego we can never gain. We get thrown into that vicious negative-to-positive-to-negative spiral I talked about earlier.

The *Course* teaches us that "anything that causes fear obeys the laws of division and separation." This is the root of guilt. However, our true Home, or heaven, has no root. The *Course* goes on to teach us, "We cannot ask the Holy Spirit to dissolve our fear, because fear does not exist." But we can ask Him to release us from the illusion of fear.

A Course in Miracles was written as though Jesus is speaking to us through the author. But in no way is the *Course* a worship of Jesus, but merely a lesson from him. He tells us that if he intervened between our thoughts, such as fear and the results of fear, he would be tampering with a basic law of "cause and effect." His lesson, or *A Course* if you will, does not want to denigrate the power of our thinking. But the *Course* does want us to look at our errors as lessons, whereby we can come closer to understanding true cause and effect. There is no such thing as a "bad experience," but rather an opportunity to be ready for the next step.

With cause and effect, simply try to remember that "Cause" is God, and "effect" is His creations. The rain shower can be seen as "Cause" and the blooming daffodils its effects, in this sense. However ... with a different scenario, could we possibly say the daffodils might be "Cause?" Cause never stops extending and is infinite. Given that, can we ourselves also be considered "Cause?"

Of course we can, because we are all of the One Mind that extends itself. We are, all of us together as a whole, the "One Begotten Son" that God so loves. The Bible has tried to communicate this to us, but because of ego interpretations the focus has always been on a physical body. An individual body is all the ego knows.

The *Course* calls God's only son—the collective humankind—the "Sonship."

Jesus, in contrast, tells us to look up to him as our "elder brother" and respect should be given to an elder brother who looks out for all of his younger siblings. Jesus, the man who walked this earth, did experience for our benefit the dream of time and separation, and he had the knowledge of this through the Christ Mind that is in each one of us. But let's not confuse Jesus, the man, with Christ, even though he has been called by many "Jesus Christ." The Christ Mind is the Oneness of all minds together, including that of Jesus, our older brother, who no longer dreams of separation, but is with us in spirit. God created the Christ Mind from His Mind; therefore, each of us is of Christ.

When Jesus entered the dream and walked this earth, he was aware of his own body and lived in right-minded perception always. But while perceiving from his right-mind, he was also living among us in the Christ Mind, which is the awakened or non-separated. He was able to see both sides, or both worlds.

The Holy Spirit is the Spirit of God, which watches over the entire process of the Christ Mind and the wholeness that the Sonship entails.

The slow awakening process is the Atonement, or "At-one-ment," and Jesus—his awakened self, who no longer dreams—is in charge of the Atonement process. For visual purposes, we can imagine an interlocking chain of minds with Jesus as the first link. He maintains the end position in case we fail and must start over, which is what has been happening since the resurrection. The resurrection began the process of Atonement, and it will continue until its completion.

You may or may not be a bit confused by now. But in either event, please do not try to get hung up on dissecting the words, such as Christ, Jesus, Oneness, dream, separation, or any others that try to push their previously learned meaning on you. Rather, simply read on and allow the new meanings to sink in gradually and be absorbed like a sponge. Try not to allow your past meaning for these words to take charge. As you move along, the meaning of the words will unfold as intended for you and will be further revealed in how your awareness reflects them.

Jesus was not born into this world to save us from sin, because there is no sin to the unseparated mind; and how can someone who dreams sin? Rather, Jesus was born into this world, or entered the dream, to witness for himself. Having the Christ Mind, he was both of the dream and not of the dream while his body walked this land. His goal was then, and still is, to bring all our minds together within this interlocking chain, and this is the reason for time. Full Atonement will mark the end of time, as well as the end of the dream.

We cannot be led to the Atonement as long as we live with wrong-minded perception and thoughts, which bring on illusion such as the ego and its antics. Jesus, as our elder brother, is leading us to welcome the Holy Spirit who abides in our right-mind. The Holy Spirit's function is to undo all our errors and free us from illusion. He is here in our separated mind, guiding us to right-minded thoughts. We will touch on this more in an upcoming section. For now, try to keep in mind that the undoing of errors is an essential key to unlocking right-mindedness.

Cause and effect play a vital role in assisting the Atonement process and are why you are reading this book at this particular time. I can also tell you that most likely I would never have written such a book had I not gone to prison. At this time in your life, you may or may not be ready for its content or wish to go further after this experience. But either way, you were led here and something will result.

There have been times in my life, however brief, when I felt an amazing presence urging me toward my destiny. I can see now, as you may have as well, times a voice, or sensation, or a feeling tried to show me a direction. Once again, don't think too hard about this right now, but simply absorb it; otherwise, the ego will surely try to intrude by telling you how crazy you are or how crazy I am. (Remember, the ego likes to point the finger.)

There is a lesson in the workbook for students of the *Course*, which I revert to often. It teaches me where I am at now and keeps me planted and instills in me my purpose. It is Lesson Number 224, and I'd like to share a portion of it with you:

> My true identity is so secure, so lofty, sinless, glorious and great, wholly beneficent and free from guilt, that Heaven looks to It to give it light. It lights the world as well. It is the gift my Father gave me; the one as well I give the world. There is no gift but *This* that can be either given or received. This is reality, and only *This*. This is illusion's end. It is the *Truth*.

The Atonement, or to Atone, means to "undo" the separation by this chain of forgiveness in our minds. Remember, we said to forgive is to "look beyond." That connection you feel at times, even if only for an instant, is your thought interlocking with the chain of oneness. It is your pure thought. This connection strengthens in time, making instants turn into moments and moments into longer periods, and as you welcome spiritual vision, it strengthens the links. What is spiritual vision, you may ask? It is the part of you that can look within and understand that all that your physical body seeks will inevitably dissolve. But let me warn you, the ego is fearful of the word "inevitable."

Spiritual vision is the awareness within you that realizes the ego in you tries to hold you back from seeing and learning what is beyond your perception. Spiritual vision is simply your realization that sometimes you do have small glimpses of the "real you" that is behind your body. The Atonement cannot occur without your spiritual vision.

Pain and loss can also lead to spiritual vision, where a loss is found to be not a loss at all, and the pain is seen as "not really painful at all" when you understand that an unseparated mind cannot feel or have pain. This leads me to a brief story an old friend passed on to me a long time ago.

One of the great Zen masters of old, named Gutei, made a habit of extending his index finger whenever a disciple asked him a question about Zen. A time came when a young follower took to imitating Gutei. When the Master extended his finger to silently respond to a student, it meant the student was ready for realization or awakening. Behind Gutei's back the young disciple jokingly extended his index finger. This caused the other disciples to start laughing.

In time, however, Gutei caught his mimic. Without a word the Master took out a knife, gripped the young disciple's hand, cut off his index finger, and threw it away. The maimed pupil went off howling in pain.

"Halt!" Gutei shouted to him, and he extended his finger. Without realizing it was no longer part of his body, the disciple extended his finger as well. Then, suddenly, a beatific smile spread across his tear-stained face. The disciple was ready.

Jesus tells us through *A Course in Miracles* that "A sense of separation from God is the only lack you really need to correct."

Of course, we are not going to sacrifice our finger, or injure our body, in order to have spiritual vision. But the very fact that you are aware, that you are sensing more and more that you are beyond your body, proves that you are ready.

Part IV

The Oneness of Having and Being

Chapter 13

A Sense of Who You Are

For the remainder of this book you may notice I repeat myself, using certain words, ideas, and meanings, and even revealing the same message as before, but with a different circumstance or example. This is necessary in order for you to absorb the real message, unaltered by the ego, which it will do at any given chance. So let me start this section off by asking you a couple of questions, and as I ask simply notice your initial response. Do not criticize, just notice how you respond.

How far back in your life can you remember? Are there a few brief moments from your adolescence that now seem like a dream? Would you dare to go back even further—perhaps before your birth as a body into this world?

I'll bet that by now the ego has jumped in as a voice in your head, saying: "What are you talking about? Before my birth? This is impossible!"

The ego in you continues to say to you, in more ways than one, that it could not possibly have existed before your physical birth here on Earth. The ego is correct for a change, because *it did not* exist before your birth. But you did! All the ego knows is the body, and it will not allow you to go back any further. Your belief in the body is so strong that your ego has built a solid concrete wall in front of your mind. Any thinking you do inside your mind about your existence prior to your birth just pounds at the wall like a dull jackhammer and gets nowhere. You cannot go through it by *thinking*, but you can go around it by *sensing*.

The real you that extends beyond your flesh and bones cannot be realized by thinking about it, because thinking is always rudely interrupted by the ego. The ego survives on its incessant thinking. When you think about your past, you are thinking about your body, and your body only goes back so far. The past is an illusion that doesn't exist, and so is your projected image, which is only a part of your physical vision.

However, when you are able to "sense" what you are, time and projections—such as your past—mean nothing and are of no concern. Therefore, what you are is what you have always been. In this "sense" I ask you, What is it you have always been? The *Course* answers this for us by teaching us that "You are the Will of God. Do not accept anything else as your will, or you are denying what you are."

As soon as you start chuckling to yourself and thinking how foolish this all sounds, the ego in you has begun to chatter in your mind, which means you are thinking too hard about this question, rather than merely "sensing" who you are. Surely you will hear the ego as you think, but your own *sense* of who you are does not have to listen. You choose to believe what you want. The ego believes what it wants until its death, which is its end. The ego knows this, which is why it tries so desperately to hang on to you.

Here is another question for you to think about, or let me say "sense" about: When you experience the fragrance of a beautiful flower, do you initially think about its fragrance, or does it first hit you as a "sensation" that is wonderful? Of course you sense it first; then thinking sets in to tell you it is a flower, because in your past somebody taught you about a flower.

This is why in an earlier section I asked you not to think too much about my words. Now I am asking you to simply use the words in front of you much like you would a highway sign while traveling, and allow your unique "sense" to continue the journey. If you stopped the car and took the time to read and think about each highway sign while driving, you might never get to your destination. There is no name for your unique *sense*, other than "you." The ego cannot name it, because the ego has no *sensing* capacity. Therefore, it doesn't know your real mind nor your true Source.

By allowing your thinking to subside from time to time, by quieting your mind, you can begin to have glimpses of the Truth about you or the connection to your Source. We will discuss this more soon, but for now try to understand that these glimpses will strengthen, and once they are no longer considered to be just isolated glimpses, new fresh glimpses will come to you, and so on and so on. These glimpses are in your real Mind, with no ego involvement. For example, in his book *A New Earth*, Eckhart Tolle writes about a flowering consciousness, which sent me dreaming. Or was I really dreaming?

What I mean is, let me share with you a glimpse I had in my real Mind—a sense of that day some 233 million years ago, at sunrise, when the first flower to ever appear on Earth opened to receive the rays of the sun. (Note: Your ego has most likely interrupted you already. "Come on, millions of years ago? What's he trying to do here?" But once again, just acknowledge its interruption without buying into it and move on.)

Prior to this momentous event, which brought about an evolutionary transformation in the life of plants, the planet had already been covered with vegetation for millions of years. I remember my impression that that first flower did not survive long, but it gave hope to the few more flowers following, which remained rare, since conditions of the ground were not yet favorable for widespread flowering to occur. Later, though, on another sunny day, the ground, now fertile, suddenly gave way to an explosion of color and fragrance all over the land. This critical threshold was reached in plant life everywhere. I saw this clearly, though at the time I thought I was dreaming.

At this time, thoughts were spreading from the Oneness of the Loving Thought that sustained everything. Back then, a sensation caused us to call this Thought our Mind, and to call this wholeness of Being, or this "Oneness," God. We did not yet have, before the split, any awareness of having a body. Therefore, the statement "God created man in His own Image and Likeness" did not mean an image of flesh and bones, as the ego wishes to read from Scripture. It needs to be understood that "Image" is "thought" and "Likeness" means "of a like quality." God surely created spirit in His own Thought and of a like quality to His own. There can be nothing else. God extends his One Thought, or Divine Universal Law; this is creation.

Even before humankind was embodied, during this time of flowering, our thoughts as a whole started splitting away and were no longer whole. But these separating thoughts that began occurring were not real thought at all. They were born of a daze, a dream of sorts, that we were separate and that separate wholes had formed. In this dream, flowering was taking place everywhere. The dream was becoming deeper, and more thought continued to dream. It started fragmenting and splitting away from Oneness. These fragmented pieces of thought, or separate dreams, believed they could individually imagine a bigger and better thought, or a paradise, if you will. Of course, the Real Wholeness never really did split at all, and it watches on as the fragments continue their dream.

As the dream deepened even more, the peace of mind, or paradise, we once had seemed to be gone—although, despite having been dazed, a part of the split mind called the right-mind began sensing that it was rooted to a place beyond the dream. It felt as though it needed to wake up. It started resisting any further fragmentation.

Aware of the right-mind's resistance, the wishful splitting aspect called *ego* began to pursue "this" and "that" and continues to this day to believe it can convince the right-mind that it has a better way. The ego tells us that all we have to do in order to gain "that" is to sacrifice "this" and that we must do it in a hurry because "life is short, then you die." The ego's motto is "Somebody must lose in order for somebody else to gain." The more we pressed on in the dream to gain "things," the more lonely and fearful we continued to feel.

By this time the ego was more independent and separated, but lacked identification. It started to dream even deeper and started projecting an image of what it thought it looked like. It formed an identity. As its identity of a body developed, along with its continual splitting mind, flowers were the first thing we came to value that served no survival purpose. The awesomeness of the flower struck a chord. With our right-mind sensing the beauty of these flowers, it found a way to silence the ego, however briefly, giving us pure joy. That joy is a glimpse of our Source, or our real Home.

This type of an awakened moment, or feelings of joy and love, is our "sense" of connectedness to our real Mind, or God. This is your spirituality. As soon as our ego sees this, it gets afraid and pulls back to its identification with the body. This is why you choose to think about the believability of what I'm trying to get across to you.

Without one fully realizing it, the fragrance from a flower can be like a bridge between the world of form and the formless that allows us to *sense* the formless truth. That delicate fragrance we can say is spirit in itself. However, you will never convince the ego of this.

If we used the word "Heaven," or "Kingdom" in a wider sense than the traditionally accepted one given to us by religions, we could look upon flowers and nature in general, with its ethereal quality, as the "kingdom" of pure life. When we can sense this formless essence it becomes holiness, and it doesn't require statues, or beads, or special oils and waters, accompanied by a formal procession, ceremony, or ritual.

So when you are alert and experience the beauty of a flower, or other breathless experiences of nature, without naming them mentally, it becomes, however briefly, the Light beginning to radiate your formless self into the realm of your own spirituality. You can learn to radiate and shine into others, where it will not be your own, but will be shared as one Light.

The Love of God, for yet a little while, must still be expressed through one body to another, because right-minded vision is still so dim. You can use your body best to help yourself brighten your own perception so you can achieve real vision, of which the physical eye is incapable. Perception is not to be confused with knowledge, however; knowledge is where fear and loneliness do not exist. Knowledge abides forever just beyond your right mind. This is where I'm going to take you now.

Chapter 14

Allow for Hope and See the Light

Have you ever observed the numbers of colors that are in the rainbow? How about the types of wildflowers in a meadow, where you left room for question in your perception? From perception to knowledge, two distinct thought systems arise that are totally opposite: the real and the unreal.

In the realm of knowledge, no real thoughts exist apart from our Creator, because God and His creations share one Will.

The world of perception, however, is made by the belief in opposites and individual wills in constant conflict with one another and God, which became the separation. You might perceive seven colors in the rainbow, whereas I might perceive only five. We might both be ready to defend our perceptions as the only reality. What our perception sees and hears is projected into our awareness in a way that conforms with our wishes and beliefs. This leads to a world of illusions, a world that needs constant defense precisely because it is unreal. Our separated mind of different perceptions has been caught up in the world of multiple points of view. Thus, we're caught in a dream we can't escape without help. Everything we see witnesses to the reality of the dream.

God has provided the answer, and the only way out is through the true helper. It is the function of His voice, which is the Holy Spirit, who will reverse our thinking and help us to unlearn our mistakes. This process of "undoing" errors will help us to escape the dream and reawaken back to the unseparated world where we safely rest. We have not really left our Home. But out wrong-minded perception, which is our ego, holds us in the dream with defensive thoughts.

This always brings on anger and attack in some form as the result. Even a perceived defensive thought can be harmful. Any anger we incur involves our projection of being a separate mind from that of God's. This makes us fearful and is why we have attack-type thoughts.

It is important that we trust the power of our real Mind, or pre-separated Mind, in order that we may see the problems in our life as unreal. We use the concept of the Trinity for better understanding of the One Mind, because of our perception of time and space.

The Trinity portrays the One Mind of all creation in a symbolic, vertical configuration. At the top of the triangle is God, the Creator. Below God is the whole Son, or Sonship, led by the mind of Jesus, our elder brother. The Bible states, "For God so loved the world He gave His only begotten Son, that whosoever believes in Him should not perish but have everlasting life." Even under the roof of religions, the ego interprets this to support its fear tactics. But the Holy Spirit through our right-minded thinking reinterprets this for us to mean, "God has only one Son, and if all of humankind are His children, every one of them must be an integral part of the whole Sonship." This takes "flesh and bones" out of it. We are God's only begotten Son (or daughter).

Additionally of this One Mind is the Holy Spirit, to whom Jesus, as our elder brother, leads us for communication, healing, and guidance. This comfortable guidance is necessary so that we can sense God's Will for us, which is our own true free will. The ego, again, tries to frighten us by interpreting another Scripture as "All are called but few are chosen." But the Holy Spirit reinterprets this and redirects our protected thinking to the meaning "All are called but few have listened." The Holy Spirit in us is our healing power, which reverses all illusory thoughts of the ego by abiding in our right-mind, the step below the One-mindedness that Jesus achieved. When this happens within us, the ego will be completely obliterated.

In the creation God extended His Thought, called the "Christ Mind," which is the only real thought there ever has been and will ever be. Jesus, the man, came to experience this Truth of mind, and leads all his siblings, or the entire Sonship, to the same knowledge and full awakening from the dream. Keep in mind the word "son" as used here is not physical; nor are the words "brothers," "sisters," or "daughters" in this context. When I write of the *Son*ship, or Jesus' *brothers*, I use the words to mean all of us, as one. The completion of this interlocking chain of minds will be full Atonement, an event also known as the "Second Coming of Christ." In relation to time this will take place in millions of years, or, in reality, only an instant away in the dream, just as the separation was that long ago. All time, in reality, can only be comparable to an instant. Even while we are here, time doesn't have any meaning to us, other than for communication purposes between our bodies.

Regardless, you won't have to wait to experience the wholeness of right-minded vision, the first step before you can start approaching the One-mindedness of Christ. All aspects of the One Thought that may be necessary for this process are communicated through our bodies individually by the Holy Spirit, as well as into our minds. I sense this process to be much like the way, years ago, I would whisper loving thoughts into the ear of my once-little girl while she slept, and she would smile because her mind realized the presence of my loving gesture even while she dreamed. Now that she is grown and teaching school, she in turn extends herself by sharing her experiences.

The Holy Spirit uses the universal law of *cause and effect*, which requires the use of time, to help in the awakening, or healing, process. Awakening and healing are the same, as our split mind shifts back to oneness. Cause and effect is what makes events occur. Total healing of the split-mind, transforming us to right-mindedness, is the Holy Spirit's goal on this level; ultimately His goal is One-mindedness with Christ.

Likewise, Jesus, who experienced full healing for our benefit early on, leads us by example and watches over the atonement process. Thus, the Trinity concept serves as our Light that radiates confidence within us to face the darkness in our lives, making adversity work for us, rather than against us.

Another way of looking at the "dream of separation" is to consider a small part of the whole Christ Mind nodding off into a daydream of sorts, where the dream leads us to perceive that we have a separate will from that of God's Will. In comparison to time, this whole dream of the whole of humanity occurs in about an instant. Consider how often you have said to yourself, and to others as we are growing older, "The past seems like a dream that happened in a flash."

Wrong-minded perception, which is the part of consciousness where the ego abides, leads to the adversity we live by. It brings on attack thoughts based on how we see the world. We then project anger and perceive hostility coming at us from a world we fear is about to strike us at any time. We perceive our own attack as self-defense, thus joining the way of the world in an increasingly vicious circle. Our only way out is to change our mind about the world. Otherwise, thoughts of attack and counterattack preoccupy our thinking, as well as the thinking of much of the world. This process must be reversed, and this is why the Holy Spirit is a part of all our minds.

This savageness of the world sparks a part in the "dreamer's" mind to naturally want to wake up, which is the result of cause and effect. This is not a joyous feeling much of the time, but, even briefly, surely you have often realized that escaping this madness is inevitable. Once again, when the word "inevitable" sinks in, the ego becomes frantic in telling you something like "World peace is impossible." Does this sound familiar?

If so, take a look at the world you see, and realize that everything is one day going to perish; nothing will last. You may also have noticed that something has forever been "whispering" into your "dreaming" mind, lovingly telling you that "You really do know this is not the world you want."

If you simply go ahead and accept a bad situation for what it is, this will allow for hope, seen as light. From that point belief in growth will embed itself in you, becoming knowledge. You will "know" your growth because you will see it happening. Your hope will be known as real. With time, you will begin to see opportunities that open up and lead you away from loss. Then, all of this will only be an instant of your past. This is why it is so important that you go ahead and live your true free will. This is where your joy is and certainly your freedom as well.

Chapter 15

Truth Is Our Choice

Freedom can never be gained, because you always have it. But it can be impossible for you to perceive this if you see your body as all there is in being yourself. Your body is full of limits. If you look for freedom in a body, you are looking for it where it does not exist. The mind can be made free when it no longer identifies itself as a body, firmly tied to it and sheltered as though the body is the master. But identified with the body, we feel vulnerable to outside influences that dictate and try to rule us, leaving us feeling afraid to act without approval.

Expecting more pain and fear in our lives will only allow the ego to take advantage of us by placing blame and becoming defensive. The ego's help will only keep us in the vicious circle we talked about earlier, taking us on the ride of "around and around" as we try to figure out where to get off the insane roller coaster. This keeps us always turning to the ego for peace and security, as though we're constantly asking, "When am I going to find it?" The more we depend on the ego in this way, the more fearful we get.

The *Course* teaches us that "the abilities we now possess are only shadows of our real strength. All of our present functions we make divided and open to question and doubt." If we don't realize our present abilities, such as our right-mindedness, we simply will not advance in anything we pursue. We must realize the opportunities we have in all areas of our lives, or at least realize the step we're on now at this moment before we can move up to our real potential.

The experience of prison has been a reality beyond anything I have ever known before. For me it required learning a new way of merely *being*; that is, who I really am in a violent environment. Many times, especially in the beginning, I would feel myself on the edge of panic, trying in my mind to squeeze myself past the steel bars. Screeching and screaming often echoed all around me as I continued scolding myself. My own fearful muttering would sound as desperate as I felt.

There came a point when I learned to get a grip on myself and quiet my mind and maintain a serene state of being. I became like a zombie much of the time. My mind started turning inward. There was a definite force building inside me that was telling me, "Don't give up." Then my own voice would respond by saying to myself, "I can't give up; I have no other place to go." A strength was building inside me like nothing I had ever surrendered to before. As I look back I am convinced it was the Holy Spirit, opening my eyes to a gift I've always had. About the best way I can explain this is to say that my inner journey felt as though I had discovered a wisdom. I continue to learn from it. It is a power that was new to me, and this wisdom seems as if it is finally free to be itself. Only my true self can tap into it, and the wisdom itself is called Truth. This wisdom is very simple, and it tells me that anything not of Truth is not real, and therefore, must be illusory, made by the ego. Many times "strength" is thought to be built on these illusions and fears, but quite the opposite is true.

It didn't take me long to look fear square in the face when I realized that Belmont Prison's reputation for being a "Gladiator School" was no joke. Everywhere I looked seemed to be kids, young men barely out of high school, and many who had never attended high school, let alone graduated. These young "gangsters"—literally, members of gangs—stood out and ruled the place.

I stood out as well, and the few men of my age bracket were often called "Pops" or "Old School" or just plain "School" for short. At this particular prison the age of fifty was surely "old school" and this "Pops" age bracket was definitely a minority.

But there were no senior privileges; everyone and everything was fair game. The racial mix was 70 percent black and 30 percent white and Hispanic. This set the stage for the gang warfare that was fought daily. Gangs were of a fraternal order that populate prisons all over the country.

The unwritten rule at Belmont was that you fell into one of three categories. First were those who either owned or had under their chain of command other, weaker inmates who had to earn their way to their level or beyond. Second were those fighting their way up the ranks and were considered owned or ruled by another. Lastly, if neither of these appealed to you, your only option was that of an independent status. This option was called "traveling alone" or being solo, with no protection other than your own "solo" way of dealing with problems.

The inmates like myself, who traveled solo and wanted no part in gang activity, gradually became aware of one another. One would be able to notice fellow independents who just wanted to be left alone. It would take some time to prove your devoted independent status by "not giving in" to the gangs and their enticement tactics. Many independents looked out for one another in certain ways and warned others of trouble ahead. An independent has few, if any, friends, and you are cautious in trusting anyone.

Each gang basically has its own gladiators who have many responsibilities, and one of those tasks might be to drag an independent into action somehow. This is usually some kind of recruitment measure or threat, to give you a sense of the importance of having protection. Only after a few to several bumps and bruises, if you're lucky, and your own voice being heard strongly enough, does the message get out that you are a waste of their time. This pertains only to a certain degree, but a livable one. However, you are never totally out of the game. They always seem to test you when you least expect it.

On a bitter cold morning just after breakfast, when I least expected having a problem, a show of illusory strength was displayed against me while I was walking the prison yard. A blow to the back of my head by a young gladiator slammed me straight to the ground. I didn't know what hit me. The next thing I remember is sitting on a gurney at the infirmary, having a blood-spattered gash stitched up.

After sixteen stitches and a bandaged head, I found myself in segregation, also known as "the hole." I would spend eleven days in the hole, wondering, *What the hell happened?* while an investigation was launched. This was routine and basically was meant to determine which gang I was tied to, if any. It was discovered that a young "wannabe" gladiator seeking membership into a well-known gang had used me as his prey for initiation. The gangs call this "earning your bones" for its new members.

My thoughts dwelled on the cowardly action of the new gladiator. Unfortunately, much of the world understands strength as being outwardly physically powerful or forceful. But when we have inner strength, we live from truth. In any situation we have a choice to act from a position of truth or falsehood. If we choose truth, our true essence will be revealed, and our decisions are made from our right-mind. Our thinking will sprout from this. We will also see any obstacles from a right-minded point of view.

During those eleven days in the hole, only a few weeks prior to my stumbling into *A Course in Miracles*, I felt as though a part of me was watching over my thoughts. I had experienced this "watching-over" of my feelings and thoughts and decisions, even in my childhood. But now, in prison, and in the hole, I was trying to find my way through my frustration and took this observer of my thoughts deeper. There were no books, magazines, radio, not even a Bible. The hole had a thin foam mattress on the concrete floor, a toilet in the corner, and a solid steel door with a slot near the bottom for a food tray to slide through. Believe me when I say that this type of dark confinement can bring much that has been held inside to the surface.

My inward thoughts focused on a world that invents terms and procedures it wishes to be true, usually for the sake of some form of gain—a world that believes it can create its own truths built on its own judgments. I found that if someone convinces me I am untruthful, be it morally or otherwise, he has denied me of my own truth. This, then, has me living according to his judgment of the way the world is to be. Still in shock at the mere fact of being in prison, I also recognized my own illusions that led me to make decisions for material gain, and I rued the harm this had caused me to cause others.

On day six in the hole, I heard the sounds of chains dragging along the concrete floor in the hallway outside my cell. The steel door to the cell next to me clanged open. I heard the chains being unlocked around the ankles of another inmate, as the guard directed him to enter the cell. After a few hours my new neighbor was shouting through his food slot to find company in me. I responded to his call. His name was Steve, a white man of forty-seven, and like me a victim to a gladiator "earning his bones." He'd been stabbed in the thigh with a shank by a young black man, he went on to tell me. He had just returned from an outside hospital and would remain in the hole while the investigation was performed.

Steve and I made some casual conversation through the food slot as he told me about his six-year prison term for burglary. He had only ten months remaining and would go back to his job as an automobile mechanic. Steve was helpful to me regarding what I should expect from gang activity, as he was aware that I was just beginning my ten-year term. That fact in itself was constantly haunting me, as was my concern about surviving the decade stretching before me, with an ever-renewing population of angry young gladiators with something to prove. Therefore, I eagerly digested his information with an eye toward my own survival.

On day seven in the hole, the horror continued. I heard an outpouring of enraged shouts, along with the sounds of chains, as yet another inmate was dragged to the hole and thrown into the same cell with Steve. It was quiet next door as Steve and his new cellmate had no choice but to get acquainted. Alone in my cell, I prayed it would remain that way. I couldn't bear the thought of sharing that tiny hole with another prisoner, who would possibly be a young gladiator who could stir up more trouble.

A few hours later I heard strange and unusual crying for help, along with accelerated pounding on the steel door next to me. I recognized the voice as Steve's. The pounding and crying and choking continued, then slowed its pace, and finally stopped. I could only hear the commotion due to the concrete wall separating the cells. I lowered myself to the floor, hoping to see a clue through the food slot. Realizing there was trouble, I screamed and screamed for help, louder and louder, through the food slot in the door. Three guards arrived after several minutes of my shouting. I stuck my arm out of the food slot and pointed to the cell next to me. I was out of breath from yelling. One of the guards opened the door and, realizing an inmate was unconscious and bleeding from the head, he excitedly called for medics.

The hallway had many cells lined in a row, much like you would imagine death row. It's normally chaotic, with insane, vulgar, animalistic sounds echoing off the block walls—a loud, ceaseless, hollow-type sound. That day the hole grew silent. A guard snapped handcuffs onto the new inmate, pushing him into the hallway. Through the food slot in my door I watched as the young black man fell to the floor, only to be dragged away.

My initial thoughts were that Steve was hurt bad. Within minutes medical staff had arrived with a gurney. They spent several minutes in the cell. It was quiet and cold when the gurney left with Steve's body, his face covered up with a sheet. He was dead.

The dead man, Steve, age forty-seven, whom I never did actually meet face to face, but had talked with through the slot in our doors, had been beaten to death in cold blood by a twenty-five-year-old youth. Rumors in the weeks ahead said that the incident was gang related and racially motivated. Later I would also discover that Steve was a high-ranking icon in a white supremacy gang. A contract had been put on Steve's life, which does very often happen in gang wars. The two men should have never been in the same cell together.

I was asked a few days later by prison officials to give a statement as to what I heard. However, based on the conversations I'd had with Steve prior to his death, I knew it was in my best interests not to make a statement. I'd also learned that a statement from me wouldn't have carried much weight anyway, being that I was also a prisoner.

Five days later, after twelve days solo, I was released from the hole and declared not guilty of any foul play in the violent attack on myself that had sent me there.

Any false strength we conjure up is nothing more than fear masquerading as something powerful. This is created by the ego and bears no likeness to who we truly are. The young inmate desiring a gang membership only provided himself with a false identity he thought that he needed in order to make him feel strong. In reality, this illusion only made him more fearful.

We get upset and angry at the world for not being fair, but we project that image and continue to contribute to its inequities. We are all starving for love that the world is afraid to give us. This brings on violent action as defense, because we are so afraid of losing more love. Do you see how the ego creates a never-ending cycle of weakness?

The ego believes it is all-powerful until faced head on with the Light we have radiating within us, but we are often afraid to let it shine by being our True Self. The ego is afraid the Light may shine into its hiding place, which is anchored in misconception. But upon this misconception of self, the world smiles with approval. It guarantees the pathways of the weak are safely kept, and those who walk on them will not escape, nor will they find right-mindedness, let alone eternity, or One-minded vision.

Of course, I'm not blaming the world for my own mistakes caused by my own lack of vision. But I do know that the world cannot force its images on me any longer. I refuse to accept them. The time has come for me to see exactly *who* and *what* I am connected to. I hope you feel by now you are beginning to know me—and your True Self.

When the people of the world have "earned their bones" to the point where they start questioning the world's fake concepts, then truth will set them free to face the world without fear.

A Course in Miracles wants us to learn that "the [illusory] world's purpose is that we arrive without a self, and the world helps to make one as we go along. So by the time we reach maturity, we have perfected it to meet the world on equal terms, seeing truth as we see fit." This was so with the prison officials at Belmont when they decided that the truth would be "Steve's death was accident related."

Chapter 16

The Abstract and the Concrete

Being that the ego was made by the dream of humankind, the content of anything the ego strives to construct really doesn't matter. Why? Because there is no truth to it. It's not real. The efforts of the ego eventually will perish, and the ego itself faces ultimate death. Then why does any of this really concern us, as the ego and what it makes us do seem to be quite real?

Our mind is naturally abstract, meaning it is of a concentrated essence—the essence of God, who created the mind as whole. What is the essence of God? It is the One Thought of the One Mind that sustains everything. This Thought of God that created our own essence within this wholeness is hard to understand for the ego, which can only see the concrete.

Essence, of course, is not concrete. Therefore, the ego part of the mind splits off from the abstract. We see this every day when we refuse to believe what is not normal, or "concrete." The ego depends on the concrete, or only what it can understand for its own benefits. In the split mind, the ego part is separated from the abstract or formless, because of the ego's unwillingness to understand the confusing abstract. Why do we make it so confusing? We don't; the ego does. The ego tries to make a concrete image of the formless abstract, but every time it looks at it, a different image appears.

We have learned to feel separate from everything, including God, who additionally we have learned to fear. An old adage goes, "Everyone wants to go to Heaven but nobody wants to die in order to get there." The ego sees everything as a separate entity, including in our closest relationships. The ego's only use for communication is for establishing separateness. What is "yours" and what is "mine" never seems to truly equal "ours."

Just take a look at ugly courtroom battles over "who" gets "what." The ego's only concern is to protect itself, and it has no need otherwise to communicate. It will fight to the bitter end to defend its ideas and its separateness when it feels threatened, but it will work diligently to be accepted. This is why it feels the need to "earn its bones."

Have you ever decided not to speak to someone who has upset you because you don't like his position on a controversial matter? His stance seems to threaten you and your position; therefore, you immediately start thinking of ways to defend your ground. Or have you ever recognized some poor behavior on your part, so you begin to conjure up excuses? You do this until all excuses possible have been exhausted, and then you come up with your only last defense: "This is my story and I'm sticking to it." Does this sound familiar? Next, you feel guilt or shame beginning to penetrate your awareness, so you become even more defensive and fearful of what others might think.

This is quite the opposite with Spirit, which reacts the same way to everything it knows is true and does not respond at all to anything else. Nor does Spirit make any attempt to prove something to be true, because it doesn't have to. Spirit knows that what is true is everything that God created, and with this knowledge there is no reason to prove otherwise. Spirit is direct and complete communication with every aspect of creation because it is one with its creator.

Let me explain by offering a picture. Imagine it's winter and you are sitting on a bench in a serene park setting. Snow is falling gently all around you in big soft, beautiful flakes. Crystalline snowflakes are landing one by one on your dark coat sleeve, each one quite different, which you see as awesome. You're in a peaceful mood as you contemplate the perfect flakes each of a unique design, which slowly melt into your wool coat. Are your immediate thoughts involved with the meteorological aspects, such as cloud cover and atmospheric conditions, that play a role in this type of snowfall? I doubt it, at least not at first. Instead, I'm sure you are initially caught up in wonder, however briefly, at the act of nature itself. The unexplainable God essence of the snowflakes flowering the landscape is what brings you Home. It's that unexplainable awe with no thinking.

This is your abstract communication with the Oneness of God of which you are a part. This explains why you were in awe: it's because you are *of* the awe. God created every mind by "abstractly" communicating His mind into it, and our minds are forever a channel for receiving His Will. The ego in all of us decided not to accept God's Will, since the ego relies on a separate will made by itself. The ego can only "make," but your will, which is also God's Will, *creates*.

Perhaps some of you are thinking something like, "I love my independence, and it is my will, and I do not want to be controlled." And as you think about this, you then add: "This is not the type of thing my true God would want of me."

But freedom is obtained through wholeness. What I am really describing is having the independence you truly want, because it is your own free will. But to truly be your free will, it must also be God's Will that He gave you in the creation. It is always God's Will first, because He must have it in Him before He can give it to you. Any will that you merely "make up" will make you frantic, or fearful, or doubtful, or guilty, and cannot be a free will. What is free is not fearful. If your will springs from a feeling of lack or fear, it is simply a will of your ego that is necessary to maintain your separateness, where ego-based wishes begin their drive. This surely is not *independence*.

Realizing your true free will could be stated literally as "waking up and smelling the roses." Your free will is your kingdom, and it does not require thinking to find it. In fact, it's not lost, so it doesn't need finding. It simply is, and what "is" is "you."

This is what it means to have everything and to be independent. This is the way we were all created—to have everything, and to share what we have, which increases joy in others. Nothing real can be increased or decreased by sharing, and this is also our will, to take joy in sharing.

Consider this: We all deep down within want to help in some fashion because it makes us feel good as we share the essence of who we are. We don't have to "think" about it, as it just feels good. For example, how often have you been quick to give directions to a total stranger who is clearly lost in an unfamiliar area of town? The desire to help seems to rise to the surface in almost everyone. Yes, even in prison, believe it or not. We may not offer help much of the time, due to our fear of losing something. But we still feel our natural inclination to help.

This is what *Oneness* means. The "how" or "what" and to "whom" are irrelevant, because the real creation of the Oneness that we are gives everything, always. In the kingdom, where you sense Oneness, there is no difference between "having" and "being," as there is in a concrete, separated mind.

Isn't it interesting, as well, that when you receive directions from a total stranger, you trust them when they tell you to "Turn right at the next traffic light?" In this state of being—Oneness—your being, or the real you, also gives everything always, even when you're receiving.

The Bible repeatedly states that we should "praise God." This certainly does not mean that it's necessary for us to tell God how great and wonderful He is. God has no ego that needs stroking. Acknowledging our part in the Oneness of all that exists is how we praise God.

God is praised whenever any mind learns to be wholly helpful. This is impossible without being wholly helpless, because the "helpless" and the "helping" must coexist. The truly helpful are invulnerable to the ways of the ego, because they are not protecting their egos; therefore, nothing can hurt them. When we praise God in this way, His praise is returned by the joy of our attitude when we are helpful, or when we are grateful that we were helped. This is how you can truly say to another, "Praise the Lord." This is how you know His kingdom. A single snowflake can signify who you are.

Part V

The Shift to Right-Mindedness

Chapter 17

Your Invitation for Guidance

A Course in Miracles gives us a lesson deep within the student workbook suggesting we study a fact of the universe. "What shares the purpose of the universe, shares the purpose of our Creator."

When we discuss the universe throughout this book, I'm not referring to the physical universe we initially think of, with the stars, planets, and all its glory. (Note: Your ego may have briefly raised its eyebrows to question this. But that's okay; simply notice this interruption and move on.) The universe you see with the body's eyes, even in all its splendor, is a projected image, and the awe you sense is from your right-mindedness. So go ahead, by all means, and accept this beautiful perception of a starry sky, full moon, and a possible shooting star for what it is: it's awesomeness, wonder, glory ... and not the physical. Allow your right-minded view of beauty to send you joy.

The universe I'm talking about is the essence of all that exists, which of course includes the joy you receive from your right-mind of that star-filled evening or the snowflake in the example I used earlier. It includes the receptivity and gratitude you felt, with no questions or doubts, when you received directions from the total stranger. When we revel in the wonders of the universe, this naturalness is where our own healing takes place.

Hang on as we go a bit deeper into our total right-mindedness.

Healing is the process where two minds begin to perceive their wholeness. This is where the minds can merge together as something strong, yet both nurturing and nourishing that interlocking chain in the atonement process. In that constant cracking apart of the concrete, so to speak, is where abstract, right-minded perception flows into the gaps and fills them with Truth, which gives us joy and the confidence that touches others. By reaching others, we are reaching deeper within, to the Sonship. As we consistently allow the gaps in the cracking concrete to fill, God's Oneness is communicated and wholeness is known.

In the example where you asked for directions on the street, which got you safely to your destination, that brief moment showed a wholly joyous Oneness serving its purpose. The individual giving you the directions did not think twice before offering accurate and helpful thoughts. It was natural of him to help you and was an abstract response where oneness became automatic.

Remember that Spirit truly knows not a single difference between "having" and "being." The abstract mind responds automatically to the laws Spirit obeys, which are the laws of the Mind of God, which we are a part of. To Spirit, getting or gaining is meaningless, and giving (being) is all there is. When you received the directions on the street from the stranger, you had to actually "give" automatically in order to receive.

What did you actually give, you may ask? You gave your real self and not an ego; therefore, his real self could not refuse you. You touched the stranger without an ego, and he merely responded automatically from his real self. Of course, this kind of thinking is totally alien to having and getting things in the eyes of the ego. Ego-based thought does not share ideas unless it sees possible gain.

Consider when you share a material possession fifty-fifty. You are sharing its ownership. If you share an idea, however, you do not lose it or decrease its value. All of the idea is still yours, even though it has been given away. Further, if the one to whom you give it accepts it as his, it reinforces the idea in your mind. If you can accept the fact that the world is an idea in which we all participate, the whole belief in the untrue association the ego makes between giving and losing is out the window.

In order for you to fill in the gaps of the concrete in your mind, let's start your own healing process, which leads you to wholeness. It begins by creating a new vision for yourself of the real universe with just a few concepts you'll want to absorb like a sponge. Go ahead and take a few moments, or however long it takes, to review these from a place of inner Truth, which includes that abstract awareness and alertness you are capable of.

- Thoughts increase by being shared as an extension.
- The more who believe in these extended thoughts, the stronger the thoughts become.
- Everything is an idea.
- With all this understood, then how can giving and losing be associated?

These few simple concepts for a strengthened attitude of willingness to heal are your invitation for the Holy Spirit to be your Guide. You will experience Him simply by asking for guidance. He is in your right-mind and fills the gaps in the split-apart concrete with right-minded perception first. Your new perceived notions will smooth over the gaps, where right-minded thinking will become abstractly automatic. Your mind will increase in total right-mindedness, outweighing the wrong-mindedness that makes illusory projections in order to cover up the ego's guilt.

As you continue to heal in this fashion, you will notice fewer and fewer wrong-minded views of what you once thought was your reality. The Holy Spirit was in the mind of Jesus, the gaps nonexistent because there was no concrete thought. As a man, Jesus actually manifested the Holy Spirit as a model for our own healing. His vision was in the abstract, but was able to understand our concrete projections.

The Bible says, "May the mind be in you that was also in Christ Jesus." The Holy Spirit interprets this for us, regardless of what the ego says, and our thinking is redirected to understand this Scripture to mean: "If we allow our minds to heal, we can then think like Jesus thought, and join Him in the Christ Mind."

The Holy Spirit is referred to as the Healer, the Comforter, and the Guide. For centuries, the Holy Spirit has been described as something "separate" and apart from us and God. Past generations have given us their projected image of a white dove as the symbol for the Holy Spirit, as though something outside us brings communication into our heart, between God and all of us.

As a man and also one of God's creations, Jesus' right-minded thinking, which was of the universal inspiration known as the Holy Spirit, taught him first and foremost that this Inspiration is within all of us, and is not separate or located "out there." Jesus would not have been able to have this inspiration himself without knowing this. Once again, please do not try to think about this in physical terms, but instead, allow it to flow into the gaps of your healing mind. If you are ready to proceed in healing your separated mind, simply give the Holy Spirit in your own words an open invitation to be your Guide.

The Holy Spirit will remain a part of all of us everywhere and in all walks of life, as long as healing is needed. He will keep us pointed in the proper direction to the Light of joy. He points us to the way beyond healing and leads us to love life according to our free will. He cannot go wrong, because our true free will is God's Will. You can live your free will by understanding that everything you need is within you.

Consider it this way: You have your true self as the commander of your journey, Jesus as your model, and the Holy Spirit as your

Guide. Additionally, this all rests within the One Thought of God and is His idea of your free will. Now in readiness, let's move on and witness the Light shining the ego out of the picture.

Chapter 18

Your Spiritual Flashlight

The magician David Copperfield made the Statue of Liberty disappear back in the 1970s on national television at prime time. I watched this event, as did many others from around the world, fascinated and excited by an illusion everyone knew could not truly be real. Although it seemed real, he used a method to obscure our view of the statue and divert our thoughts into the dark New York City sky, projecting an image of an absent Ms. Liberty. The world wishes that illusions can give us something, but they never do.

It's the ego's world, because the ego dreams of ways we wish things to be. The ego is a thought system separate from the One that created us. It is a choice we think we have that doesn't exist and has no meaning. It's a thought that humanity has chosen to keep since the dream of time and space began, believing it can determine its own immortality and ways to get there. The ego contradicts itself by believing in immortality, while it fears its own death. Because of its twisted madness it doesn't really believe in anything, and like all dreams it will end. The ego knows this, and out of its guilt for separation from the One Mind of Truth, it fears its own mortality and maintains the attitude "Get all you can now." All this chosen non-sense is for one purpose, and it can only be for its own gain.

Earlier on, I mentioned that we need to notice our feelings of guilt, to observe them. Our guilt and fear are areas of darkness in our minds where the ego sits and looks on, continuing to worry about its own existence. The ego is afraid of light, because light exposes darkness, and the ego fears being exposed. It feeds on your fear to help it hide. If you don't face it head on, fear will remain to feed its existence.

You might be ashamed of your own guilt, but these feelings must be exposed or the ego will use these guilt feelings to strengthen its foundation. By exposing it, I'm not suggesting that you go out and announce your guilt to certain people you meet. In fact, this is the worst thing you can do, because it will only expose your ego to other egos who think their way is better. Other egos will wish to destroy your ego so their own ego will feel stronger. Then you will be a target for comments and ridicule that will only make your ego feel defensive and thereby feed your ego, not dissolve it. Isn't this an unsettling or fearful thought in and of itself?

But what you can do is to simply intimidate your own ego by looking directly at it. Yes, stare at it as you notice the feelings of guilt and fear it was trying to project onto you. By doing this you're letting the ego be aware of the real you, exposing the ego for what it is. Do not criticize or condemn it, just simply notice it. Look at it, much like you would your child who has misbehaved or is being a brat. Don't scold it, but merely look at these feelings of fear and guilt, which make the ego what it is. Let it see your presence.

By doing this, the ego is getting the message that you are not a part of its antics. The ego will think and wonder what it is you're up to. It will produce more feelings of fear, and then you will need to look at them as well. The ego will worry because it knows it cannot survive without you. When the worry sets in, observe it too. You are no longer held a prisoner by these feelings when you do this.

Consider when a dark room is exposed to light, the room no longer is dark. Because of its exposure to light the dark room becomes nonexistent, and now it is a different room, with new meaning, one of light. What you are is truly light. The light is your reality, and when you observe the ego and its means for survival, you are bringing light to the darkness. The only way for darkness to return is if the light goes out. But your true Light forever shines and never goes out. The Light is your true essence.

Here's what I'd like you to consider doing: Try to imagine having a good-size flashlight in your mind—the kind you would use to look into a dark corner of a closet or in the attic of your house. You're able to aim this flashlight anywhere in your mind for security reasons. Use it often when you feel the ego hiding in a corner of your mind. When the ego is at work on these feelings of guilt, fear, and worry, even insecurity, merely shine the flashlight directly on these feelings, exposing them like a burglar caught in the night with the goods. Shine the flashlight on the ego's face, exposing the illusion for what it is.

Once again, do not show any emotions toward this observation, because if you do, it is another trick by the ego to pull you back in. All you want to do is to let it know that you have exposed it. There's no need to get emotional by getting upset. Once you have exposed it by shining your mind's "house flashlight" into its face, notice how it makes you feel. Observe your good feelings of joy and peace.

But now there is one more question to ask yourself during this process, as you observe yourself holding the flashlight and shining it into the ego's territory. Who is the observer, watching you operate the flashlight? Well, with the knowledge you have gained thus far from absorbing these words, couldn't we say it is the Christ Mind within you? Or, more simply put, it is "you," as the *Face of Christ*.

Look at this flashlight that shines in your mind as your *true* essence. It's the Light that you are. From here on, throughout this book, we will be referring to your "spiritual flashlight" for the situations where light is needed to sidetrack or neutralize the ego in you. Be sure to keep this close in mind as we move along, and keep your flashlight handy.

The Light that you are of will keep the ego from running rampant, as well as keep its antics to a minimum while you dream of time and illusion, as your essence leads you to reawakening. If you don't allow your true light to shine and radiate you will not be at peace or fulfilled, except for temporary periods of time when you satisfy your ego, which will reward you with pleasure. But don't get me wrong here. I am not saying that you should not have pleasures, such as a nice home, car, and the things that you enjoy. By all means, our Divinity wants us to have all of these nice things. You should be recognized in your community when this type of happiness is the result of giving of yourself and not the result of a temporary thrill made by the ego. If you have nice material surroundings, you will enjoy them even further if you understand that you come into this world with nothing and you leave this world with nothing. This type of positive attitude leaves the ego out of it. You will enjoy yourself, while you contribute to the "whole" picture.

For most of my adult life, which was just about all my years in business, I felt as though I was stuck in the dark, hiding, and afraid to come out. Of course, I was striving to go forward in a material world with my business as the focus, but in reality I was only going deeper into the dark. These temporary gains in possessions and career objectives allowed me to hide inside of them. A certain zone had a hold on me that led me to make wrong-minded decisions, which is easy to do when you think from wrong-minded perception. Deep within I really wasn't comfortable, because fear resulted, and any change, even slight, triggered additional fear of it being a threat to the complacency I thought was keeping me safe.

It wasn't long after my involvement with *A Course in Miracles* that I began learning some enlightening things about my incarceration. I was forced to accept myself as who I truly am, because there is nothing material to hide behind in prison, and nobody was going to help me in prison except my true self. The ego surely lost its stronghold, and illusions of a false self could not prevail. Prison is full of egos that are frightened. By hiding nothing, I was able to sense and trust in my own true essence, which had no need to wear a phony hat. This essence, or Light, in me has made it easier to share myself, who and what I am about, without having to talk about it. There is an old adage that has truth to it if seen in proper perspective: "Talk is cheap."

However, as I move on with my own journey, I see that understanding the essence of what I am alerts me to why people do "talk cheaply." The Light in me surely shows me that "talking" is not necessary to develop peace within and to allow myself to truly see that "there is no death." I can understand the darkness for what it is, which really is *nothing*. Overlooking the darkness, by seeing beyond it in myself first, and then in others, is true forgiveness.

It seems there is a gap between what we perceive and what is actually true. Allow me to paint you another picture: Look at this as two separate peaks to a mountain, a lower peak and an ultimate peak. The lower peak is our perception, where we perceive a direction in a positive fashion, but with uncertainty. The ultimate peak, which is higher and brighter and above all the cloud cover, is your own knowledge, and knowledge is always *certain*.

There are no doubts where knowledge rests, and truth is always abiding there. The valley between the two peaks is full of uncertainty and untruths, where the land is unkempt and the terrain is tough. Along these rough and rocky roads, the "wannabes" travel and worry about "what if," as uncertainty is constantly a battle. But when we live by our right-mindedness, it builds a bridge between the two peaks so we may travel over the valley with ease, to our destination, where Truth is waiting to welcome us. Once over the bridge, all uncertainty is behind us. The bridge, which we can call *forgiveness*, is built with the help of communication from the Holy Spirit. He has bridged the way. He is able to do this by "undoing" our past errors and mistakes. This can happen in an instant, and it starts with total surrender.

Before I was arrested and taken into custody, I had been hiding from the indictment, and then the warrant for my arrest. The news of the details in my case was plastered all through the newspapers, with the media having a feast. I was embarrassed, ashamed, and in a state of total darkness, flat broke and lost. Only when I totally surrendered to the fact I was helpless and needed a glimmer of hope that one day I would see light again— only when I literally held the loaded gun to my head—something happened in my mind that kept me from pulling the trigger on that lonely night. Now as I look back, I am aware it was my surrendered thoughts that acted as the invitation for the Holy Spirit to take over from that point.

My material dark thoughts had led me to believe that my daughters would be better off with me dead, as all I felt I was worth was a sizable life insurance policy, which was mature enough to cover suicide. The fear of my material world ending was so strong I believed that life was no longer where I belonged. Prior to this crash, I had targeted all of my energy and perseverance on efforts to please the world so I might be accepted as a leader. Trying to keep up, being a winner, was my constant focus. All of this strain was due to my attempt to give the world what I *thought* it demanded. Something told me I was tired of being held hostage. In reality, all I simply wanted was my own true free will, to be who I've always been, a part of the unseparated Mind of God, where wholeness always wins.

I know that I am following my free will, which is also Gods' Will, by writing this book. I feel it is necessary to contribute to the "whole." The words are flowing, and they seem to direct my ink pen onto the page. I'm getting surges of energy as I write, and ideas keep arriving while I'm involved with this project. My goal is to at least help a few individuals find their true Light, or a *will* that can bring them out of darkness, so they can see for themselves that the ego's hold on them is not real. I am feeling true strength, as my former unreal self is behind me. I can see each day how I am growing more and more toward total awakening from the dream. The ego in each of us individually does not like this type of growth, and at first you may feel awkward, though headed in a truthful direction. But it doesn't matter what the ego thinks, because it's only *nothing*.

What is real within us is the Christ Mind, and the face of Christ smiles to see us acknowledge the Holy Spirit as our Guide. The Holy Spirit will give you the support in anything you need to accomplish your purpose. I find it amazing and gratifying, the guidance I am receiving here in prison as I write these words to compile this book. The resources I need just seem to show up to assist me. The Holy Spirit's communication and the effects of this communication are physically visible everywhere.

Remember, as long as we must contend with the ego, our mind is split. But that's okay for now; just understand that the wrong-mindedness in us needs correction and errors to be *undone*, as we heal our mind on a consistent basis while right-mindedness fills the gaps. The Holy Spirit will transform perception to knowledge as we need it. As feelings of guilt and fear pop up along the way, simply use your *spiritual flashlight* to shine them away—to open the eyes of darkness.

Have you ever perceived something to be true but were not quite certain, only to find out later it was true? Something happened along the way that gave you this knowledge—perhaps a change of circumstances, or a different attitude, or a conversation with a friend. Whatever it was, it was not of the ego. It was the Holy Spirit using the law of *cause and effect* to turn perception into knowledge, because you were ready for it.

We have said that the Holy Spirit is one-minded and abides in our right-mind. Therefore, it is important that you start to recognize the Holy Spirit as "within" you, and not located some place "out there." He represents us and God as the Oneness we all are. Being that we are joined with God, the Holy Spirit speaks for both. He is the "Connector of Thought," or the bridge we travel on. He is the voice "for" God. He seems to be whatever meets the needs we think we have in order to perform our free will. However, He is not deceived when we perceive ourselves entrapped in needs we don't truly have. The Holy Spirit will use time to physically arrange events, or not arrange events.

Consider, for example, the experience I described early on in this book, of the way *A Course in Miracles* showed up in my life, and while in prison. How did a very clean, untarnished copy of A Course land on that bunkside cabinet the way it did, where no one had a clue whatsoever of what this publication even was? Did it appear out of thin air? Of course not. But there were unexplainable circumstances as to why and how it was left there. These are the things and events that I am not even supposed to be aware of or understand. But however this occurred, there was a "cause" that resulted in an "effect." The bottom line is, the *Course* found its way to me, and at an appropriate time in my life. I guess we can say it was because I was "ready" and "willing." Was this a miracle? What would you call it?

Remember, we said, "Everything happens for a reason," and it may not have a single thing to do with where you are at now. But there is a reason. There are events taking place at this very moment that may have an impact on an important and necessary change coming to your life soon, or not so soon.

The Holy Spirit is responsible for right-minded perception, but He also may use wrong-mindedness and wrong-minded occurrences to enhance His goal. The Holy Spirit is concerned with your true free will. Once you truly acknowledge and accept this, you have become ready, and changes will begin occurring along your journey over the bridge to knowledge.

Chapter 19

The "Dance" to a Wrong-Minded View

Our egocentric mind would rather believe in magic than in miracles. This makes sense, since magic is an illusion, and we love to believe in nothingness. We have been taught that only Jesus was able to perform miracles. Much of the world does indeed believe in the life of Jesus, and so, with that in mind, let me ask you to consider a few questions.

If a stranger showed up in your town and it was rumored that he could perform miracles, what would you say or think? Let's take this further and say this stranger was a nice, trusting man who loved children, and most everyone, including the children, was drawn to him. Let's also say that after a while of everyone admiring this man, he now made a statement that he was Jesus and that he was back to save the world. What would you think about this man who dared to call himself Jesus? Wouldn't someone, maybe even the local police, do a little investigation of this matter, just as they did two thousand years ago?

But if another man strange to your town, and also a nice man, said he was a magician, and he proved to all that his magic tricks were one of a kind, what would you think or say? Would you feel safer with the magician, or with the newly claimed Jesus in town? You can bet that most people would enjoy the magician's tricks and would condemn the so-called miracle worker. People haven't changed much in over two thousand years in the way they pass judgment.

Deep down within us all, we know that miracles are real, but we must learn that we are of the will to perform them, guided by the Holy Spirit. I'm not talking about turning water into wine; I am saying that everything we do create is a matter of our willingness to serve or to live our free will. We may not even know we are performing a miracle. Someone left a book in a prison cabinet, for example. Did he think this was a miracle? Probably not. This gesture didn't even become a "miracle" until long afterward, when the person it was "intended" for found it.

Whatever we alone *make* is of our body, in our body's own sight. We say it's real, but it is not real in the Mind of God, where our own mind rests and creates. The meaning of the Last Judgment will end the confusion.

For centuries now we've been taught to see the Last Judgment as fearsome, when really few have understood it, due to the ego's misleading interpretation. Religions have their reasons for forming their own meaning for it, most often to encourage the fear of God.

However, God's Holy Spirit in us all prepares us for the Last Judgment in that the Sonship will lead the way. It will be a final healing for those minds that have not reawakened where wholeness is needed, and it will not be a day of punishment whatsoever. This final reawakening, a joyous and peaceful event in all minds, will take only an instant, as all minds will see themselves as the Second Coming of Christ. We will all be at-one, which will be full Atonement. We will see the ego for what it is: nothing. It will be the final process for bringing everyone to right-mindedness first, setting the order for that very instant when, as a whole, we step up to total Oneness. This is when One-mindedness will be *known* and no longer perceived.

Our preparation for the Last Judgment does not entail special sacrifices or rituals. It simply asks that we start to understand the true meaning of *healing*. To heal is simply to understand that judgment of our past causes us pain and brings on illusions that we allow ourselves to be a part of. Healing is the process of trusting the Holy Spirit to *undo* the errors in our lives caused by illusory thinking. To trust the Holy Spirit in this is to trust yourself. The more we're able to see our true free will, the more our split-mind will shift over to right-minded perception, which strengthens our abstract vision. This is a shift toward total right-mindedness in our thought process.

Once again, perception of any kind is not to be considered knowledge; but right-minded perception is a stage we must first enter in order to cross over the bridge to knowledge. Therefore, when you have begun to lean toward right-minded thinking, you are in a healing mode. This is apparent in the change of mind we experience when we have times of anger, grief, worry, or frustration, and it is the Holy Spirit that has corrected our views on such matters that has helped us to change our mind.

When my oldest daughter Erin was only twelve years old, there was an issue with a boy-girl dance she wanted to attend at a local Boys Club. The Boys Club was a civic organization and was considered a safe place. However, I was against her going to the dance, because I felt she was too young to start mixing with boys. But she insisted and persisted, as twelve-year-old girls do, that she was indeed not too young. I can still hear her now, trying to convince me of her maturity level, as she stated that she was *"almost a teenager."* She claimed that all the other girls were allowed to go to the dance, and that I, as her father, didn't understand. She cried and said I didn't love her, and added as many other "boo-hoo's" as she could dream up. She continued angrily that she would get her mother to approve of the dance.

Rather than continue the heated debate, I asked that we both let this rest over the weekend. The following day an *urge* came over me to telephone the Boys Club to find out more about the upcoming dance. I spoke to the club's manager, who was a counselor for kids, as well as the father of a preteen boy, so need I say, he understood my concern. He assured me that the dance was set up for preteens only and was going to be a well-supervised event.

His confident voice over the telephone put me at ease, and now I was okay with Erin going to the dance. In fact, I volunteered to drive my daughter and her girlfriends to the dance on that evening. This, of course, allowed me to get a peek inside the dance hall so I could envision the time would be safely spent. This gave me a second assurance that everything would be okay and my daughter would do fine.

On the night of the dance, Erin looked over at me in the front seat of my car as her loving father who cared about her. I could see this in her smile. We both felt good and excited about her first dance. The next day, following the dance, she appreciated me as her father, and that her friends had the chance to meet her dad. It made her feel as though she could trust the love I held so deeply for her.

I didn't realize it then, but now I can see it was Holy Spirit within me, guiding me to make the phone call to the Boys Club, which started my change of mind. My own judgment thoughts about such a dance frightened me, and were negative, wrong-minded perceived notions of older boys taking advantage of my little girl. It was illusory thinking, to say the least. But the Holy Spirit used my wrong-minded thoughts to bring out my responsibility for protecting my daughter.

Only when I was able to realize that the dance was safe, as well as offering a growing-up experience for Erin, did my mind shift automatically over to right-mindedness. Did I ever have knowledge that she would be safe? No, not entirely; although as her father, I did shift over to the knowledge that it was in Erin's best interest, for many reasons, that she attend the dance. But my right-minded perception was strong enough to allow my daughter—and myself—to have this experience.

The Holy Spirit used time as His tool to shift my perception and allow truth to be seen. As for now, in my later years, I see this as a great example for me in understanding my own healing process, where once again, time was used within the universal law of cause and effect. Was it a magic trick? Or was it a miracle?

Chapter 20

Allowing Darkness to Find the Light

The first step toward healing and trusting your true vision involves a sorting out of the confusion between falsehood and truth. We must be aware that if we live in fear we will not be able to hear the voice for God, the Holy Spirit. He is always there, but with the fears we have, we may not be realizing His presence. At this point you will want to shine your spiritual flashlight on any fears you may have, and by doing so, these fears will be drawn to the light. As they become of the light, they fade away and the Holy Spirit will know you are ready to hear His communications. Within an instant, you will begin to notice how ridiculous your fears have been, due to wrong-minded thinking, and a shift in perception will begin.

Can you imagine the tremendous peace the world would feel if no one ever initially looked at another individual's behavior with judgmental thoughts? This is the purpose of the Last Judgment. Think about the anxieties we take onto ourselves for such things as our hair being out of place, our physique being less than movie-star-perfect, or having the complexion problems that haunt teenagers. Look at the millions of dollars spent on cosmetics and cosmetic surgery. When we are constantly judging ourselves, this makes us judge others. Of course we want to look our best and portray a beautiful image, because this gives us joy. But is it doing us any good to do this at the cost of the fear of being judged poorly by others? Do we really need the acceptance of others in order to live a joyful life?

What you can do now is start realizing that judging anybody in any fashion really has no meaning and is not beneficial to us. All of our uncertainty comes from a feeling of being under a magnifying glass. When you feel the need to judge, or even feel as though you are being judged, simply notice the ego-based thoughts by using your spiritual flashlight. Draw the ego-based feelings to the light, and get a good look at them without any further judgment. We simply do not need judgment to organize our lives. When we are *willing* to live a life without judgment, only then will there be no need to judge. Of course, to cross the street you must make a judgment—an assessment. But the form of judgment I'm talking about entails condemning or criticizing others.

We're afraid of what we perceive, and we are also afraid to accept what we view in our questionable perceptions. Therefore, we judge. Perception is never certain, and knowledge is always certain. When we are absolutely certain of a given situation, we reserve no fear. But when we perceive wrong-mindedly, it leads to doubt, fear, and judgment.

Our right-minded thoughts may still leave room for uncertainty, but of a positive nature that tells us there's no need for erratic judgment. We are aware that the Holy Spirit is behind this right-minded attitude and that any consequences of action we may take are meant to be. This is a part of the healing process.

Whenever you do use your spiritual flashlight to let the ego know it is being exposed, understand you are drawing it to the light. Then immediately ask the Holy Spirit for help by saying something like this in the form of a prayer: "Holy Spirit, my ego is making judgmental thoughts, which I refuse to judge. I am turning these thoughts over to you for *undoing*." Then be done with it; don't dwell on it and move on. It's really that simple.

The ego is at constant war with the Holy Spirit. Since it is at war, the ego must always be on the defensive. However, the Holy Spirit could care less and knows of no such war. He has no battle plan to gain or defend Oneness. The Holy Spirit is there for us, and He is us. We identify ourselves when we are operating from our true free will, which must be God's Will. So again, what is God's Will? It's His idea of you.

There are also times when we are not certain of our own free will, because we have an "authority problem." When this occurs, we're trying to be the "author" of this idea of God. We think our life is a story we can write. The world helps us with this when it tells us we can do whatever we set our mind on doing. This is true; but which part of our split-mind are we using in doing so? We often maintain that others are fighting us for this authority, and this makes us believe that we have our own power in addition to God's Will. We think God's power, or His Will, enables us to boost our own power if we only will "praise the Lord."

This rubs off onto our children in statements such as "I don't need you to tell me what's best; I'll show you." Or, "You just wait and see how my way is the best. After all, I've got God on my side." Often we will quote Scripture that may seem to take our side in proving a stance we support, and it's usually for our material gain.

We may not always say these types of things, but we do often think them, as a defense strategy. These beliefs are actually fear inducing and keep us living within the world's view of truth. This is why we feel we must prove ourselves. This can, however, be undone once we recognize it. Once you have shined your light on these authoritative thoughts, simply ask the Holy Spirit to *undo* your thinking pattern. It will be undone, and you will experience a shift in the way you perceive future problems.

Even with the littlest and simplest indecisions or power struggles, just stop for a moment and shine your spiritual flashlight not on the problem, but on your feeling toward the problem. Draw these feelings to the light. The Holy Spirit will set you free of them. There is no one who at times doesn't feel as though he is imprisoned against his own will. If this is the result of not fulfilling your own free will, then you are not free and are not seeing God's Will as your own. To feel imprisoned is not a free will, and I certainly can vouch for that.

If you are stuck in a relationship, or a situation, or a business that is controlling you, as was the case with me, it is because you are putting a conflicting will up against God's Will. It does not mean to necessarily leave the relationship, but it is a sign that you are in need of the Holy Spirit's guidance to see something you may have been missing. You might want to say something like this as a prayer within yourself: "Holy Spirit, I feel I'm off track here and getting deeper into a lost feeling. Please show me the higher ground." That's it. Put your trust into the fact that relief is on its way, and keep your ears and eyes open, along with your heart.

Take a look at your life, whether successful or unsuccessful, in whatever manner you deem success to be. Try to see, without judging yourself, where the ego has led you astray in certain situations. Just by acknowledging that the ego did set you off in a wrong-minded direction is a great starting point. Go over this with yourself without any self-abasement, and don't feel the need to share this with anybody else. Truth is what brought me to the point where I now see the Holy Spirit's guidance daily, and believe me, prison is where it is needed the most. Although the ego is still a huge pain in the mind, so to speak, it knows that I am on to its little tricks. The ego also is aware that I have the knowledge of how fearful it is of my spiritual flashlight, and that my light forever shines.

The ego is a thought system, and with the help of the Holy Spirit it is slowly fading away. It's a thought system afraid of death. Use your light, which is kept lit by God's Light, and notice the ego in you slowly fading away as you draw it to your light. This proves to you the illusion it really is. The more you notice the Holy Spirit, even in the tiniest of ways, the less you will see the ego as a threat.

In her book called *A Return to Love*, spiritual leader Marianne Williamson used an example of scenes from the movie *The Wizard of Oz* to paint a picture of the ego. I have added a thought of my own, regarding the scene where Dorothy tosses the bucket of water onto the Wicked Witch of the West. The water begins melting the witch away, as she cries out slowly and frantically that she is melting into nothing—much like the Light will do to your ego. Dorothy looks on in amazement as she sees the witch melting. When the witch is gone, all that is left, lying there on the floor of her huge castle, are her scary witch's hat and broom—material possessions. Dorothy wakes up from the dream and realizes she's been at home all along—that she never left Kansas. She was safe in bed, dreaming of illusions and frightening occurrences. The Wicked Witch wasn't real after all.

The ego is not real, and you, too, are at Home all along as you slowly, but with peace and joy, move toward awakening. You wake up, and it will all have only lasted an instant. There is no death, and you will realize that there is only a silly belief in death.

Part VI

The Light That Will Give You Certainty

Chapter 21

The Seeds We Sow

On a beautiful, sun-filled summer afternoon in 2007, when my spirits were not feeling as elegant and glorious as the sky appeared, I was sitting on the deck just off the kitchen of my home at the lake. My companion, who had listened to my whining all afternoon, despite the ice chest full of beer, did convince me that the lake that day was a serene sight for sunken eyes. As I glared at the fishing dock at the edge of the backyard, I thought about casting a line. But I came up with an excuse to stay close to the telephone—and the beer—as I waited for a promised call from my attorney with information about my inevitable indictment by the grand jury. He had suggested earlier in the week that I should expect the worst.

I was inexperienced with the judicial game and how it's played, other than what I'd seen on television. I'd been trying to hide, hoping it was all a bad dream and I would soon wake up. It was my father's seventy-second birthday. What would I say to my parents and my daughters? What were my friends and neighbors going to think? Gulps of beer didn't seem to soothe the pain, but did help in my scolding myself. My companion gave up trying to cheer me and left.

About two hours later, the beer cooler now empty, the telephone call finally came through. My thoughts mumbled something like, *Typical lawyers, always love to make you wait.* The answering machine was just inside the kitchen screen door, so I didn't bother to get up. As I screened the call, my lawyer's rapid report gave me enough bad news about the indictment. He ran the time limit out on the recorder with his fast-talking legal jargon, but what information I did hear was that local police would be by the house to arrest me within a day or two.

My frantic thoughts were screaming questions to myself. *You idiot, what are you going to do now? You just had to push things, didn't you, because enough was never enough?* The beer was gone, and I was miserable.

The stock market was failing. The portfolios of most of my clients were at tremendous lows. These additional panic-stricken thoughts poured throughout my trembling mind, even though I knew that my clients were not blaming me for the lows of the market. But what would they think now, once my criminal case hit the newspapers? I was just about flat broke and hanging on by a credit card string. The car loans, mortgage, alimony, child support, and all the other business overhead was a pressure I could no longer handle, not to mention how my recent divorce had tapped me out, both emotionally and financially, and now I was facing felony charges. Everything was quickly caving in around me, and as I found out what *rock bottom* felt like, my family had no idea. This had to be my death, I was sure of it.

I tried to put some effort into prayer, as I had believed in prayer all my life, but found it difficult. The meditation practices I had learned a few years prior helped a little, but would soon realize the depressed chatter that was in charge, and I'd struggle even further. I was literally sick, nauseated, and disgusted with myself and the world. I was a mess.

The lawyer flat out told me he could not win a trial by jury, but did assure me he would do his best to work out a plea deal. He advised me to realistically expect a few years in prison. It was a sure thing I would lose my securities license and would never again practice as a financial advisor or anything related. Things were looking gloomier and darker, more and more.

Going to prison was unthinkable. *I certainly didn't intend to hurt anyone,* I defended myself repeatedly. *My daughters need me. Hell, I'm better off dead.* Thoughts of doom arose as I started hating myself. Something told me it was time to hit the bed and start over in the morning.

The next morning arrived earlier than usual for me, and I telephoned a trusted friend whom I had known for many years. Tom was also a business associate, and I felt surely he would understand my predicament; at least he would be a good ear to bend. After talking with Tom in detail about what was going down, he seemed to have an awareness of where I was at emotionally. He lived one hundred miles away in Columbus, Ohio, and insisted I drive down from Canton to spend the weekend before being taken into custody. He suggested a few days away might help me to get a better grip on the turmoil.

That evening, when I arrived at Tom's house, he was ready to take me out to dinner at one of his favorite local restaurants that had a jazz band playing that evening. Tom was aware of our mutual groove for jazz music. He also insisted I meet Chris, a friend of his who showed up to join us for dinner. Chris was in business as an accountant and had spent two years in prison for a problem involving a real estate deal and unpaid income tax. He had served time basically for tax evasion.

Nevertheless, he had lived the penitentiary life for a while, and the point was that businessmen were indeed going to prison for their mistakes; I was not alone. Tom, of course, had explained my situation to Chris beforehand and asked him to offer me some helpful words based on his own experiences of prison. We had a frank, sincere talk over dinner, and after dinner the three of us moved to a quiet corner of the bar, where we could talk a while longer and still hear the jazz trio in the background.

Chris, who was aware of my anxiety and felt he was in a position to be straightforward, began by saying, "Okay, Jim, based on what I know about your case and today's 'tough on crime' judicial system, the judge is most likely going to send you to prison. With today's politics, he will feel that he owes the public and your community. After all, who voted him into office?"

Immediately a huge lump rose in my throat. "Prison, I don't deserve prison," I blurted out. My anxiety tripled, and I felt furious and frightened inside. "What's it like? Go ahead, Chris, please tell me all I need to know."

Chris responded carefully. "It's a true hell every single day." My eyes opened wide as I listened in shock. "But you seem strong, Jim; you should do okay. Be careful how you carry yourself and who you associate with. You will see many sick things going on all around you. For example, a guy I knew had his face bashed in with a steel tray from a footlocker while he was sleeping. It seemed he used his bunkmate's toilet paper without asking first. Just stick to yourself and stay out of the way. The young punks will test you, as their gangs are everywhere, and they mean business."

I wondered what kind of business he was talking about, but I sensed it meant danger. I quickly thought, *I'll just have to bring out the best in me.*

"The gangs are heavily involved in a huge black-white racial problem, a war of sorts among the gangs," Chris went on. "You will need to stand up for yourself right off the bat. You simply cannot let anybody intimidate you. If they even sense that there is a hint of you being weak or a snitch, you're done."

Tom, Chris, and I stayed until closing time. All along, as we talked, I would periodically glance at the television behind the bar, which was showing highlights of that day's U.S. Open Golf championship. Chris didn't seem to pay any attention to it, even with the casual comments Tom and I brought up throughout the evening about golf. Toward the end of the night, Tom mentioned that before Chris went to prison he'd been an avid golfer, and as a fan of the pros, too, he'd enjoyed following the professional golf tour. But ever since prison he no longer seemed to have an interest.

"Why is this, Chris?" he asked.

Chris took a moment to ponder Tom's question and finally answered. "For me it seemed the thing to do—golf and some other things too. I looked at prison as a readjustment to my life, but it also took much away from me. It did give me time to find out who I truly am. But much of the 'old me' and my 'old ways' are gone. Oh, don't get me wrong, I'm still the same person—just without the old meaningless ways of living each day. For me it was a conscious decision to put many things behind me and rebuild who I must be."

I stayed in town with Tom for the weekend and then headed home. I still didn't know what to do. What could I do? The things Chris had to say really bothered me. Prison life seemed like a struggle I was not prepared to handle. Was God punishing me? My thoughts certainly told me God was not helping me or answering my prayers. I started to wonder about what the Bible says about sowing your seeds, and how careful to be. Had I sown bad seeds, and now I was reaping punishment?

Since becoming a student of *A Course in Miracles*, I have learned that there is never a reason to fear God. This is a wrong-minded perception shared by much of the world. But the *Course* has shown me to notice my own perception of right-mindedness shifting over to knowledge when it's needed, or when I am ready to use the knowledge for sharing wholeness. I have no reason to fear death, because it doesn't exist. The so-called fear of God is one of the biggest illusions ever projected by the ego, which has become a terrible myth that we continue to live by and suffer from. God is all love. He is the One true Thought inside all of us. Rather than fearing God, I was really in fear of my own reality. What really scared me was realizing my true state of being.

In my pre-prison state of panic, it was impossible for me to look inward. All that time I never knew my true reality, and I perceived fearful consequences from something outside of me. I was using my ego as my guide for defense, and it did not want me to realize my true self, nor did it wish for me to look inward. I always kept my focus on promises "out there." The ego—which does not know anything, because it is nothing—was showing me that help was to be found outside of myself, which only meant more and more ego involvement.

If we look back to the symbolic Garden of Eden, we see Adam, who was the first result of the ego, look inward and perceive sin, which was not sin at all, but guilt. Had his ego-based thought not believed it was God who drove him out of paradise, the thought of fearing God would never have developed. His ego projected an outside image of God as an angered old man with a white beard who had some form of magic powers. This is yet another misinterpretation of Scripture for the ego's use as support for fearing what is real. Because of that belief, the true knowledge of our Creator was lost. Talk about believing in "false gods." What is *certain*, however, is that no loving Father would knowingly cause fear to his children. Therefore, with this certainty, we can shift over to knowledge more willingly as the Holy Spirit determines our readiness.

The Holy Spirit, being the direct communicator with God, will never teach us that we are sinful. He will, though, correct our errors, and this, of course, makes no one fearful. Rather, it gives us relief. When we have relief, don't we feel certain? Of course we do, and there's no need for you to be afraid to look deep within and actually know you will not find sin. Go ahead, look inward, and ask yourself about the errors that are sitting there bothering you. Who in this world ever taught you that these errors are sin? While you are observing these errors at this moment, your true Guide and Healer, the Holy Spirit, is undoing them. If you feel nervous about looking within yourself, simply be certain that this is the ego getting rattled. All you need to do is shine your spiritual flashlight on the anxiety you feel, and observe it. It will be drawn to the light and fade away. This fading away is the Holy Spirit, undoing.

Unlike Adam, what if we looked inward and realized there was no sin to see? Wouldn't this catch on everywhere? But this frightens the ego, as it answers directly back to you that, "Yes, there is indeed sin, and we all are sinners." Haven't we been taught by the world for generations, and over thousands of years, that "Sin breeds in all of us?" What if, for the next thousands of years, we continually in the present "*now*" had the knowledge that sin does not exist? But keep in mind, that to believe in no sin would threaten the ego's existence and put an end to its teaching devices.

My own sinful thoughts about the ordeal that sent me to prison were that I may have "sown some bad seeds," when in reality I made numerous errors in my thinking. The Holy Spirit reinterprets the ego's version of "As ye sow, so shall ye reap" to really mean, "What you consider worth cultivating, you will cultivate in yourself." Your judgment of what is worthy makes it worthy to you.

Before I was sent to prison, I had cultivated ground for the ego to guide me on; instead, I needed to have shared my uncertainty with my real guide, the Holy Spirit. He would have changed my erroneous thinking and led me in a different direction. The Holy Spirit surely tried and intended to do just that, but my panic, induced at an earlier stage by the ego, would obscure any right-mindedness that wanted to prevail. The Holy Spirit, then, had no other choice but to use my own wrong-mindedness to eventually lift the obscuring cloud cover. He used time, along with my own wrong-minded views, to guide me toward seeing a necessary shift.

I didn't "sow any bad seeds"; I merely made decisions to plant on wrong-minded ground. By constantly asking the Holy Spirit to undo all our errors and ego-based thought when we sense it, it will cause the part of our mind that we have given to the ego to merely shift over to the more comfortable right-mind. Then, what is of right-mindedness will have the opportunity to shift over to knowledge, which is certain. Whatever is certain is forgiven, and whatever is forgiven rests beyond uncertainty. Here, you know your true Home.

Chapter 22

Being Certain

During my childhood I was certain of one thing, and that was my passion to play football. I guess this is because I began learning to hold onto the football before I could walk. Old family photos immortalize these early life lessons from my father—both outdoors and in the living room of the home where my parents still reside. My mother will attest to a few banged-up sofa tables and damaged lamps, along with a constant test of the durability of the carpeting.

Using each end of the sofa to designate goal lines, my dad would show me the secrets of driving my legs toward the goal line. My dad, as the defensive linebacker, taught me not to fear. I would drive my legs, with the football properly tucked under my arm, around or over the top of his wide shoulders for some brutal touchdowns. In these trenches he would inspire me with promises that I would one day become a great halfback, as long as I remained willing. He urged me to realize the importance of the power in driving my legs, and eventually I would learn from constant practice to steer those driving legs with my mind. We would watch the big games on television, and he would point out the effortless actions of the star players.

Although I never did get my driving legs on the turf at Notre Dame, I do know that I got more from pursuing that goal and not accomplishing it than I did from many of the ones I did accomplish. And I did enjoy periods of success during my youthful career as a halfback, and now great memories, which I attribute to the days of worn-out carpeting and broken lamps.

Did my father push me? You bet he did. But he knew that I wanted to be pushed. He was aware of my determination, and he saw the joy this inspired in me. Besides, it inspired him too.

Joy is where the kingdom is, and joy is why Jesus taught the children and spoke of being like them. It's in us all, this joy that children possess, but along the way we seem to lose it.

I was fortunate to be a part of the Catholic school system in the 1960s, with their excellent football program involving all the schools in the diocese. The league was very competitive, with games each Sunday for a seven-game season, plus a championship playoff. The league was taken seriously by the players, coaches, fans, priests, nuns, and even the cheerleaders, who were polished in their uniforms and as well coached as the players.

I was twelve when our undefeated team won the league championship for the first time in the school's history. That football team and that football season definitely extended joy everywhere. Our small-town newspaper made a big deal of the victory for us, with a team picture and an article about the game that had won us the trophy. This celebrated event for the school and the whole parish brought individuals together, however briefly, and was talked about for a long time after.

My driving legs exhibited their strength with a seventy-yard touchdown run down the sidelines of the opposing team's bench, my mind steering the legs in and out of a few wide shoulders on the way to the goal line. I remember catching glimpses of the look on the faces of the opposing coaches and players as I hoofed my way past, and before I knew it, I had darted across the goal line for the score. When I turned around in the end zone to jog my way back to our team's sideline bench, I saw the faces of my teammates and coaches, cheering, and my father in the bleachers beaming proudly, the cheerleaders waving their pompoms with joy. My own feelings were overwhelming.

In the car on the way home, I remember my dad asking me questions about the game, and also about my touchdown run. He asked me a peculiar question. "Tell me, Jimmy," he said, "what exactly were you thinking about as you took the handoff from the quarterback and ran for the goal line?" It was not unusual for him to ask me questions about the execution of certain plays, blocking assignments, and such. But this time it seemed as though he wanted to know where my mind was at, rather than the technical aspects of a certain move I made against a defender.

I remember answering him by saying that I wasn't thinking at all. He replied with fatherly wisdom that I must have been thinking, otherwise how would my legs have known when to move and in what direction was the goal line? He added firmly that surely I had been thinking. But of course he was indicating to me that my brain had to be functioning; therefore, I was thinking.

I replied to the effect that my legs were moving on their own, and that the football seemed as though it was a part of me, or attached. I went on to say that, although I was not thinking about anything, I did feel like I was watching myself run for the touchdown. I continued to tell my father that there were many times when I would feel as though I was watching over myself. My dad frowned in a concerned fashion with one eye on the road and another eye on me. Then he took a deep sigh and said to me, "Don't tell your mother about this."

Many individuals have described times in their lives when they have experienced peak performance, and all of them having different ways of explaining this. But every one of them says the performance had seemed effortless, and there is no thinking involved. Just ask a professional golfer what he is thinking about in the top of his backswing. Or ask an opera singer what she is thinking about at the height of a high note. You would get the same answer from both of these creative individuals. They will tell you there is *no thinking* and, of course, no fear.

The most successful lectures I held in my years of business seemed effortless; I was having fun, and so was the group. Many times I felt I was observing myself while speaking to a group of fifty or so. But there were also times that were not so good, when it seemed I was trying to force my words into a point of view. I sensed a pressure on me to force a particular outcome, rather than just being a part of the process and enjoying it.

Am I trying to say this ability of "observing" myself is something special? Of course not; in fact, it's quite common. But I am trying to say that we all have an intrinsic way of being that can stimulate peak performance.

What I am talking about here are "moments of enlightenment." This enlightenment involves your total self. It is not "self-centered" in the sense of egotism, but rather "centered on self." Enlightenment is a recognition, not a change at all, that you are of the Light that is not of the ego-based world. It is your glimpse of *One-mindedness*, and the more you experience it, the longer these glimpses can be. Could I have been *enlightened*, or have had glimpses of *One-mindedness*, at the age of twelve? Absolutely! Why not?

We all have had these types of sensations of being beyond our body, but may have simply passed them off as luck, or intuition, or having a great day. Once again, what was it that Jesus was able to see in children, before there was enough time for the ego to take over?

Wouldn't it make sense to teach our children this in the schools, just the way we support academics and sports? Why not? Eckhart Tolle in his book, *The Power of Now*, writes about possible schools of Enlightenment, and I'd like to simplify this by extending that thought to just "classes of certainty." In other words, what if there were programmed periods in the elementary schools called *classes of certainty*, where these ideas were taught in a *nonreligious* way? Just maybe our children and the generations to come could grow up understanding what the ego really is and what it is not. The child could learn to be "certain" in what is real, and carry about a certain confidence toward enlightenment. This could be so, without participating in some fantasy or make-believe charade. Thus we could do away with the argument over religion in the schools. At first, the thought of this scares many of us. Why is this?

Sadly, at this time the world does not want this type of knowledge, nor does the world want out children to grow up "not needing an ego." Why are we afraid of this? Our real true selves are not afraid; however, our ego is deathly fearful of this knowledge.

What would you rather have your child say to you: that he wants to grow up to be a star football player at Notre Dame, or a reawakened enlightened being? What if the child said he wanted to be both? There is no conflict in total One-mindedness, yet the world does not seem to want to be conflict-free. Or could we simply say that the world as a whole is not yet ready?

Chapter 23

Trusting Your Light

On a planet with a human population of seven billion, is it a wonder we have conflict? Each of these individuals has his or her own projected image of the way things seem to be. Given the way we look at ourselves, the way we wish ourselves to be, and our separate doubts, surely the illusion of separateness seems fearfully real. Each of us, in our personal dreams, create our own conflict in the world, while in reality we are still of the whole.

A Course in Miracles comments: "The Holy Spirit teaches one lesson and [it] applies to all individuals in all situations. Being conflict free makes the power of the Kingdom yours."

The ego cannot understand what the "Kingdom of God" really is. The Kingdom of Heaven is *"you,"* the real you. The ego thinks of Heaven as something outside ourselves. As a child we may have been taught that Heaven is an actual physical location, perhaps beyond the stars. That's a lot of bodies "out there" in the universe, waiting for our arrival. But seriously now, what else but "you" could the Kingdom of Heaven be? Since you are one with the universe, what else but *you* did God create?

When your body terminates its existence, the world you now project will be gone, along with your ego. The world you physically see cannot truly be here without you. Think about that. The Truth you are *is* the universe and is your part in the Atonement. The ego can never be a part of this interlocking chain of minds, because the ego is not real. Only what is of God can be real. The ego finds this fearful and cannot understand the Oneness of any thought. But there is true oneness seen in all individuals, though our ego tries to block it. It senses this oneness, but runs away or hides from this Truth.

This brings to mind a situation I was involved in at Belmont Prison, and it occurred after my discovery of *A Course in Miracles*. I had a confrontation with a young "gladiator" who is a known bully of a popular gang with a rough reputation. The bully had a reputation for extorting other inmates who he thought were weaker or older, and using them for his advantages. His tactics were to force other inmates to buy him cigarettes, coffee, candy, or other goods from the commissary, in exchange for safety or protection. If an inmate refused his "services," there would usually be cruel and violent consequences to pay.

One day, when he and I were both alone in an unguarded area outside the library, he approached me, and being aware of his reputation, I suddenly became "ready." He firmly, but very immaturely, ordered me to take off the brand-new pair of tennis shoes I had just received from my friend Ron on the outside. He had not seen me before, and since I am at least twenty-five years his senior, he thought I would be a pushover. However, he realized quickly I was not going to give in to his demand. He was much bigger than me, and he was a black man, which I only mention because of the constant racial conflicts in prison.

I looked him squarely in the eyes, with no hesitation, and firmly said, "No thank you."

He was not able to keep eye contact with me, as he looked away and chuckled the words, "Say what?"

I quickly responded, again with firmness. "I am saying to you clearly that my shoes will stay on my feet." As he looked at me briefly with a confused and bewildered expression, I added, "Just move, because I'm sure you really do not want trouble with me."

It was that simple and all I needed to do, and I continued to gaze calmly at him until he couldn't stand it any longer. He turned around and walked quickly away, mumbling some babble about me being an insane old fool.

My spirit, or my *light*, had created a shield that his ego could not penetrate. This frightened him. Did my ego ask for a pat on the back afterward? Hardly. In fact, my ego was nonexistent; the coward that it is wanted no part in this unveiling of the Christ Mind. When my true Light stood by Truth, it was the same as the pail of water that Dorothy threw on the Wicked Witch. This is the type of strength that confuses the ego, and it's in us all. The *grandeur* of my spirit faced this gladiator's ego, which is all he could show me at the time. The sensation was too much, so all his ego could do was judge me to be insane. His own true Light wanted to come out, but was too severely obscured by the ego—just as heavy cloud cover is to the sun. We'll be talking about the "Grandeur of God" that's in us all a bit later.

But for now, try to see the Holy Spirit as the communicator of the Truth that no force except your own free will can ever understand. When the bully saw the truth about me, with no illusion for his ego to control, he was lost. His own darkness was exposed to my Light, or my "spiritual flashlight," if you will.

Although this particular physical incident worked out safely for me, I am in no way insinuating we use this Truth as a physical defense. Prison, however, is a place where I had no other choice but to stand up for myself by showing a strong physical demeanor. I guess you could say I had to be prepared to defend myself, and I was willing to accept whatever outcome resulted from my stance. But I also trusted my Light.

If you are not hearing the voice *for* God, you're not listening. His voice is everywhere you are. It's really simply being yourself without thinking or forcing a particular outcome. We do, however, seem to hear the voice of the ego, which shows up in our attitude and behavior. Our mind is filled with all kinds of schemes to save the face of the ego.

Chapter 24

Understanding the Light

The Holy Spirit will guide you in your desired direction if you will allow Him to. He will guide you to where your free will waits for you, even if He must use someone else's body in communicating certain messages to you. His concern is your free will, which is God's Will. It is impossible for you to achieve anything truly desired, other than this. Why? Because what is not your *free will* has never even been created by God, nor will it ever be. This is why you will never be at peace or have pure joy, unless it's through your own *free will*. When you are involved in doing whatever it is you love, with pure joy and with ease, and without a single ounce of uncertainty, this is your natural state of grace. Beware, however, that the world may not want you to proceed in the direction your heart is urging you, and not wanting to lose their acceptance, you may take an unwanted path. For example, I spent twenty-five years in an industry that did a good job of convincing me that this was where I belonged.

Keep in mind that your free will is not only about your chosen career path; it is about anything at all you participate in. In other words, it's about how you live your life. But when my own inner self tried to argue against the flattery of others, my ego-based thoughts always reminded me of the bills to pay, the deadlines and commitments, and the pressures of keeping up with the Joneses. The world convinced me of the rules that dictate "We do what we must do," and then we take some well-earned time off to reward ourselves with whatever we really love to do.

"This is how life works," the ego convinced me, and that anything desirable was located "out there"—outside ourselves. Am I blaming the world? Not at all; but this belief we choose to make out of fear makes it impossible for any of us to operate from a true state of grace. Until I began to open myself to right-mindedness, I always seemed to be looking "out there" for what might make me whole or feel complete.

We all have our own natural state of grace, and there is no reason to hide a single thing about who we truly are. When you are in your true state of grace, you will discover that you don't need what the world dictates. This is where I'd like you to answer a question within yourself; please do so honestly, without leaning toward what the world would prefer you say.

What else could you desire but the truth about yourself?

Your answer to this question is your true free will, and you share it with your Creator. This is the "you" that is the kingdom. In answering this question you come to remember God. This is where you are at one with God's Mind, and His idea of you does not ask for what the world teaches. We all have our state of grace, and we must share it. But this does not mean that you should go around telling people throughout your day, "The Grace of God is with me," nor does it give you the right to dictate what others should do.

When you know it enough in yourself, others will pick up on your radiance, and they may or may not get the message. The Holy Spirit will speak through you by your example, as well as through the examples of others, depending on the level of readiness of those involved. The Holy Spirit will use time, and at the appropriate moment He will know what to show or offer. Messages will be given and received based on the level of readiness for that particular situation. This is how we extend ourselves.

I remember a business relationship I had with a small technology company that was experiencing tremendous growth. I had given the small firm a financial planning presentation, as my goal was, of course, to obtain the company as a new client. I would advise them on investment decisions to accelerate the company's portfolio, as well as the individuals' personal portfolios. It was a good-size account for me, and my efforts paid off; they signed on.

The company president, Bart, whom I had known for a few years, was in the same golf league as I was. Bart pulled me aside one day while I was gathering a census at the company's main office, which I needed to prepare my data. He saw that I was busy, but asked that I step into his office for a moment. He seriously asked if he could ask me a personal question. I said, "Of course."

He hesitated, then proceeded. "Jim, without offending you, what are you doing in the financial services business?"

He continued that he and his partner respected my knowledge and expertise, but they both felt I belonged somewhere else. He assured me they were sticking by me in our business arrangement, but also wanted me to be aware that one of the reasons they went with me was that they "understood." Baffled, I wondered, *What is it they understand?* I never did ask, and neither of them volunteered. I simply nodded my head in agreement and went back to what I'd been doing. It wouldn't be until much later that I would realize what he meant.

When we extend our grace, or radiant Light, we're simply extending that light over any darkness that remains, along with the light of others, which is the same light. This is so because of His Source. But you cannot think about this in order for it to happen. Just as the opera singer releases her high note, it is effortless. It's effortless because your true light is who you are. The others who live in their true light alongside you actually connect and form one Light, which is accepted and "understood."

One Light is all there is. Those who live in darkness will cover their eyes to you, because initially they are suspicious and fearful. This is only because these individuals are not on the same healing, or readiness, level; nevertheless, they are still at one with you. It is only that their light is obscured at some level for the time being. But don't allow this to get in your way while the radiance that you are radiates, because your radiance is surely intended to help shine through their obscurity. You receive radiance from others this way as well.

Those who can glimpse your light will gradually begin to see their own light, which will gradually touch yours and connect to it. You also found or realized your own light through the influences of someone else, whether you are aware of it or not. No one likes to step out of the dark and abruptly into bright light. By coming to an understanding of this concept of light, you are doing your part in the Atonement. You are both giving and receiving.

If you recognize the light of another, you will also be acknowledging your own light. Nothing is easier than recognizing Truth. If you're not operating from truth, you may temporarily fool others, but you will know this, and I'm sorry to say, so will other true radiant individuals, who will see that you are lost.

If this is the case, that you are not seeing truth, you will not be able to see or hear the Holy Spirit's guidance, or recognize His voice through others. He can only guide the truthful. But don't be too hard on yourself if you do realize that you have not been honest with yourself and that you have not been living from your state of grace. The very fact that you recognize this is *Truth* in *itself*, and this recognition is the beginning of the undoing process by the Holy Spirit. This is your knowledge now, and the Holy Spirit led you to it. Therefore, be real with yourself by accepting this knowledge as your first step of leaving the dark. The obscurity starts to lift.

Now you have the knowledge to move forward as slowly as you need to, and understand you are moving in the right direction, or a "right-minded" direction. But also understand that "slowly" is an illusion, because there is no such thing as time in regards to "slow" or "fast" in Oneness. Therefore you may want to ease up on yourself. Accept the fact that this hold of the ego has been a difficult release, especially with no support from the outside world, and go ahead and give yourself some credit as you give the Holy Spirit a little smile, letting Him know you now *understand*.

By this point in this book, you should know the feeling of Truth. But if you have questions or reservations about whether or not you know for sure, or have a doubt about a particular situation or circumstance, you can be sure that your doubts are due to the ego flexing its muscles for defense. Also keep in mind that your doubts or questions spring from the environment you were born into. But these doubts are nothing that your spiritual flashlight cannot handle. Therefore, shine it directly on those feelings of doubt, and get a good look at them for what they really are. Allow your doubts to approach the light, and as they do they will fade away. Once again, remember to use your spiritual flashlight without being emotional, and simply be done with it by moving on.

You will be truthful with yourself when you realize that you are healing another mind when that person recognizes your own radiance. And you are being healed, as well, when you recognize the radiance in others. We were created as a wholeness we are not even aware of. This healing within the Sonship is acknowledgment of our power to co-create with God. What else could we call this healing Light, other than the power of our creation?

Jesus tells us through the *Course*, "Only the whole Sonship is worthy to be co-creator with God, because only the whole Sonship can create like Him."

Here in prison, I recently received a letter from Bart, the president of the technology company. Through modern technology he was able to research the facts about my incarceration. He wanted to let me know how sorry he was to hear about my problem, and he informed me that he had always looked up to me. His letter was deeply encouraging, and believe me when I say that receiving a letter of this fine magnitude while behind bars is tremendously uplifting. The letter also arrived during a dark time, when I was able to see his light. Bart went on to say how he'd sold his share of the company to his partner and no longer had any dealings within the business, nor any regrets.

Bart sold his home, as well, and moved to Florida, where he purchased an old, rundown golf course. He tells me he has fixed up the old course and is having the time of his life. He has invited me to play his *updated* golf course "on him," as often as I would like once I am released from prison. Now I realize what Bart meant a few years ago, that day in his office, when he told me that he "understood."

Part VII

Grandeur or Grandiosity?

Chapter 25

The Grandiosity of the Ego

One of the many things the *Course* has done for me is to open my eyes to all the nothingness that consumed much of my life, and the little tricks the ego uses to guide me toward the grand promises it can't fulfill. How could it? For the ego is a false image. Now, it's easy for me to see that the grandest the ego could ever be is grandiose. Grandiosity is the ego's limited kingdom. Grandiosity is expressed in competitiveness; it always involves attack, and it acts out its pompous and exaggerated form of importance or dignity. Its goal is always about "outdoing," but never "undoing." In its attempts to win at all costs, the ego will vacillate between suspiciousness and viciousness, getting nowhere.

Even at the slightest presence of the real side of your split mind, however, where you display the grandeur that is your state of grace, the ego in you automatically feels abandoned. The ego becomes threatened by how meaningless it finds itself when it looks at the Grandeur of God that you are. The ego believes it must somehow retaliate and will attempt to offer gifts to induce you to return to the ego for safety.

The ego continues to remain vigilant and suspicious, especially when a part of you seems to be trying to figure things out. This frightens the ego, and it shifts to viciousness when you calmly decide not to tolerate its abuse. It then makes efforts for its own relief, whereby you begin berating yourself. Have you ever called yourself an idiot, or possibly worse, for something stupid you felt you did? I sure have.

Have you ever set your mind on doing something magnificent, something you have always dreamed of doing? How about something such as writing a book? Then, possibly, you put it off, saying, "one of these days" I will write that book. You may even add to the comfort of your procrastination by saying, "But when I do, it'll be a bestseller." Maybe the day finally does come around when you have the momentum to get started, but you begin telling yourself that "You'll only be making a fool of yourself." How many times have you done any of this, about any type of project or goal?

Additionally, how many times did you ever really end up making a fool of yourself? Probably hardly ever, if at all. But you'll surely be jealous of the ones who, without any announcements, did go ahead and write their book or "follow their bliss." Next, the ego may say or think something like, "Well, if I really set my mind to it, I surely could write an even better book." Does any of this sound even slightly familiar?

Even if you find your way through the ego's obstacles and finally do start your project, you may start hearing voices in your head, such as: "You idiot, who do you think you are to write a book and host lectures around the world?" With that, the ego continues. "What in the world qualifies you as an expert to write a book about spirituality?" The ego is not done yet. "You went to prison, and that alone makes you a loser!" And if that's not enough, "Do you realize what a fool you will look like when nobody cares to read your book, let alone purchase it? What publisher in their right mind would take an interest in what you have to say?"

Ouch! Wow, did I belittle myself, or what? By now you should be able to see that in this case, my ego was begging me to crawl back to it, where I can feel safe. Need I say that my own spiritual flashlight gets quite a bit of use? But not to worry; the batteries in your own spiritual flashlight will never die, because its power to shine Light has an eternal Source.

We've all heard it before and have seen it written repeatedly: "You are what you think." *A Course in Miracles* takes this deeper by teaching: "What you are is unaffected by your thoughts. But what you look upon is their direct result."

Chapter 26

The Grandeur of God, Which You Are

When we can sense ourselves as being the magnificent Grandeur of God, which is untouchable by anything outside of God, we then carry with us the radiance of grandeur. Grandeur is something real and is not flaunted. It shines. But when we walk around in a boastful, arrogant, false self, high on our body's achievements, with promises (or threats) of more achievements, we're on a grandiose fishing trip, using a lure that catches more ego.

The ego can never understand the difference between grandeur and its own grandiosity, because it sees only images that it wishes to project for personal gain and adoration, whereas grandeur portrays inward beauty and exemplifies pure joy. The projections of the ego lead to attack now or a scheme to attack later.

The grandiose simply cannot understand God's Grandeur because grandeur sets us free. The ego doesn't want us to be free. Please keep in mind, I am talking about the grandiosity and grandeur that is in each one of us. So other egos outside yourself will also sense the grandeur that you are, and will immediately warn others that you are insane, or that you are in denial, because you are not seeing reality. Does this denial thing sound familiar?

It always seems we are accused of being in denial when we "go against the grain," so to speak. Have you noticed this? But other egos are correct, and your grandeur certainly is in denial. The grandeur that you are is in denial of the illusions projected by the world's ego, and knows that true reality lies within and does not need to be boastful, or pompous, or demanding.

The ego's grandiosity is a common obstacle in the jealously guarded relationships between a man and woman, or in the love-hate battle. I remember issues with a woman I was deeply involved with for many years, where I was often accused of being involved with other women, which was absurd. It seems that when she was a child, her own father confessed not only to her mother, but to the entire large family, that he was having an affair with another woman. This tore the family apart, and sure enough, the marriage ended in divorce. This family split apart in the days when divorce was shameful and not nearly as popular or accepted as today. It humiliated the children, especially among their friends. I was able to understand this, because I can remember this same thing happening to a friend of mine's parents when I was growing up.

There would be times in my relationship with this woman when I would work long hours, or choose to be alone, or maybe go out with a few of my male friends. At times, when I was away from her, her fears and insecurities led her to think I was with another woman. It got to a point where she would follow me around to places where I would meet with my friends. After several episodes of our bickering over this ridiculous assumption, I became defensive to a point where I realized this had to stop.

I simply decided I no longer needed to defend myself, and remained quiet while she grilled me. I would try to overlook her behavior by considering its source. The more I remained defenseless, the more she would become emotionally upset and suspicious. Back then, of course, I wasn't able to see this "dance" for what it was. But somehow, some of the times, I seemed to know what to do to calm her fears. Nonetheless, we engaged in a vicious circle. Once her accusations would start up, and sooner or later run out of steam, she would then turn back toward more suspicion. Of course I was no angel myself, in that I, too, would start to become suspicious of her ulterior motives, if any.

Rather than understand that space and time might have helped her to sort this out, my own ego would become defensive when faced with her unjust attacks, and the result would be an ongoing battle between both our egos. We accomplished nothing, other than to increase distrust, doubt, and fear. Hiding out until the next time, our separate egos would privately simmer, building grounds for the next grandiose defense.

The *Course* teaches that "From your grandeur you can bless, because your grandeur is your abundance." What does it really mean, to bless? In the example here of my past relationship, to bless might have meant allowing my grandeur to be touched by her grandeur, or for mine to touch hers. In this way we can bless each other. Neither party needs to be aware of what's happening. If I can recognize the grandeur in her, a blessing has been made. We do this by holding it in our minds and keeping our vision whole as we overlook illusory behavior.

In other words, I could have said to her, "Honey, you are mistaken about what you are accusing me of, and I do understand your concern. Please believe me when I say there are so many lovely things I see in you." Once this gesture is given from your heart, be done with it, and if necessary leave the scene temporarily, allowing her time and space to absorb the forgiving words, which is healing time. When we bless we are simply extending our love.

Grandeur is about pure truth. Truth does not get suspicious, nor does it become vicious. Truth, being what it is, cannot vacillate. How can *oneness* vacillate between something other than being at-one? It is very easy to distinguish grandeur from grandiosity, because love is returned and pride is not.

Consider a clear night when you are enjoying the stars and full harvest moon in a calm sky. Do you cover your eyes to shield the splendor? Of course not. You accept the beauty for what it is. But since the beauty of the star-filled sky is merely your separated mind projecting an image while you dream, the starry sky itself cannot possibly be the grandeur you sense. The grandeur is within the splendor of your real mind, which reflects its image of the night sky. Your dream-filled mind may very well see the stars and moon, but the real unseparated you beholds the grandeur that the dream portrays. In other words, "a sweet dream." Anyone who dreams of love will be drawn to grandeur, which has no need to hold pride.

Only love and good can result from grandeur, because if there is no love there can be no good. We see this represented symbolically in *The Wizard of Oz*, where Dorothy could not have ever awakened out of the dream of Oz if her good and loving home in Kansas were unreal. The Holy Spirit will only recognize what is real, which is our *God-Given Grandeur*, and it is an extension of God. He gave us this real value; we did not proclaim or establish it falsely, like the charlatan Wizard of Oz did. Our grandeur needs no defense, nor does it need a curtain to hide behind. Grandiosity is no match for who we truly are.

Is it arrogant to recognize and radiate our grandeur, you might ask? The ego thinks it is. But our grandeur is what it is. To accept ourselves as God-created, we cannot be arrogant; rather, it is the denial of arrogance. But to accept the ego is arrogant, because it means that you believe yourself to be truer than God.

Chapter 27

The Ego's Plan for Grievances

Believe it or not, the ego has set up a plan for you to help you find your way in this world, and it's a grandiose plan for salvation. The ego's plan is the opposite of God's plan and is full of stress. The ego's plan centers on holding grievances. It maintains that if others acted differently we would be profitable, or the marriage would work out, or the budget would be balanced, or the right amount of weight would be lost; and the list goes on. The ego's grievances make a never-ending chain of events that "could be," "should be," only if "things were different," or "if he or she would only change." The excuses and blame pile high.

This is why the ego's plan is always "Seek but do not find"—thus assuring us we will not find the life we are seeking. With all the talk about salvation, do we really know what it is we are trying to be saved from? Grandeur does not need saving. We've already discussed that salvation is being able to acknowledge that you are being guided by the Holy Spirit as you live your own true free will. He helps you seek out only what you will absolutely find. Otherwise, your purpose becomes divided and relies on fantasy wishes.

The ego's plan for forgiveness is also fantasy and is surely grandiose. In our culture the quest for forgiveness and healing is undertaken by individuals who are unhealed themselves, but claim to be *healers*. These "unhealed healers" try to heal what they have not healed in themselves by using external means. The priestly class may wish to believe in special oils or waters, or other such forgiveness/healing fantasies. Some may claim to draw spirits through themselves, or may use chanting or ceremonies said to draw the attention of spirits, saints, or God, as though the *Divine* is outside of ourselves somewhere and requires convincing to come to our aid.

Another approach toward forgiveness and healing is taken in a therapeutic fashion, by therapists and theologians. A theologian may insist that every one of us is a sinner and use the fear of condemnation while urging us to repent to effect healing. The therapist will charge you for hours on end to listen to you in an office setting. The goal is to cut through past experiences that have led to current depression. A psychotherapist is more likely to make us believe that our attack thoughts are real, as both therapist and patient work to uncover the dark sources of our unhappiness.

The theologian instructs us to look for a distant light "out there," while emphasizing sacrifice so we may be rewarded that the light will shine upon us. The psychotherapist wishes to help us find our light by analyzing the darkness. However, both are missing the point, and certainly missing the Holy Spirit, who cannot be found "out there" or in the darkest realm of the psyche: the ego-based world of fantasy.

Healing begins by perceiving the Light, then translating that perception into clearness of mind by continually extending it and accepting the clarity for what it is. This clarity leads to certainty. There is not a single ancient writing that can prove your certainty. But there are present effects that assure you of it.

The *Course* shows us how the ego is off in too many directions, seeking for what it will never find. It really doesn't want salvation, which is why it cannot explain or understand being saved. "The Holy Spirit is the only Therapist. He makes healing clear in any situation in which He is the Guide. All you can do is let Him fulfill His function."

Consider that if the ego is unreal, and its thoughts are illusory, which leads to false beliefs, then how can something that is unreal be "uncovered?" It can only be acknowledged as unreal by the grandeur that you are.

Chapter 28

Your Grandeur Will Speak for Itself

If we advance confidently with the grandeur that we have always been and will be, in the direction of our true feelings of purpose and not fantasy wishes, stepping through the fog that obscures our way, we will live the life we imagined. The fog will lift, and only then will we find unexpected successes. We will be guided by our own grandeur to put some occurrences, situations, and events behind us. We will see the path that leads us beyond the world's boundaries, where new, universal, and more liberal laws will begin to establish themselves around us and within us. Or the old laws will be expanded and reinterpreted in our favor in a more liberal sense, and we will live within the realm of a higher order of beings.

This is the *undoing* of our errors that is the Holy Spirit's function, which leads us to reawaken from the dream of a separated mind—a fantasy that will never be real. In proportion to all of this, we will simplify our lives.

The laws of the universe will appear less complex, and the errors we make will be corrected automatically. Our weaknesses will not drain us, and all that used to seem like effort will become effortless. All you have to do is tell the Holy Spirit that you are ready for His guidance and simply ask Him to be your foundation. From this foundation you will know eternity without fear.

Remember this when you hear your heart beating for your purpose, and the ego tries to hold you back. If you're having a problem identifying with your life's purpose, simply discuss this with the Holy Spirit. You can easily do this by focusing your thoughts on the following words in the form of a prayer.

What would you have me do?

Where would you have me go?

What would you have me say, and to whom?

Give the Holy Spirit full charge of your thoughts throughout your day. Allow Him to tell you what needs to be done by you in His plan for your purpose. He will answer in proportion to your willingness, and your readiness to hear His voice. Keep your ears and eyes open. The very fact that you have been along with me this far into this book, for whatever reason, helps both you and me to prove our willingness, and this makes us both ready to listen. For you, it is enough to get you started, and for me, it's enough to keep me moving along the path with you.

Throughout your day tell yourself often that you are absolutely sure that the Holy Spirit is at work to help you find and fulfill your function. You will see your clarity increase and lead to certainty as He sees that you're ready for this knowledge. In the meantime, your sureness leads you there. This is the process; be assured that without *your* function or purpose there would be a missing link in the interlocking chain for Atonement. In order that the Sonship become completely whole, it needs your purpose to be fulfilled.

The Holy Spirit is determined to get your part aligned, so you can fulfill your purpose in God's plan for our reawakening. This is the Atonement process. Be alert, be ready, and allow your grandeur to speak for itself.

Chapter 29

Letting Go

How often have you said to yourself, or even heard the statement from others, "Life is passing me by?" When we can realize and acknowledge within ourselves that there is more to our thoughts than our struggles for survival, then the question of the purpose for our life becomes our life. Many individuals are so caught up in the routines of daily living, it seems to deprive their life of purpose. This is why "life passes us by."

This was no different for me, feeling life pass me by in the "dog eat dog" world of the business *I chose*, which then consumed me. I, too, always thought there would be more, and when there wasn't, I thought there *should* be more. Somewhere along the line bits and pieces of my own life's puzzle seemed to begin fitting together when *A Course in Miracles* entered my life and started teaching me that the true and primary purpose of my own self cannot be found outside myself.

I am realizing an inner peace, which opens my eyes to my purpose as clear as day. It is for me to look at myself as one with the real world within the realm of my mind, and to extend more deeply inward, and outward to others, the grandeur of my loving thought. In this way I'm able to help others. I must let the world see me for what I am; then those who accept me will also be sharing who they truly are in that same thought. This is how we achieve our sense of wholeness.

I'm able to see how I share this purpose with every person on this planet. It is the purpose of our being, or as we said earlier, our true essence. It is total right-mindedness. My inner purpose, as well as your inner purpose, is essential to the purpose of the Sonship. It is the directions on the "back of the box" for healing our split and separated mind.

I can hear you saying that "This all seems great, but what is really in this for me while I'm here in this body on Earth?" The answer is simple. Finding and living in alignment with your inner purpose is the foundation for fulfilling your physical, or outer, purpose, which is concerned with doing things, such as your career, your role in the community, your family and your children's future, and enjoying the finer things in life. Your inner purpose will pave the way for your outer purpose, so you can enjoy life. While dreaming, it should be enjoyed.

To begin awakening means to begin acknowledging the split-mind, the dream, and your attempt to heal yourself and others as a whole. This will give your physical life the success it deserves, as well as grant you inner peace. These truths, I believe, are what Jesus and the apostles had conversations about while out on Peter's fishing boat. Inner peace is the bed you lie on while in the dream of life. When you do reawaken, your bed, or inner peace, will still be in place with you in it. No dream can take that away. The ego can only obscure it. But the obscurity never lasts. "This too shall pass."

Meditation can be an excellent tool for tapping into your Home, inner peace. It will support your outer purpose. I'd like to share with you a meditation practice I discovered years ago, and since my connection with *A Course in Miracles*, I have enhanced this meditation from lessons in the *Workbook for Students*. Here it is:

I lie flat on my back on a comfortable surface. I sense every inch of my body gradually sinking into the surface, as if my body is making a mold. Starting at the tips of my toes I notice a sensation of aliveness flowing through me, upward toward my head and into my brain, where it swishes around, and then, like an ocean wave, heads back toward my toes.

This gets me to notice my breathing. I breathe in through my nostrils, holding for a second or two, and release slowly and effortlessly through my mouth. I focus on the breath and notice the contraction and expansion of my chest and abdomen. I sense my inward breath filling up every bit of space within my body. I visualize the breath being absorbed throughout my entire flesh and bones, into every nook and cranny between nerve endings. I take this sensation into every cell and atom.

I imagine an ocean wave swishing from toes to knees and back, then from toes to hips and back, and again to the shoulders, with added force in the swishing around of the wave, until finally it reaches its peak in the brain. The wave pulls away from the head area with gentle ease, as in a subsiding wave, all the way back to the toes, where I repeat the motion. It's important to gain a rhythm in this motion of the waves: back and forth in a cleansing motion.

Next I put my mind onto the breath and let an outward breath carry all thoughts out into the space of the room. The inward breath becomes automatic as it fills my entire body. The right-minded thoughts of my outward breath radiate and extend, never stopping. The wrong-minded, ego-based thoughts, such as guilt and fear and attack, gradually with ease fade away into the nothing they originated from.

Whatever these thoughts are, without judgment or harshness toward myself, I let go, and I know that I am being honest and true about their ego-based nothingness. With this knowledge they are gone, never capable of being received by anyone.

Letting everything rise through space, as I focus mostly on my outward breath, feels like I am communicating with other minds, who realize or have glimpses of their connectedness to the whole. While inhaling there is a sense of opening up without fear, and receiving into my mind, by way of my body, all thoughts intended for me from the whole. I sense a receiving and a giving from and to the love of the entire Sonship. Every part of the whole is accepting my own thoughts, along with my gratitude for the thoughts I receive.

If my mind wanders off, I simply return my focus to my breathing; my inward and outward breaths seem to naturally put me back on the path. The thoughts I am receiving are not intended to be consciously looked at now, but merely to rest in my mind, where they will expand over time and will be seen by my light when I'm ready for them.

I keep in mind that these thoughts are eternal, and time is only used to get me to the eternal essence I've always been. But even now, this moment, is eternal. I find it difficult to have nagging stray thoughts if I focus entirely on my breathing. The breathing allows me to feel the healing process, and it teaches me that it is Truth.

I find it healing to recognize all the ways I've tried to fool myself by believing the illusions that have resulted in my errors, to realize the attack thoughts I've held inside. I look at all of this with a sense of humor, along with kindness to myself. By feeling sure of myself, I am becoming certain of the whole, which welcomes me; this is how all healing takes place.

A normal meditation for me usually lasts about twenty minutes, and when I come out of my meditation I feel a belonging to something close, safe, and certain. I feel relieved of any physical stress or anxiety and feel connected and not alone.

We all face problems in the world and we're all in this together, whether ready or not ready for healing. When I realize I am talking to myself at times, I look at it as healing in motion. If I feel I'm changing some old, stuck patterns that are shared by individuals everywhere, this gives me room for compassion and honesty, along with my understanding of how we are able to get stuck.

I'm finding out for myself, and so will you, if you have not already, that when we truly acknowledge the healing process, we are told by something divine that it is "okay"; our errors are being undone, so relax and trust.

For me, my meditation sessions have given me the support to just "let go" of the ego. When I do *let go*, the Holy Spirit simply continues to undo what He deems to be necessary in order for healing to be complete. I must admit to myself that my incarceration is a part of the Holy Spirit's undoing process in me. He now knows of my readiness and the truth I see. My imprisonment is what brought out my willingness to just let go.

The meditation will allow you to relax and be still, letting things flow naturally. As with anything else, for meditation to be successful you must participate consistently in this stillness-of-mind practice and experience the inner peace it offers. You and I are not alone, and the way things truly are cannot be taught. There is no formula, it merely is.

I'm hoping to impress upon you that, through still and quiet meditation, we all can pull together at releasing and letting go of certain things, while other things move up to the front. Acknowledging your own *God-Given Grandeur*, and the healing you are constantly involved in within you, is a good example of "things being moved up to the front."

In order for the world to speak as a whole, we first have to see how hard we struggle, and then "let go of it." The ego will be frightened, but that's a good thing. Then we can open our minds to the *Oneness* we truly are, and our hearts will follow while the ego begins to fade.

Our wrong-minded habits of thought will be replaced by our right-minded qualities and intentions.

Chapter 30

The Conflict of Having Two Teachers

If you're searching for a formula for success, it is in healing; and inner knowledge does not pave the way for healing. Rather, it's the reverse. Peace is always first, before inner knowledge; then stillness comes, along with silence. This process of quieting the mind worries the ego. This is why I urge you to practice meditation. Peace is the grandeur of the Kingdom and is the quality that directs healing to take place, ultimately leading to knowledge. There is no such thing as conflict within peace; thus conflict is not of the Kingdom. Peace is the condition for the Kingdom of Heaven, and grandiosity can never understand this. In a section just ahead we will discuss in more detail what actually is the Kingdom of Heaven. But before we do, try to really get a sensation or feeling deep within you about the grandeur that you are. Hold onto that Truth.

For now, let me ask you: If you have an argument with your spouse just before bedtime, what are the chances of finding the peace of your kingdom in the bedroom that night? Regardless of how you view your kingdom, you are going to have to meet the conditions for peace within yourself. God's Will is peace, and if you oppose His Will, how can this be knowledgeable? The goal is knowledge of Oneness, and peace will get you there through healing.

When we have the knowledge, our entire being operates from truth. This is inner strength. If we had the knowledge of how our own healing and the healing of others affects the way we see the world, we would not be so ready to allow the ego to consume us. The argument at bedtime may have been avoided if either party had been alert enough to consider any ego involvement, for whatever reason; then peace could have been offered. A healing mind could have understood the conflict the ego desired, light could have been shed, and the entire conflict defused.

The ego's distractions may seem to interfere with healing, but can only do so if you give it the power to do so. The ego's voice is not real. We can't expect it to say to us, "Hey there, just in case you were doubtful, I'm not real after all." You don't need to evaluate the ego's voice when you hear it, but you do need to acknowledge its false presence by shining your *spiritual flashlight* directly on it. Look at it closely, notice it without judgment, and also observe the feelings and how they make you feel; then be done with it by letting it go.

If you don't want the ego's voice chanting in your head, depriving you of peace, then it will be removed from your mind. Simply by understanding that the ego is intruding means you recognize that peace is being deprived. You are then in a position to ask the Holy Spirit to intervene and to remove the ego from your mind. This is the power of your knowledge that started with the perception by your right-mind that the ego was intruding. Truth is now known to be within you, and it becomes your inner strength.

The message I'm hoping to convey in this chapter was portrayed in an old, old movie I watched while in prison. Saturday night at Belmont Prison is normally a time when we are offered a movie programmed by the recreation department. It is the option of each inmate to watch the movie in the crowded dayroom, where we sit elbow to elbow on steel benches bolted to the concrete floor—not a very comfortable setting for entertainment. Nevertheless, on a particular Saturday evening I decided to watch the black-and-white film about the days of the New England settlers and their survival building a life in the New World. With all they struggled with, it struck me that much of their constant threat from and conflict with the Indians resembled what many in prison are up against with the gangs and the struggle for mere survival behind the walls of prison. Depending on the length of one's sentence, you do try to make some type of a life for yourself. This is an essential part of survival in prison to keep one from losing himself.

On the frontier, the first generation of Pilgrims experienced rough times with the native Indians. On one occasion during a hostile Indian threat, local authorities urged a community of Quakers to enter the local army fort for protection. Considering this a retreat behind arms, the Quakers maintained their spiritual commitment to nonviolence and chose not to enter the fort. They continued their normal activities.

One day, while they were sitting in silent devotion in their house of prayer, a party of Indians suddenly approached the building. The Indians were painted and armed and ready for the work of slaughter. They passed back and forth before the building, war-dancing by the opened door of the church, peeking curiously inside, until having sufficiently encountered the quiet worshipers. The Quakers went on with their worship without defense or anxiety, just as though the Indians were not representing a threat. The Indians realized the Quakers were not a threat to them, and in time they respectfully entered the prayer house and joined the Quakers.

The Indians were greeted by the elders of the group of Quakers with an extended hand of peace, and were shown to such space available in the house, which the Indians occupied in reverent silence until the meeting came to a close. They were then invited to one of the nearest dwellings by the leading elder of the society. On their departure, the Indian chief took the elder aside and pledged him and his people perfect safety from the red man.

The Indian chief said to the elder, "When Indian come to this place, Indian meant to tomahawk every white man for his scalp. But Indian find white man with no guns, no fighting weapons, so still, so peaceable, worshiping Great Spirit. The Great Spirit speaks to Indians' heart and tell Indian 'No hurt white man,' so we decide not to bother white man, and we like peace, as you do."

Okay, it was an old movie with clichéd dialogue. But what was obvious here was that the Quakers did not allow their egos to acknowledge the egos within the Indians. When we respond to our own ego, growing angry or fearful or judgmental, it makes it that much easier to engage with other egos, due to the ego's need for defense. This is not only a call to war against whatever enemy you believe to be outside of you, but is also a call to war within yourself—a call for inner conflict. But the only opponent for war is your physical self. Those whom you perceive as your opponents are part of the peace you are giving up by deciding to attack them. How can you have peace if you attack it? This is not part of your kingdom.

Realizing your part in the Atonement gives you the opposite perception of what most have been learning, as well as an opposite outcome: peace for everyone. And giving it in order to receive it is the way to Atonement, not by fighting over individual peace. Anything individual is identified with the ego, and the ego is not capable of ever having peace. Why? Because it's not real. If the outcome of your life has made you unhappy, and you want it to be different from what it has been, a change in your learning pattern is necessary. We can all do this; every one of us is learning all the time.

First you must change your direction, and be consistent with one solid learning pattern. If your learning is planned by two separate teachers who believe in opposed ideas, it cannot be integrated as one pattern. If you depend on two opposing teachers simultaneously, each one merely interferes with the other. This leads to fluctuation, but not to change. If you become volatile, you have no direction. You cannot choose one because you cannot relinquish the other, even if the other doesn't exist, meaning the ego. The ego sows confusion by teaching you that many directions exist, while giving no rationale for choice.

We must recognize the total senselessness of this before a real change in direction can become possible. No one can learn simultaneously from two teachers who are in total disagreement about everything. They would be teaching us entirely different things in entirely different ways, which might be possible, except that both are teaching us about ourselves. Your true reality is unaffected, but if you listen to the ego your mind will continue to fragment, as the ego likes to do, giving you additional false realities to deal with. Remember, our goal is to undo the false, not to make more of it.

The Indian chief and his warriors chose their direction once they had knowledge of what they truly wanted. Peace was already part of their grandeur; therefore, they acknowledged it and chose peace over war.

The Quakers had not a single doubt in their minds, regardless of the Indians' decision; peace was their teacher then, and remains so. The Indians did not want to fight against peace, their true teacher. We can say that in the realm of One-mindedness, the face of Christ chose for the Indians and was the Grandeur that made the decision of a direction resulting in peace. Did the Quakers set the example by sharing in the Christ Mind? Of course, and it was so because of the example they followed from the Christ Mind in the man, Jesus, who once walked this earth as a part of the dream, giving us all this same lesson.

The ego, which is unreal, can never be one. But your free will, which is of peace and brought to your attention by the Holy Spirit, is one and is not fragmented. Your true free will is a direction that has one teacher and one purpose. However, you must first be on the same page with yourself, before you can begin to fulfill your function guided by the one teacher of the entire Sonship.

He can do this because He is of you, and you are of Him; One Mind that constitutes one whole, therefore impossible to be located "out there." Your own acknowledgment of all this is your holiness. Just as in the story of the Quakers and the Indians, it lets *you* teach the world, which is one with *you*. You cannot do this by preaching it, but merely by your own quiet recognition that in this holiness all things are blessed along with you— except for the ego.

Jesus, as our elder brother, makes this quite simple when he tells us through *A Course in Miracles*: "Every brother you meet becomes either a witness for the Christ in you, or for the ego in you. It is your choice."

Part VIII

Peace Is in Who You Are

Chapter 31

The God of Sickness

Wouldn't you agree that we are truly under no laws but God's? Of course, I am not trying to say we should ignore man's laws of the land in which we live, which are designed to maintain order and peace—at least the lawmakers' version of peace. I'll leave that "can of worms" unopened, though I may decide to open it for a future book. When I say there are no laws but God's, I'm also suggesting the ego-based fallibility of all of the grandiose beliefs that have written our books of laws, both religious and civic. We've created a magical body of guidelines for humanity to adhere to in order to be a "God-fearing individual." Well, fearing God surely is what mankind has done to himself. If we fail to lead a life within these laws, other men who are organized to "know" tell us we will "burn in hell."

The *Course* teaches us: "All magic is an attempt at reconciling the irreconcilable, and all religion is the recognition that the irreconcilable cannot be reconciled." What is the *Course* trying to get across to us here? What this means depends on which thought system you choose to use. If you use the real thought system with which the Holy Spirit guides you, then your understanding of what *A Course in Miracles* extends to you will be interpreted in your own unique and truthful way. There is no right or wrong way, such as a correct or incorrect answer to a test. Your right-minded thought system will yield only truth as you know it, without ego involvement. It reveals the core of who you are, and not who I am. We do both share the same guide, however; and since I am the one writing this book, you get to have a glimpse of how the Holy Spirit is guiding me, and our shared guide of inspiration may communicate to you through these words in some fashion.

Keep in mind that I am not in any manner picking on religion. I am personally grateful to the many teachers, nuns, priests, and others who helped in giving me a foundation for looking at myself and the world. But the ego is in the mind of all of us for now, and it often finds its way to control or govern groups by promoting the concepts of sin, guilt, and hellfire, especially when we have conflicting beliefs. Purveyors of this religious doctrine have never gone to great lengths to teach us that there are no such things as sin, the devil, or the gates of hell. This set of rules would rather have us believe that our "all-loving Creator" would cast us out of His arms and into a fiery pit to eternal suffering. The Truth, which was placed gently into my "essence," tells me I have no reason to ever believe these tactics of a "nothing-based thought system."

Once again, these byproducts of the dream of separation, which include this doctrine, seem to be fearful things—illusions made by the ego to continue the separation and the fantasy. Our real mind is already at Home, while a separated or split-off portion seeks for a better world. For this very reason, sickness and perfection can never be reconciled, and will forever remain irreconcilable, because a Mind of God that is perfect can never be sick.

God created us perfect, so we are all perfect. But illusion will tell you otherwise. If you believe in sickness, you have placed your sickness first, before God. He created you first; sickness did not. By believing in sickness you have placed yourself at the mercy of false gods, or a sickness you wish to kill. You may have trouble seeing this clearly at first, as we have all been taught to place way too much emphasis on our body as who we are. But being angry at a sickness is the belief in an idol, which has turned on you.

Sickness is merely a happening of the body for a period of time, and time does not really exist. That's why sickness doesn't last. It does not own or control you. It is no threat to who you are, or your Oneness with God. Remember, you continually live on and on, regardless of any attacks on your body.

Does all of this mean that if we take prescribed medication in order to fight, say, an infection, or high blood pressure, or diabetes, or have surgery to treat cancer, that we are attacking an idol, or believing in sickness? Or does this mean that if we meditate, eat a wholesome diet, or exercise to keep healthy, we are granting reality to illness? Absolutely not. It is important that we do our best to maintain a healthy body. Such temporary conditions as colds, high blood pressure, and even cancer can be helped by medical treatments. This help comes from within the real world, where wholeness is the answer. We'll go into this more a bit later.

For now, please keep in mind that as long as we are of a separated mind, with two distinctly opposite thought systems, the mind is never clear of ego interference. To know this and to realize what is real, we must be able to judge within ourselves what we perceive to be unreal. When we are truly judging within ourselves about the real and the unreal, the Holy Spirit is actually doing the judging for us. When you overlook an ego-based thought, the Holy Spirit is judging it correctly for you, and it means you need to "let it go."

If your mind fills up with ego-based thought, or illusion, you cannot have knowledge about these thoughts because knowledge is Truth, and Truth is never illusory. Therefore, Truth and illusion are irreconcilable. They simply have never coexisted as one, and what you and I are is one with Truth. Neither you nor I can be partly true or partly false. *We*, together, are both true without variances. One day our bodies will turn to dust, and where will *we* be then? I hope by now you can answer this. Well, okay, I'll say it again: We've never left Home.

If you believe you are sick, you are believing that part of the Sonship is sick. We discuss sickness here, but this is the same for any other illusion. The Sonship is all Truth and is what we all are, whether awakened or unawakened. We cannot be partly sick, or partly angry, or partly attackful, and so on. A false god cannot choose one part of the Sonship and make him sick, then heal him. If the Sonship is one in all aspects, it cannot be divided into separate parts.

If we perceive a sickness as an invasion to who we truly are, our mind is split into more fragments, making more ego, which certainly means we are not functioning wholly. This is the control and power the ego seeks. Our bodies will from time to time have ailments, and will one day not recover from a certain ailment, which will merely stop time from operating your body. This is what we decided would happen when we separated our thought from God's. We gave the thought of sickness to ourselves, as a separate illusion our fragmented minds hold onto, and with separate definitions and degrees of sickness. In other words, it is our split mind that believes it has a body that is sick.

To believe in a sickness as "before" God is to believe it is "before" Oneness, or everything. This is impossible. God's laws are of freedom and love, which is total Oneness, and neither comes from your body. Somewhere along the way the world has taught us the laws of bondage, and we continue to believe the path of the ego will lead to freedom. Freedom and bondage cannot be reconciled, although many struggle to do so in the form of religion, by thinking that freedom and bondage work hand in hand to promote God's laws. Bondage and freedom working together can only be beneficial to continually and consistently fragment our mind, and in this manner, bundles of ego-based thought are made. It's truly that simple.

Chapter 32

Finding Peace with the Real Thought System

I may have come across to you so far as being against religion, and before we go any further, let me say this is not the case. How we choose to look at our chosen religion, or that of others, or religion in general, once again depends on which thought system we are judging from. If the Holy Spirit is doing our judging, then we are against nothing and can only be on the side for *Truth*. In reality, what does it truly matter which religion, if any, individuals choose to participate in, when they know from their own heart what is right for them? No one has the right to tell you what should be in your heart.

But if we believe we have sinned, we are adhering to—even worshiping—the only thought that makes us feel unaccepted by God. What else but the idea of sin brings into existence our attack thoughts? What else but our belief in sin then becomes the source of guilt, demanding punishment and suffering? Additionally, what but the concept of sin can be the source of fear, obscuring Truth, making love seem like some higher characteristic of fear, and of attack? Sin is an ego-based thought, and this thought can only develop in a separated and continually fragmenting mind.

As a child growing up in the Catholic school system, I was taught that if I sinned I must do penance handed down by a priest—a form of punishment in order that I might be forgiven. A typical penance might be to say ten "Hail Marys," maybe three of the Lord's Prayer, and almost always an Act of Contrition. I wondered why I would be given a punishment to say prayers. Even as a child I asked myself, "Shouldn't prayer be something I want to do because it gives me peace of mind?"

If we participate in a belief out of fear—say, the fear of going to hell—then this is not freedom, but merely a disguise for bondage. The laws of freedom that are made by man can often be, instead, the laws of bondage, written by fragmented and splitting-apart, wrong-minded perception, believing that this is where power lies. But Truth is the only power there is, and our right-mindedness tells us that bondage is not truth.

We've seen it often: the devout churchgoer who, once away from the steps of the church, criticizes or ignores the beggar who is hungry and homeless. The thinking seems to be, "If he'd only get off his rump," or "If he'd put the beer bottle down long enough he could work for a living like normal people," or "If he won't help himself, why should I?" This type of thinking leads to more separation—more bondage in the mind—and the hour or so at church each week is an attempt to buy freedom. Another vicious circle. Those who believe this type of freedom is available are trying to purchase it from false idols, only to add to the chains that already imprison them.

God has protected everything by His laws, which are the laws of love. There are no laws for deciding what is appropriate to love. When we choose fear and separation, we have given our loyalty to the gods we chose to dream up, but they will not be there to accept it. Therefore, how can we find peace with this type of a thought system?

As a prisoner in this prison system where I do my time, we literally are packed into a warehouse-type setting, with rows of double-bunked beds stacked like cordwood. Each double bunk is placed thirty inches from the next. There are few places to sit and write or read. In fact, as I write these words into my journal, there is an inmate on each side of me, our elbows touching by hair or skin, and loud, obnoxious, and vulgar conversations going on all around me. There is no privacy, even when showering or using a toilet. We are in one another's faces constantly, all day long and well into the night. We literally view the world from the inside-out in many respects.

The relentless closeness of living space is the main reason for violence in prison—not unlike what happens with animals when you keep them locked up together in a too-crowded cage. I once witnessed an older inmate grab a younger inmate by his long hair and slam his face onto the concrete floor several times. Blood spurted everywhere. It seems the younger inmate thought he could get away with moving his bunk over by a few inches into the older man's space. The young man was actually trying to steal six precious inches of territory.

Yet, this physical closeness will, at times, bring out some sharing of another's anxiety, loneliness, or despair, and can open up a limited line of communication, often with some somber conversations.

The most common problems of despair and anxiety come from home, and are shared among inmates who have obtained a certain trust level with one another. The "let down," or disappointment, from family and friends can be brutal—especially family, which seems to hit the heart the hardest.

I have seen this heartbreak on the faces of many prisoners of all different ages, when a family member has turned his or her back. The family takes the attitude that the prisoner's situation is not their problem, nor do they want it to be. "He made his bed; now he must sleep in it" is a typical response from many family members. I have seen the letters from home that others have confided to me, and many family members act as if the inmate has died. Many fellow prisoners have expressed their grief and disbelief in this distancing of their family. Some lament the hypocrisy of those who espoused their "church following" ways prior to their son, brother, father, even grandfather going off to prison.

One man's adult daughter wrote to him saying she could no longer be in contact with him because of his *life* sentence in prison. She didn't see the use in maintaining a relationship with a father who would not be able to involve himself physically with the events in her life and that of her children. She said she could not bear the fact that her kids had a grandfather who was doing life in prison. This tore the man to pieces, and later he was found dead, hanging by a bedsheet tied to the end of his top bunk.

Another man tried to choke himself to death, and a prison guard had to quickly remove a mop handle from his throat. His wife of thirty years had divorced him without notice—no letter or phone call. The divorce papers were finalized and mailed to him by the court. He will be on suicide watch for the remainder of his eight-year sentence.

Another prisoner used a torn-apart twin-track razor to slit his wrists while in the shower directly next to me. Medical staff arrived in time to save his life. His mother had died suddenly of a heart attack, but no one in his family wrote to tell him. He was notified a month after her death by the public defender who had represented him in court.

I could go on and on about this, as the stories may seem unbelievable, but are all true. I write to my own loved ones, telling them of this ugliness, and I have no reason to exaggerate. These things happen all the time in prison, and all too often.

When I first entered prison and started to hear this kind of talk about families turning their back, I felt disbelief. I said to myself how certain I was this would not be the case with my own family. I saw this as a problem I would not have to face, even though I had been warned by others this response was common. Sure enough, I was wrong. Some members of my own family distanced themselves and became nonsupportive. I was kept out of the loop on many family issues. I was shocked, and hurt, and still to this day feel the pain. But once again, the pain is only as bad as the thought system I use to feel it with.

I consider myself fortunate to have the support of others in my family, who seem to understand, or at least want to try and understand. They know I appreciate them, and my love goes out to them. For the ones who have chosen not to stick behind me, my love goes out to them, too, and I am able to overlook their decision, because I understand the ego hold on all of us. I don't try to understand their feelings, because their feelings are their own. But I am grateful I am able to look beyond, because a few years ago I would not have been able to do so. Now I deeply understand that there is a *cause and effect* to everything. And I am able to see the healing taking place in one individual, though all I can do is wait until she is ready.

Since becoming a student and now a teacher of *A Course in Miracles*, I understand that false gods don't bring on chaos. How can they? But we choose to make the chaos, which makes the gods seem real when they surely are not real at all. In the case of families who have distanced their family members—whether in prison or for other reasons—they have their own set of rules that we cannot change. What anyone can do in a similar situation is to accept the fact that nothing but God's laws have ever been and will forever be. Simply trust His laws.

When we can forgive, we're not only overlooking, but also "letting go" of things, and this allows us to look beyond the body. This is how the Holy Spirit can release us from the ones we have forgiven, and we put it in His hands for undoing. This in itself becomes a great act of faith, because it is your recognition and acknowledgment of the power of the One Mind that is eternal.

Chapter 33

Heaven

Heaven is within the realm of a powerful thought that is of itself. This would be you. It is the ceaseless, uninterrupted One Thought of love in all of creation, in all situations. There is no beginning or ending to its flow. It is not an energy, but is simply all that there is. It is your essence, conflict free, where all efforts are effortless. Its results are at such a maximum that the body cannot understand it—although in the Kingdom of Heaven there is no such idea of a maximum or a minimum. But since we can only comprehend what is of time and space, the word "maximum" offers us a sense of measurement. All this effortless power is yours, and everything you touch, see, hear, and love is of maximum beauty and joy and peace, and therefore, is beheld and experienced with the Christ vision within you—the One Mind that is your true identity.

Jesus had the knowledge of this, which is why he said, "I am with you always." He meant it literally; therefore, we are "the way, the truth, and the life." As our elder brother, Jesus individually is our model and is a manifestation of the Holy Spirit. This was intended so we can see that we, as well, manifest the Holy Spirit physically in our own one-minded actions, even as we dream in our separated state of mind. These actions and reactions, which are our manifestations, are a result of the Kingdom within us, or simply put, Heaven.

These manifestations of the Holy Spirit arise not within your body, but with *you*. All that your body can do is act them out. So when you overlook the behavior or attitude of others, in this forgiveness you are acting on behalf of the Holy Spirit and are a physical manifestation of who you truly are. The more we forgive, which is to overlook and look beyond ego-based thought, even within ourselves, the less ego involvement there is in our process of making atonement.

When you see yourself as separated from who you truly are, you experience your body and yourself together as unreal. This is why the ego is insane and teaches us that all we can ever be is our body. This is why we fear death. This is also why we interpret the Second Coming of Christ as the arrival of a man's body.

Who you truly are is not a lesson some other individual can sit down and teach you. It is merely known by you, once you lift the obscurity of the illusion of you as your body. You already do see without this obscurity quite often, though you may hardly realize it. This cannot be done by effort; it can only be done by "undoing." The Holy Spirit leads you to these moments, but in time the ego is alerted and interferes, only to bring on more obscurity.

The reality of the Kingdom is where moments are not questionable, because the Holy Spirit's function is to undo the questionable and make it certain. Your oneness with all of creation is perfectly certain and perfectly calm, and you experience these moments without doubt. Your mind holds onto perfect peace and serenity, because that is what you are.

Because of our separated mind, and since we are dreaming of time, these moments when we experience the Kingdom seem to be quite brief. This is because the ego is alerted and interrupts to remind us of being in a body. However, during those moments when the ego is silenced, time is irrelevant, because in that moment there is no beginning or ending. In other words, time does not exist. A present moment will remain a present moment until the ego speaks up to remind us of its past.

Absorb now what I have to say very carefully, with all of your awareness. Have you ever had a flash, however brief, of awe and amazement, a moment of *"no-thinking,"* and merely total alertness and attention? Although it does not last, you may indeed have experienced this many times without realizing what it is and its importance. This is what you need to become aware of, to sense the fact that you are safely at Home in Heaven, while your separated mind continues to dream. The beauty, the majesty, and the sacredness of nature has a way of whispering without conflict into your dreaming mind, giving you glimpses of an awakening light.

Have you ever gazed up at the infinity of a quiet night sky, in awe at the splendor of the stars and moon glowing its vastness directly into you? Or have you ever stood at the edge of the woods facing a green meadow as the sun is swiftly setting and heard the hammering sound of a wood hen echoing in the forest behind you? Or have you ever been out in the middle of a calm lake, with the water still and glistening like glass, as a gentle rain silently ripples the lake into motion? Have you ever stared into the eyes of a wild animal, such as a squirrel, or a fox, or deer, as it gazed directly back at you as though it were trying to tell you something?

Beyond the beauty of these external forms and within the experience itself, there is more to be found. Something that cannot be named. Something ineffable, some deep inner holy essence that shines through somehow. It only reveals itself to you when you are calmly alert to a present moment, with no chatter going on in your head from the ego. Your mind is perfectly still and quiet and peaceful. It may only last a second or two, but it is there. This nameless essence and your presence are one and the same. It could not exist without the Oneness of a single Thought that holds it together. This One Thought is Heaven, and the Mind that sustains it is God.

The very instant the ego recognizes this, that heightened present moment becomes a thing of the past, and time once again is suddenly ticking away. But with the guidance of the Holy

Spirit, time can be used to *lengthen* these moments of pure thought, without ego interference.

We all fear and wonder about the end of the world, due to our tremendous hold on the body. However, if some cosmic convulsion or nuclear greed brought an end to the entire physical universe, with the earth and the stars and the sun exploding into nothingness, the real universe would remain totally unaffected. At the moment your body dies, the ego is silenced forever, and you become that present moment. Life continues, without interruption.

Chapter 34

Participating in the Holy Encounter

A Course in Miracles offers us a glimpse of Heaven, in that "everything God values rests There, and nothing else. Heaven is perfectly unambiguous. Everything is clear and bright and calls forth no response. There is not darkness, and there is no contrast. There is no variation. There is no interruption. There is a sense of peace so deep that no dream in this world has ever brought even a dim imagining of what it is."

If you can begin to realize that any conflict within you is there because of variations, or real and unreal powers, you would see your freedom and be able to attain and maintain the peace Heaven offers you. Its gifts are yours, because you are what makes Heaven.

Everything you need in this world has already been given to you. You are lacking nothing. You might be using unreal power to achieve your goals and the gifts you desire. But if you will truly confide in the Holy Spirit your yearning for the light you feel you are lacking, then you will learn that you indeed have a glow. Your Creator is Light, and He has lit your lamp from His. It will never burn out, but it may become dim due to your own obscured thoughts. The Holy Spirit merely uncovers the obscurity so you can see your own light. He is the direct communicator between your mind and the Mind you emanate from. If you want to experience Heaven, you can learn to make the decision to hear from the teacher who knows all about you. All you have to do is sincerely ask, and then start opening your eyes to the world around you.

There is no limit to your learning, because there is no limit to your mind that has been extended you from God, and equipped with the Holy Spirit as the mediator of true Thought. How could there ever be a limit to this perfect Oneness? What is it exactly that is involved in this limitless learning? It's pretty simple. It is the Knowledge of your Oneness with God and the Sonship. Dr. Wayne W. Dyer states in his book *Real Magic*, "When the student is ready, the Teacher will appear." You are the teacher and the student. If you are ready, which is what we have been discussing all along in this book, then you will see the Holy Spirit's lessons everywhere you go and in everyone you encounter.

But if what you wish to experience is not of the Will of God, you will only be blocking out these lessons. Let's be real here. If you are pursuing something that is not truly good for you, then how can you be happy? You can't. The Holy Spirit understands that the Will of God cannot be forced on you. He also knows how to teach you and guide you toward God's Will; but you may not know this, at least not yet. There may have been some unfortunate happenings in your life, just as my own incarceration has been to me. The Holy Spirit had no other option but to use this route in order to get my attention. Think about this deeply concerning your own misfortunes, which may well lead to your fortunate true purpose. Or something may already have worked out for you as a result of what you once thought was a costly mistake.

The Will of the Father, and the Son, which is you as your part in the Sonship, is One extending Thought. It allows you to extend yourself as well, when it is of your *true* free will. Your will is His Thought, and the Holy Spirit's task is to deliver it to you. In the process, your free will is extended and received into the Sonship.

This process may entail new physical occurrences, such as an unusual meeting of another individual or something new among your normal and usual acquaintances. Situations or awkward circumstances may pop up unexpectedly, simply because your physical appearance was needed for something you may never be aware of.

For example, you may overhear a conversation in a coffee shop, where a complete stranger mentions key words that have an impact on a particular decision you are making. Then, once the decision is successfully made, it may impact a problem in someone else's life. Your individual will is the Holy Spirit's goal, because His ultimate goal is the Atonement. We separated our thought from God's by dreaming, and this is why He placed the Holy Spirit in the dream.

Your brothers/sisters of the entire Sonship, as well, have an individual free will that the Holy Spirit foresees, and His function is for the will of your brothers/sisters to operate along with yours. It must, otherwise it could not be the One Thought of God. This is perfect creation, which is what you and I are. The Holy Spirit assists you by using time to precisely have each *effect* serve its *cause*.

Therefore, do not discount "hunches" or intuitive feelings toward an action you might be considering. If you act, and if it comes from your heart, you cannot go wrong. If your hunch is off track, don't be too concerned, because if you acted from truth and your free will, you cannot be harmed. Besides, it is possible your hunch was right all along, but it is not time yet for the results to manifest. As well, be on the lookout when you meet someone for the first time, and remember that it is a "holy encounter." How is this, you may ask? How you look at him or her is how you will think of yourself. There is nothing else for you to look for, or no other thought to have. The goal here must be to "know yourself."

We are all looking for our own purpose while we are here on Earth. Even if we think we've found it, we still leave room for question or for ways to improve. But consider that since you have only two thought systems, and one of them is the illusory ego, then the Holy Spirit must be where your Truth abides. Your mind is acknowledged by you as either wholly of God, communicated through you by the Holy Spirit, or it is of the ego. There is no other, nor a combination of the two. Therefore, which of the two is the real you?

With this understood and accepted, whenever you are with another person, you have the opportunity to find them, rather than fear them. The ego will try to judge them, whether good or bad. It will always be for how you may benefit or prosper by knowing this person. Keep in mind the old adage about "judging a book by its cover." Your ego will immediately wish to size up a new person you encounter, but only has the experience of "nothing" when it comes to judging. Its credentials speak for themselves, since the ego is nothing.

Whenever you are with another person you are learning what you are, because you're teaching what you are. Keep in mind, you are either projecting illusory images or extending one-minded thought in all encounters. The ego projects; the real you extends. Whomever you encounter will respond either with fear or joy, which is the same as untruth or truth, and this will depend on which teacher you are listening to—the ego or the Holy Spirit? They are both within you, but only the Truth is real.

Your encounter will either imprison you or free you. Bondage or freedom will be based on how you decide. This is a huge responsibility you have to yourself, so that each encounter can be in line with the Atonement, or "nothing" at all.

This is why it's always important to keep the ego out of any encounter you have, which will keep it a "holy encounter." Having understood this, now you can see why you once believed that when you first met another person, you thought he was someone other than yourself. Every *holy encounter* that you enter into fully will teach you this is not so. And try to remember this when you catch yourself "judging the book's cover." Even in a holy encounter, once the person walks away from you, their own ego may turn on its projector, and so may your ego begin projecting images. But that's okay; at least you will have initially seen that person for the truth.

Since you and your brothers/sisters are of one Thought with God, you can only encounter part of yourself, because God is everything. God's Thought is everywhere, and you cannot exclude that because you are included in it. The ego will teach you that you think you are alone for your own purpose and that your purpose is for you alone. How often do we hear the advice "Look out for number one?"

The Holy Spirit, the only real aspect of you, will guide you to see that your strength lies in the strength of praising His Thought. How do we truly "praise God?" It certainly does not mean you should go around town telling everyone you run into "Praise the Lord." The Holy Spirit has given you this strength to fulfill your own free will. So living your daily life by pursuing the purpose you truly see fit for you is most certainly your way of "praising the Lord."

Our all-loving Father does not want us to suffer for a wrong decision, and He certainly doesn't punish us for any such wrong turns on the world's roads. The ego wishes us to "burn in hell." God has given us the Holy Spirit to undo our wrong-minded thinking, including the thoughts of a fiery hell.

Wrong decisions are taken care of in such a way that they have no power. Anything not of power cannot be a Will of God, therefore will never know the Kingdom of Heaven. If you encounter God's Will everywhere you go, then you will know your purpose.

Chapter 35

Being the Truth That You Are

Are you able to live a life that is not about who you truly are and still be at peace? We might try to justify within ourselves that we do what we must in order to survive. We pay the bills, or we live up to the family name, or like many, we believe we are not good enough to lead the life we truly desire. So we remain stuck in a mold that the world has set for us. But can we really blame the world? Or is it really that we remain stuck in the mold so we may please the world, avoiding conflict for fear of attack? Is this fear of attack, such as thinking, "What would people say?" simply another excuse or an untruth? If so, what is it you really fear? I can hear some egos saying right now, as you flex your muscles, "I don't give a darn what people think." You want to bet? We all do, at some level. We all want to be loved and accepted.

Of course, love is what Oneness offers—is what Oneness *is*. Nonetheless, we decide to remain living the delusional, where we judge truth as something we don't really want. It's as though we're afraid of it. We're afraid that if we go with our "gut" feelings, in other words, go with what is really within us, then we would be in denial or accused of being in denial. This would single us out for all to see us as a failure, or a rebel, or nonconformist, causing us much embarrassment and anxiety, and possibly loss of the ones who we think love us. This is what we think might happen, but rarely does.

Could we be afraid of losing love? As we discussed earlier on, the only denial in this sense is the denial of ego-based thought and refusal to live a life of illusion. We get comfortable and complacent living according to ego-based gossip and illusory ways of portraying who we truly are. We block all knowledge, except for the knowledge that keeps us comfortably satisfying the ego.

There is a way out of this trap, but once again, you must be operating from truth. It must be total Truth and not a partial truth, nor can it be a truth that is "stretched." So before we move on here, please ask yourself one simple question: Why am I afraid of the Truth?

Since you must operate from this one and only Truth, bring out your spiritual flashlight right now. Go ahead, I'll give you a second or two to reach for it. Okay, let's go. Shine the light directly on the Truth you see and notice. The one Truth seems to be a very lovely pathway. This is the path of your desires that need to be a part of you, more than just goals. Look at these true desires—not fantasies, but sincere, honest desires—which portray who you truly are. If you sense a swift tug by the ego while doing this, it is normal. You need to cast the light onto it and simply suggest that it needs to move aside. Let it know that as of now, in this present moment, you are operating from your own true free will, which is God's Will.

Let the ego understand this without having to explain yourself, as you shine the Light on your resistance or indecisiveness. Then immediately begin to trust that the Holy Spirit will be leading and guiding you on your way from here on. Notify the ego that you are now using the Light to cut through the obscurity the ego has made for you. You might visualize this much like the light on a locomotive, confidently cruising down the track through the fog. You must stand firm, and keep your spiritual flashlight handy to shine away any further antics of the ego.

Alone you can do nothing, because all you'll have within is the ego, which is nothing. But together with the Holy Spirit, as well as with your brothers/sisters of the Sonship, and their guidance, too, from the Holy Spirit, you can fuse a power far beyond any power you could ever master alone. This power is invincible because it is undivided and is of the Mind of God.

The only way to know your own will as God's Will is by surrendering yourself to it. Yes, by totally being a part of the undivided will of the Sonship, which is of your real mind, wholly of God. This is your freedom, where the prison door swings open.

How do we become whole? By being your true self in all that you do, and by understanding that healing is the process of making whole. Therefore, to heal is to unite those who are like you. You don't have to "do" anything. Perceiving the likeness is enough, and is to recognize the Creator of this undivided whole. You recognize God by feeling safe and guided, or by being at peace, just as when you heard the wood hen hammering away in the woods or wondered at the vastness of that starry sky you know so well. Yes, it was a projected image, but the sensation you felt was God. Even while you dream of separation, you are realizing that you are being guided back Home. It is a safe and joyous journey, and man, is it ever Heaven!

So relax, because when you recognize this undivided whole, however briefly, as one with God, you are recognizing yourself. This gives you the confidence to step out of the mold the world was happy to see you fit into. You will also be able to immediately recognize the ego in any given situation, and notice the discomfort it gives you. You will know how to force the ego to back off, as you alert the Holy Spirit to undo any ego-based thought patterns. Once again, practice using your spiritual flashlight, the Light that you are. The process will become automatic whenever you sense the ego sneaking into a position to pollute your thoughts.

Your union with the Sonship is beyond the ego in you. This is why forgiveness gets you there, because you've "looked beyond" by "overlooking." Your success in putting the ego behind you is guaranteed by God. While you are here in a body, the ego will still be there, but behind you as a follower and a wannabe. Its nothingness cannot match you. Nothing can prevail against your united will with everyone and everything. The Holy Spirit will not allow it.

Leaving your comfort zone may initially frighten you, if this is what is necessary to get started on the road to peace. Just go with your heart. The ego will attempt to join you on your journey, but you cannot allow it. By sensing defeat and becoming angered by it, the ego will regard itself as rejected and will become retaliative. You may hear negative "self-talk," telling you that you are stupid or worthless. The rejection may seem to hurt, but it's not real pain because it comes from nothing. When you feel such pain, immediately place your Light on the pain itself, look at it, and feel it for what it is: nothing.

As mentioned earlier, let me caution you again not to express any anger or hostility or fearful emotions while using your spiritual flashlight, because this is how the ego can sneak in the back door on you and come up from behind you. This is another trick up its sleeve. It's important that when observing the ego, or the emotions or thoughts it gives you, that you merely observe by using your grandeur. The ego's grandiosity won't stand up to your *God-Given Grandeur*.

A good example of how you could look at this is the manner in which you take out your trash. You don't get angry or upset or fearful when the trash smells terrible; you just notice it and drop it into the trash can and are done with it. You feel no loss. So use your spiritual flashlight on the ego, much like taking out the trash. If the ego finds that its sneakiness can upset you, it may try to set another mold for you that it thinks might suit you better—but that is just another detour on a wrong path.

The ego's way is not the Holy Spirit's way, but it is also not your way. The Holy Spirit has one direction for all minds, and the one He teaches is of the Sonship, which is what you and I are at one with. Never allow the ego to interfere with your journey. Go ahead and notice it, because not noticing the ego would be denial. When it reveals its guilty and jealous face, let it become aware that you hold the Light of Grandeur over its nothingness. Is this arrogance? No, but thinking that you are something that is really nothing is.

Part IX

Knowing the Whole

Chapter 36

Knowing the Whole Entirely

Arrogance can be seen as an ill attitude toward the body, which is expressed when you attack. When the ego judges anything, it first looks at what it believes its use can be in order to benefit the body. It believes that you are your body and teaches that you are meant to attack with it. The ego does not view your body as the true source it's meant to be. In the real world the body is a communication source while you dream of separation. Your body is the means to unite with your brother, by communicating through it. If God's children are going to dream about the fantasy of a separated thought system, He wants them to have the means to help one another to reawaken.

By communicating with one another, we can bring illusory thought to the real One Thought of God. This is the true journey we are on, as the Holy Spirit guides us to the goal. The body is an illusory projection of who we think we are; however, it's not the source of its own health. Your body's condition lies solely in your interpretation of its function. If you believe in sickness, you are supporting sickness as inhabiting your body. Your body does not determine the functions of anything that is real.

Your functions are part of your being, since they arise from your being. But your being certainly does not arise from your function. For example, your occupation does not define who you are. Therefore, why should a certain sickness define who you are? Your true essence, or being, is first. Your being is of God. The whole, which is of God, defines your part, but your part does not define the whole. God is the whole and is not separate from you. This is the confusion in the world of ego-based thought. However, to know your part in the whole is to know the whole entirely. This is so through your understanding of the difference between knowledge and perception. God is 100 percent knowledge, and our knowledge is Him.

When you first perceive a picture of the whole, you may think of it as built on separate parts joined together. You may think you can pick and choose from these parts, to determine who does what, or who does more or less. But with true knowledge of the whole, you will see it as *never* changing, and with no separate parts.

Consider a vase that holds and protects flowers. The vase has its base to enable it to sit securely on a table; it has a midsection, which leads to its rim; it has an exterior and an interior, designed to receive water and allow the flowers to reach to the light. The vase is one whole vase and will not serve its purpose if it is split into separate pieces or parts. There are no interchangeable parts, and its separate parts if broken apart cannot contain the beauty. So it is with us—with all of creation.

In order for us to achieve total knowledge of the whole as it is, it must be through the Holy Spirit. He will teach us the degree of its completeness, which can only be whole. This knowledge is necessary to keep the *voice of indecisiveness* out of your head. We seem to have two voices fighting over different uses of our body. If this perception is true, our body has the capability to shift its allegiance from one voice to the other, making concepts of both health and sickness meaningful. Thus the ego gets confused between our body's means and its end. Regarding the body as an end, the ego has no real use for it.

Have you ever noticed that when you set out to achieve something, and you finally reach your goal, that a part of you is still not satisfied? This is why we become so indecisive when considering one goal or another. It's that ego confusion over the body's purpose.

Isn't it difficult to overcome the belief that when your body dies you will no longer "be?" Conversely, isn't there a constant urge in you that tells you there is more to you than a body? This is why the ego likes it when you get sick—because when you are sick you shift your attention to your body and you feel vulnerable. The ego likes this, because then you will be in need of what it can offer you. The ego wants you begging.

Chapter 37

Extending the Present Forever

It's difficult for us to look at a sickness, whatever it might be, as a false witness to who we truly are. Why? Because we want the ego's comfort.

I remember as a child, about age seven, having a terrible accident while playing a game of hide 'n' seek when visiting another family who were close friends with my parents. Their children were of similar ages as me and my siblings, which made for fun times. In my efforts to find a good hiding spot in a shower stall tucked in a dark corner of the basement, I tripped and fell, landing on a broken shampoo bottle. In the 1960s, if you can remember, bottles were always glass—and my arm was badly cut. This resulted in a trip to the emergency room, where I endured about fifty stitches up and down my left arm. Need I say this interrupted my parents' card game with their friends?

Not too many years later, companies switched to plastic bottles for such products as shampoo, for economic as well as safety reasons. But this is not my point here. Although there is a certain *cause and effect* to everything, even with the identifiable scar that remains on my arm today, I haven't recognized the effects of this mishap, if any. But then, maybe I'm not supposed to.

After the accident I was pampered by my mother for several weeks, and of course I enjoyed being treated as though I was special. There was plenty of blueberry ice cream, and I was relieved of my chores. An infection set in to delay my recovery, adding to my pain and fear, but in due time the stiches were removed, and the healing eventually moved along to completion.

For too long after the stitches were removed, I continued to be obsessed with the pain in my left arm, pouting that the ice cream seemed to be not offered any longer. My mother caught on quickly to my antics and made a decision for me, by calling an end to my pain. She declared me no longer an ailing invalid, and my father teamed up with her to convince me further I was not in pain. In fact, he mentioned having a method to end my pain quickly. He joked about grabbing a saw from his workbench and sawing my arm completely off. His theory was, "No arm, no pain." He added that "What no longer exists cannot possibly hurt." I was able to see the love in his joking and did get the message that I had been healed, and I was soon back to terrorizing my sisters. Even as a child we learn of the ego's comfort.

Allow me to move along to 1990 and share a brief story about my friend and business partner, Mark, who left this world after a fight with cancer. Even though Mark's body died, he won the fight with cancer by displaying his power over it. The cancer lost total control over him.

Mark was undergoing treatments for two years for an aggressive form of lymphoma. It got to the point where doctors gave him the news that they were losing the battle. Mark was asked to consider experimental treatment that would be extremely tough on his body and would offer hope of a cure only for future patients. The treatment was promising not for Mark, but for others, although the treatment would prolong Mark's life for a while longer. This was fine with him. In fact, Mark jokingly went around telling people he was a "guinea pig" for cancer research.

Mark didn't give up hope within himself, but he did accept that his body was going to die at a younger age than normal. He was twenty-nine. He gained momentum in a commitment he made to help out medical research and was glad to contribute to what he said he "knew" would save others one day. This became

Mark's passion, and he felt as if he were a member of the medical team—as though he had become a part of science. He quietly gained the knowledge that he had found his purpose and was now fulfilling it.

Of course Mark still hoped his own life would be spared, but he never dwelled on his cancer, because it wasn't his, he "did not own it," I remember him once saying. He saw himself as wholly of the research to kill the beast, and this was Mark's way of saying, "Praise the Lord." He was able to speak of how "God works in mysterious ways" through his actions and his thoughts. He did not have to parade around town, or get on a pulpit, or run a newspaper advertisement to do this. He was extending himself, rather than projecting images of pain and suffering, and as a result brought loads of joy to the others he was being treated alongside of.

We can say that Mark "forgave" himself and the cancer inflicting his body. He forgave himself for a number of factors he might have been responsible for, that might have brought on the cancer. He overlooked and forgave any environmental issues, rather than trying to place blame. He chose to focus on what he could do now, in the present moment, to help others, and he had the knowledge that eternity was his.

The Holy Spirit teaches us to use our body to reach others, which Mark chose to do by using the cancer that consumed his body, so the world could see there really is nothing to fear. Mark was not, in any fashion whatsoever, in "denial" of his cancer, but he was denying it as being a part of who he was. He denied the cancer ownership over his life. He removed the ego's claim on being real, and Mark actually lived to see the ego fade away. The Holy Spirit had a lesson that was taught through Mark, as He does with all of us. The lesson is not to allow the body to be a mirror for the split-mind, or the carnival mirror of this world.

Health is seen as the natural state of everything when you leave its interpretation up to the Holy Spirit and not to the ego. Health is a result of using the body to communicate love, which is wholeness. This is what Mark did with his own cancer treatment. His mind was centered on giving and receiving, and if his own body had been spared, it would have been a result of his own giving on a "wholly" level. The cancer merely passed through his flesh and bones, and the Holy Spirit was aware of it but did not change it, because time was not a means for this lesson. Mark didn't get any "raw deal" by getting cancer. He lives, and forever.

Mark's dealings with cancer did teach me an important lesson from the Holy Spirit, and now I pass it on to you. I have learned that each instant is a clean and untarnished birth, wherein, being a child of God, we are able to emerge from our past into the present—and that the present extends forever.

Chapter 38

You Are Presently Eternal

Now is a good time to shine your spiritual flashlight on the doubts you have about your own mortality and eternity. As you place the light on your doubts, sense the Holy Spirit being your answer to all there is. After all, He is the Spirit of God and is within you. This is the answer to all your questions.

The ego does not even know what a real question is, although it's always asking plenty of them. When you are sick—say, with a simple cough, sniffles, and flu-type symptoms—don't ask the Holy Spirit to heal your body. By doing so you are only accepting the ego's belief that the body is the proper focus for healing. Instead, ask that the Holy Spirit teach you the right way to perceive your body. Ask that He undo your vulnerability to the ego.

In the previous section, Mark showed us how he perceived his body. Many might say that he had no choice, as death was surely evident. But this is ego-based thinking. He did indeed have a choice. He could have moaned and groaned while berating the world, asking for all kinds of pity and attention. Rather, he chose to see what the Truth within himself had to show him.

As for your flu symptoms, you may decide to rest and eat chicken soup, or visit a doctor for the appropriate medication, which are the responsible things to do. But in addition, you can simply ask the Holy Spirit in the form of a prayer something like this: "Holy Spirit, I realize I have temporarily lost touch with the wholeness I know I am. Please help me to maintain the knowledge of my body's purpose. Whatever it is that my body is going through at this time, I release it to you."

When we perceive something as being wrong, we're actually wishing that things could be a different way. However, the "way" is who you are. The conditioning of our awareness of sickness is really what ails us. Remember, this awareness of being sick has the strength of generation upon generation of lessons. It's as though we have learned to make sickness a reality of who and what we are. We must change our perception so we understand that our true reality will "find us" when we are ready and that the Holy Spirit is our true reality. This is the "whole"; nothing else, and certainly not a sickness.

You do not have to be sick. Just because you experience some conditions with your body does not make *you* sick. Release the symptoms to the Holy Spirit and He will help you bring the whole to you. Something will show up. Your little part is so powerful; so accept it and let the whole be yours. Ask yourself a question about how you viewed the story with Mark: What showed up for him?

Wholeness heals because it is of the One mind. All forms of sickness are physical expressions of the fear you have toward reawakening. Mark chose not to see the cancer in his body through the carnival mirror. Most of us feel that to reawaken will take us out of our comfort zone. But what really is awakening? It's simply when you can finally acknowledge that you have been operating from a split-mind and that you are now allowing healing to take place, which is a continuous process. While we are here on Earth we are always healing in some way. The Holy Spirit is constantly undoing errors that have kept you asleep. The ego tries to urge you toward believing that what you caused cannot be undone. The Holy Spirit knows better, because anything that is real, you did not cause. It has always been. The ego wants you to remain asleep, where you will not realize what the Holy Spirit is showing you.

This is why, somewhere along the line, the ego came up with the phrase "Rest in peace." How insane can this be, to ask that a dead body get some rest? "Rest in peace" is really a blessing for the living, not the dead. A spirit is always at peace, and there are no evil spirits, as the ego would like you to believe. Rest comes from waking, not sleeping. Sleep is withdrawing; waking is "joining." The *Course* workbook illustrates that "Dreams are illusions, or fantasy of joining," because they reflect the ego's distorted notions about what joining really is.

The Holy Spirit does have good use for sleep, however, and can use dreams on behalf of waking if you will let Him. How you wake is a sign of how you used your sleep. Under the influence of which teacher did you sleep? How do you feel once you awaken? Only when you awaken in a good mood with a positive outlook, even under your dreary eyes, have you utilized sleep according to the Holy Spirit's purpose. When you are healing, which we all are doing always, will you be released from the fear of waking to a disastrous day? Your decision to awaken in a positive state is a reflection of the will to love and to forgive. You can easily overlook the ego's attempts to influence you and look beyond its influence it has had on others as well. This is all it takes to forgive, and by forgiving, you are automatically loving.

The Holy Spirit doesn't distinguish between degrees of error. If He taught us that one form of sickness is more serious than another, He would also be teaching that a certain error can be more real than another. His function is to distinguish only between the false and the true, replacing the false with only the true.

The ego is always trying to weaken our mind by telling us that our bodies are being destroyed. The ego wants you dead, and yes, it believes it is also protecting the body. You may have an inclination to think this book is a study of the ego. Of course, this is what the ego would think. But this is far from the truth; rather, you need to be aware of the ego and its trickery, so you can have inner peace. But the ego's idea of peace is having your allegiance to the ego. It despises free will and intelligence and sees them as weakness, even though it makes every effort to make us weak. The ego thinks it has the power to attack, and it takes pride in this.

The Bible tells us to be perfect, to heal all errors, to take no thought of the body as separate, and to accomplish all things in the name of Christ. In the *Course*, Jesus teaches us that this perfection is not to be in Him alone, but in all of our names together, as *shared identification*. Every one of us together is the Sonship, and if we can picture a "self" of the Sonship, this "self" is the face of Christ. We are Christ as the "shared identification," which is the Holy Spirit manifested, not one particular man. But Jesus, as our elder brother, brought the realization to us, and he is first in the interlocking chain of Oneness.

The name "Christ" has no exclusive rights by religion; this name refers to God's only begotten "Son," which is the Mind of God. It is His creation and not a projected image of one individual. Everything of the Mind of God is the present moment. In this present moment you are eternal, and in the eternal we "rest in peace" as the Christ, with our Father.

Chapter 39

Your Brother and the Christ Within

When I am discussing the Christ in you, I'm not meaning actually "in" your body, but I do mean in "you." The Christ in you is not outside yourself. Anything physical about your body—your skin, your internal organs, even the cells and atoms themselves—are outside of who you are. The smallest cell in your body is a part of your physical flesh and bones. These microscopic body parts are not who you are, but rather they form the framework to the physical structure you project of yourself. These cells and atoms don't have eternal life. But you do.

Your holiness is not your flesh and bones, but your holiness is who you are. This is Christ. This is the *you* that will never die. Your body is merely a temporary structure, a communication device the Holy Spirit uses. Who and what you are is at one with Christ, whose purpose is to make manifest the One Mind, or allow it to be seen through you by those who don't know He exists. How you reveal Him is in the way you reveal your true self. Those who do understand this, by realizing this knowledge, will see Him through you as well. Likewise, you will see Him reflected in all others you meet.

Maybe now you can see a meaningful light when you hear the phrase "Christ is everywhere you go," and it does literally mean physically "everywhere you go," at least while you occupy your body. However, once communication has been linked up by the Holy Spirit through the use of your body, you do indeed go places without your body.

How many times, when facing an important decision, did you remember something that an old friend or family member once said, not necessarily a lesson, or good advice? It may have been bad advice, for that matter, but it may have been a set of words that spurred or triggered a thought you needed to make that decision. Or have you ever been thinking of someone when the telephone rang unexpectedly, only to be that person? The response we have when this happens seems to almost always be, "Oh my God, I was just thinking about you!" Then we are quick to shrug it off as coincidence. Usually it is only coincidence—but what, really, is coincidence? Isn't it only a word and a meaning derived by the ego?

Do you, as a child of God, and not meaning of flesh and bones, abide everywhere? Of course, you certainly do. This must be so, because the Christ Mind that you are a part of—the "shared identity" we previously discussed—is everywhere. If you still feel a bit confused here as to how you can be everywhere, it is likely because you have too much attachment to the body, or ego. Try to think of yourself this way: When your body turns to dust, where will you then be? This will make more sense to you in time, which the Holy Spirit is using at this moment on your behalf for this very purpose.

God is not separate from us and is the Love we have inside us. He works through the Christ Mind that we each are, using the Holy Spirit to get the message out when it is needed. This occurs in the realm of cause and effect. All communication takes place within the Christ Mind, at-one with God, who is the maestro of this one magnificent symphony orchestra.

I'd like to share an experience with you, in which I witnessed this orchestra perform. The maestro pulled the strings together, as He conducted the brass section where my longtime friend trumpeted his way to my aid. The music continues to play to this day.

Ron and I became friends some twenty-five-plus years ago, through my business activity as a financial advisor. Over the years we witnessed each other's children grow, and we were helpful to each other when both of our wives passed on in separate years. Ron and I have seen each other's good times and bad, and our thoughts were always shining bright for each other.

Things grew busy in the material world for both of us, and we both seemed to have gotten "caught up" in the world. Suddenly there was a gap of a few years where we had not seen each other. "Time flies by," as the adage says, and it surely whizzed by the two of us. But we did keep in touch periodically with e-mails and cards at Christmas, and we always had the good intention of making time to play golf.

When I was initially incarcerated, I needed much help getting personal and business arrangements squared away. I was totally helpless from behind bars. Prisoners always need help from the outside for many other reasons as well, including dealing with and communicating with lawyers. And of course simple interaction with a good friend can help keep spirits alive and positive, through the letters and the limited phone calls an inmate is permitted to receive or make. However, I completely gave up. I felt like crawling into a hole and dying, and I decided just to be alone.

When I was charged, indicted, and arrested, I thought about my good friend Ron often, but I didn't want to trouble him. I also didn't believe my case was as serious as it turned out to be. Ron lived 150 miles away, so he didn't see how I was chastised by the local newspapers. He didn't have a clue what was going on.

After being in prison for a few months, and before my encounter with *A Course in Miracles*, feeling the most destitute I'd ever known myself to be, I began wondering more about Ron. Something sparked inside me and was longing for a bit of encouragement and positive outlook from Ron, who was an excellent source for what I needed. I thought about writing him, but my lowness ran so deep it could not get out from under a rock.

During the time all that was going down with me, I was not aware that Ron had mailed a short note to my home, which had already been seized by the courts, informing me of his move to Florida. This was something that he and his deceased wife, Joyce, had always planned on doing. He mailed the note only after realizing my telephone and e-mail service was disconnected. His letter to my home was returned to him by the post office, due to lack of a forwarding order. This concerned Ron, as he was aware it was not like me to leave town without at least notifying him.

During this time Ron's new doctor in Florida had given him the bad news that he had serious intestinal cancer and that surgery was necessary in the weeks ahead to remove the cancerous section. "Coincidentally" this was also when I decided to write Ron a letter explaining my whole ordeal. Of course being unaware of his move to Florida, I mailed the letter to his Ohio home, but I did not remember his entire address and sent the letter off without a zip code, in hopes I would get a little help from the post office. No such luck. The letter was returned to me in prison. My wheels started to turn in different directions, trying to locate Ron's zip code. The prison library was no help. Finally my lowness gave up on that, too, and I proceeded to sink even lower.

However, the Light began shining through my own cloud cover. To my elation, a few weeks later a letter showed up for me, addressed from Ron. Tears sprang to my eyes as I gazed at his return address in Florida. My hands were trembling as I held onto the envelope. As I wiped my tears with the back of my hand, I noticed his handwriting was scribbly and unlike him. I sensed something was wrong. I soon found out he had written that letter from his hospital bed while recovering from surgery and while heavily medicated. He was aware I needed help.

It seems a past mutual business acquaintance had sent Ron a newspaper article about the drama the press had conjured up about my case, as well as my prison sentence. Ron immediately had his daughter find out more on the Internet, especially the name and address of the prison where I was being held. From his hospital bed, this is what my good friend had to say in his barely legible handwriting:

Dear Jimbo,

I pray you are okay. I just found out through Mac what happened. I know you need help. I will take care of whatever it is I'm able to do. I just had major surgery and I am weak, and still in the hospital. They tell me I'll be okay. Give me about 10 days or so to recover, and I'll be in touch. Help is on its way. Hang in there buddy.

Your pal,

Ronnie

Need I say more about where this message from my old friend took me inside? Ever since, he has been heavily involved with lawyers, other friends, and all that it takes to help work toward my release from this inappropriate prison term. I can honestly say that without this man's help, I would not have had the resources, while in prison, to begin this project. This man has helped me to accomplish much more than a positive frame of mind.

Ron visits me consistently, even though he lives in Florida and the prison is in Ohio. He tells me it gives him an excuse to visit his aging mother and his daughter, who both live within a short distance of the prison. His letters continue to arrive, full of encouragement and optimism. There is definitely *Truth* inside this man who seems to be on a mission.

A Course in Miracles teaches us that: "Such is the mission that your brother has for you. And such it must be that your mission is for him. The mission unites together when you realize the Christ who you both are."

Chapter 40

A Meditation for Communicating with the Whole

I wrote earlier of my sincere belief in the practice of meditation. It is an amazing technique for bringing about inner peace, especially in this world that so desperately tries to deprive us of it. The previous sections guide me to want to end this section with a meditation I have put together, based on various lessons from the workbook for students in *A Course in Miracles*. The *Course* does not promote meditation because that is not its purpose. However, the *Course* gives us every opportunity to take its lessons to whatever level we deem necessary, in the stages of our development to Oneness, or "One-Mindedness."

This meditation works for me, and its purpose is to help you see Truth, or One-Mindedness, in all that you do throughout your day. You will learn firsthand through your encounters that giving and receiving are both aspects of the same thought. This will help you to see "holy encounters," rather than just "running into" an old acquaintance.

True light, or in other words, your true state of mind, makes true vision possible. I am not describing the kind of light you see through the body's eyes, but merely a state of mind. Our goal through this meditation is to achieve a state of mind that will become so unified that darkness, or wrong-minded perception, cannot be perceived at all. What is seen as the same will be seen as one, while what is not the same you simply will not notice, because it really isn't there.

Your true light will bring peace of mind into other minds so you can share it and experience the whole. You may be asking, How does this happen? It happens when your mind learns to extend thoughts, rather than the way you were taught by generations upon generations to project images. Our extended thoughts spring from Oneness and remain one with us; the images we project are ego-based thoughts, sent forth as separate entities. Wrong-mindedness projects; wholeness extends.

Remember, projecting an image only benefits how you see the body by using the body's eyes. But extending thought strengthens the whole, which of course includes you. Because you will be sharing by extending, you will become of the whole, and healing will take place. Once you are able to have a vision that giving and receiving are one and the same, you will be witnessing the whole, which is Truth.

Begin by using the meditation technique I described in chapter 29, with the focus on the outward breath. Before you start the meditation, while in your favorite comfortable position with your eyes closed, repeat the following words to yourself while trying to see yourself at-one with your own words.

- To give and to receive are one in Truth. I will receive what I am giving now.

Say these pre-meditation words several times, as needed, until they become a part of who you are.

Close your eyes and begin your meditation. Remember, there is no right or wrong way to position your body. I prefer to lie on my back, but you may wish to sit in a chair or cross-legged on the floor. Next come three short statements to say to yourself while focused on your outward breath. Try to create a rhythm in how you breathe in and out, as you repeat these words:

- To everyone I offer quietness. To everyone I offer peace of mind. To everyone I offer gentleness.

Repeat these sentences on each outward breath as long as you wish in the meditation. Pace yourself so that during an inward breath you feel yourself receiving the gift you have previously given out. The key here is to give it and then receive it back with a blessing from the whole, along with gratefulness for your giving and receiving. When you do receive the gift back to yourself, say, "Now I accept your quietness/peace of mind/gentleness," and focus on receiving what it is you need most at that particular time.

As you receive the gift, you will want to hold the breath for a few moments, within your comfort level, and feel as though it is radiating throughout every cell of your body, just as you radiate your gift outward when you are giving it. In this way we are simply using the physicality of your body as a window to your mind. So be sure not to get stuck on the words themselves, such as quietness, peace, or gentleness, for they are merely signs that your physical nature understands. As you do with the highway signs when traveling, just absorb the words for their purpose. The Holy Spirit will translate them to your mind. Once again, this is also how I hope you are reading this book—like a highway sign on your way to somewhere pleasant.

Feel free in your meditation to use your own chosen words once you get used to the idea. You may need help in a given area, so go ahead and use words appropriate to what you want to give and receive.

For example, if you're feeling emotionally weak and having some rough times, you may want to try this method: "I give you my love and faith, and I gladly receive your strength." What you give out is accepted by the whole, and you will receive what you need. Also, do not worry so much about what it actually is that you have to give. This doesn't matter; the Holy Spirit already knows what it is you need. Keep in mind that the whole is constantly giving and receiving. It is abundant, and so are you. This is why it is "whole."

If you will practice this meditation daily for only a few minutes each day, as the days, weeks, and months go by, it will become automatic. You will feel yourself connected to other minds, and will have created a steady, radiant glow about yourself. Your radiant light will bring together other radiant light, where oneness belongs and where true healing abides. The radiance in you is the Oneness of the Christ-Mind.

Part X

Truly Giving and Receiving

Chapter 41

A True Act of Giving Heals

Would you dare to think that love is what's lacking in many people today? Love is what we all really desire, even if we're afraid to admit that love is the primary need for all of us. Why are we so afraid to admit this? Because it's a sign of weakness. Love is the only way to know truth and experience the Holy Spirit. Everything in our lives is a result of either love or fear. There is nothing else. Consider all the feelings and emotions you experience that stem either from love or fear.

When we are not finding love in our lives, it's because we are constantly concerned with loss, which stems from fear. It seems that we initially hesitate to show or give love as a defense against loss. The traditional law of the ego is, "You must sacrifice in order to gain," and this law has its *doubt-hold* on us when we have an urge to express love. We feel as if we will be penalized if we love too quickly.

However, when we think we have found love and display a bit of excitement or joy, we eventually begin to attack it, and this is what penalizes us. If we must attack it, then it really is not love. Thoughts of control are nothing more than preparation for attack, which is counter to love. All that the Holy Spirit can do in this situation is *undo* your thoughts of false love. Remember, love is whole, and wholeness cannot be attacked, because the attacker is an illusion to wholeness. In other words, wholeness is not attackable because it is one with love, and this is all it knows. Besides, how can love attack love? Remember this as well: Anything not of love must be fear, and fear is not real.

By your understanding this, you will know the Sonship as the Wholeness that cannot be attacked, because the Sonship is aware of His Father's love. This is what Jesus displayed to us in the crucifixion. The love of the Sonship, and the love we receive from the Father as a whole, gives us perfect peace, because we understand our own free will. There is no doubt that many do have a vision of their own free will, but are afraid of it. Offer love, and your free will is drawn to itself, like magnet to metal.

What does an offering of love entail? First of all, it surely does not mean to go around all day hugging people and telling them how much you love them. Also, can you get downright angry and still love? Yes, you can, as long as you understand what's going on. Let's talk about being mad at yourself, rather than being mad at another individual, because it is the same—isn't it?

If you are mad at yourself for allowing the ego to get over on you, then you have merely fragmented more ego. The ego has come in through the back door and has you imagining you are mad at an already existing, separate ego. The ego is a vicious circle. There's no *oneness* involved, only selfishness. The anger comes from the ego, and when you can understand this as it is happening, you can quickly overlook it, which is forgiving yourself, and allow the ego to fade away. But it fades into the background only until it finds its way back to you. This is why you have your spiritual flashlight—so you can keep the ego at a distance. It cannot be active without your participation.

The *Course* tells us that "You think with the mind of God. Therefore, you share your thoughts with Him, as He shares His with you. They are the same thoughts because they are thought with the same Mind."

Nothing you think you are angry about is actually a real thought. This is so because God does not have a single angry thought. Remember, we said earlier that God does not get angry at us, so there really is no reason to "fear God." Love is all you are. There is nothing but love in the unseparated Mind of God. Therefore when you are mad, this is not a real thought by your true self. However, from your right-mindedness, you are capable of witnessing these unreal thoughts. Your awareness of these unreal thoughts is the "vision of Christ" within you. This is who you really are.

When we can realize that our function is fulfilled by this vision, we will not be afraid to give and express love. This vision takes fear out of our thought, leaving us with right-mindedness in how we perceive and think. Fear can only arise from a wrong-minded perceived notion. Of course, even right-minded perception will still have to contend with the ego knocking on the door, but we have the strength to not answer. This is the starting point for accepting truth, and it leads to knowledge. Remember, right-mindedness is the road to knowledge, and the Holy Spirit bridges the valleys. When you truly have given, you will have the knowledge that you, indeed, have given.

Mother Teresa once said it best, when she talked about giving all you can from your heart to those who need help. She asked us to "look and hear their plea for help." You can do this by using your Christ vision, without a single thought of "what's in it for me."

Does this mean opening your checkbook at Christmastime to the organization that rings its bells the loudest? It could. But this is not what Mother Teresa meant. Many may respond that they have no money to spare, or the time to volunteer when they have their own family to take care of. Or they may say that they already sent a fruit basket to the nursing home or hospital, and that is the best they can do. This is fine and can be a great act of giving, if it was a real act from your heart, rather than to satisfy the ego only because the calendar says it is the "giving season."

What Mother Teresa meant was, for example, regardless of the time of the year, to visit your friend in the hospital or duck into a coffee shop and buy the homeless person you just passed a sandwich. Or—my favorite cause these days—take ten minutes from your day and write a letter or a short note to the family member in prison. It need not be long and full of dishonest sentiments just to satisfy your own guilt. Be real in your act and in what you have to say. Only you know what the truth is inside you. If you are in fear of losing something due to the effort of a simple gesture, then you will know it.

Whoever it might be, and whatever the reason for their turmoil or despair, simply ask them, "Is there anything I can possibly do for you?" Do you realize how powerful and healing it is to ask someone who is in deep despair what you can do for them? But many are afraid to do this.

Or, even easier, you could ask your friend or family member a simple question after you tell them that you can be a good sounding board: "Is there anything you would like to talk about in confidence?" That's it. Do you realize the love you will have extended to this person by such a simple act of kindness? These acts of giving are huge links in the chain for Atonement. It's not what we give from our material world, but more importantly, it is the giving of who we truly are.

It has been said and written about that Mother Teresa could often be seen in the streets of Calcutta, stooping over to talk with a beggar or disabled person resting on the street side, or up against a building, and giving that person some form of hope. These types of giving do not cost money and are certainly signs of love. The words "I love you" do not even have to be spoken. They are only words and are often without meaning.

Here, in such gestures, you will see the Holy Spirit making physical arrangements through "cause and effect" for your free will to be fulfilled, and thus making a difference in the world. Any negation whatsoever to ego-based thought is a difference made in the world and is one step closer to awakening.

The *Course* goes on to teach us that "when we make visible what is not true, what is true becomes invisible to us." This sadly describes the way many of us are living our days. We are so busy trying to bring the false to our eyesight. By opening your checkbook at Christmastime, for example, just so you can say to others, and as well to your own ego, that you did your fair share, you are shielding the ego from the truth. This is nothing more than defending yourself against true reality by making yourself appear to be loving, caring, and giving.

Remember, our all-loving Creator did not give us our split-mind. Our unseparated mind truly knows what love is and what it is not. We all have this knowledge, but are afraid to awaken to it. The Holy Spirit operates only with love, and He uses the physical realm, as well as the spiritual realm, for undoing our errors. This continual process by the Holy Spirit uses our true free will toward the goal of full Atonement.

Chapter 42

My Dudes in Prison

As I am writing this chapter in a wide-ruled composition journal, it is the Christmas season, which is the loneliest and toughest time emotionally for many prisoners. There is absolutely nothing joyous and peaceful about the holidays in prison. The talk is always about just getting it over with. I mentioned earlier how often I see prisoners who have been abandoned by family members and friends. It's sad when I walk around the cell block and bunk areas, which is one huge cage holding close to three hundred men. Many are slumped over as they sit with arms across their knees on footlockers, or are lying on their bunk, staring at the walls or ceiling in total dismay.

I find this a form of punishment no individual should have to deal with. I am not saying that an individual who committed a crime and violated another should not have to be responsible for his actions. But should abandonment by loved ones be a part of the punishment package? We all need love in this world. Especially those who live behind bars, caged in like animals, deserve some sincerity and honesty from the ones they long for.

In prison every inmate is assigned a job, which keeps the facility running. A job could be anything from working in the chow hall, laundry, or library, to cleaning, mopping, sweeping, scrubbing toilets and showers, and so on.

An inmate is compensated fifteen dollars per month, which is automatically deposited by the state into the inmate's account held by the prison. With this salary we are responsible for purchasing through the commissary our personal hygiene products, such as soap, deodorant, toothpaste, laundry detergent, underwear, socks—just about everything that a person on the outside would have to buy for himself. The commissary also sells additional items of pleasure, like snacks, radios, headphones, soft drinks, tobacco, candy, coffee, and many other items to help make time seem bearable. Needless to say, fifteen dollars per month does not carry very far. Many will go without buying the proper hygiene products in order that they may afford some of the enjoyable items.

An inmate's family and friends are welcomed by the prison to send in money directly to an inmate's account so he can spend more than the fifteen dollars per month state prison pay. A gift of a mere few dollars can help tremendously. Many inmates have no one sending them any money at all, not even a few dollars to help cushion their state pay. This poverty leads to theft, extortion, violence, gambling, and quite often homosexual acts in a prostituted manner. It is unbelievable, the extremes a poverty-stricken inmate will go to for a six-dollar bag of coffee. This is where gang activity thrives, by rewarding the poorest inmates in return for favors to the gang, such as theft and plenty more. All of this leads to violence and "earning one's bones," as we discussed earlier in this book.

Most everyone seems to have a group of two, three, or four people they can talk to on a regular basis, perhaps share a few commissary items, or have a casual conversation. But there is an unwritten rule about placing too much trust in any one single inmate. We're always looking over our own shoulders. There are no friends in prison; at least this is the unwritten law. A casual conversation today can lead to your locker box being broken into tomorrow. Sometimes companions do last, but still with a bit of guardedness. The companions whom we feel able to trust on a limited basis we call our "dudes." A "dude" will look out for another, but dudes also come and go for various and obvious reasons.

For example, at this time there are three other inmates in my loop that I call my dudes. When I gather with them to converse, we call this "kicking it." When we are "kicking it," often emotions are shared about many of the struggles and pitfalls we all face daily with prison life. But once again, we are careful as to how far we will trust. We all seem to have our own barrier to stay safely behind. Still, I have seen dudes share more with one another than they care to admit. I'll let you analyze this, or read between the lines as we move along, based on what you've read so far.

The little bit of sharing that can take place within a group of dudes can sometimes include letters from home, involving events of children, grandchildren, wives, girlfriends, siblings, parents, grandparents, cousins, you name it. All too often the subject is family members who have turned their backs, with no support of any kind. Friends, lovers, and wives hardly ever last.

Take the situation with my dude Paul, who is in a group I often "kick it" with. Paul was given a fifteen- to fifty-five-year prison sentence in a plea bargain. The "bargain" was a promise from his lawyer he would only have to do seven years of actual incarceration. The parole board was to strongly consider him for parole. His case involved a seventeen-year-old girl he had helped out of a drug addiction. One thing led to another, and a sex charge was filed against Paul. This was twenty-two years ago, and he's been in prison ever since. Our egos would ask us what was he doing with a young girl in the first place, but this is not the point here.

Needless to say, Paul has much on his mind to talk about. Before going to prison he had a thriving business in a retail outlet. The store also employed his son and daughter, both in their twenties at the time. His children, now in their forties, now own the business, which gives them a nice income to support their own families, have a nice home, and enjoy the finer things in life.

Paul says this is the thirteenth year that neither of his children has written him or contacted him in any fashion. He learns of their success in business from his eighty-four-year-old mother, who does write Paul often. Paul's wife of thirty-two years divorced him soon after he went to prison. Paul remarks that it's as though he has died in the eyes of the children. He has written to both of them over the years, never to get a reply. Paul has given up on life.

I see so much of this type of thing, it is truly upsetting, and makes for a tremendous struggle for many who must carry on behind bars. I wish to share with you three separate letters written to my dude Russ. Two of the letters are from family members, and display the type of family abandonment I have been discussing. The third is from the only friend who stuck behind Russ. All three letters were received at Christmastime.

Russ was found guilty by a jury in a car accident in which the other driver was killed. Russ was under the influence of alcohol and received a nine-year prison sentence. Russ is age fifty-four, and he says he will live the rest of his years in total remorse. Does this make it okay that he got behind the wheel of a car after drinking alcohol? Of course it does not. But Russ is aware of his problem with drinking and his error that was responsible for a man's life. The Holy Spirit is in the process of using time to undo Russ's error. I am certain of this, because I feel I know Russ.

This letter is from Russ's brother, who is only a few years younger than he.

Dear Russ,

I wanted to let you know that we all got together with Mom and Dad over Christmas. Turkey, stuffing, Mom's pies, the whole works. You were brought up in a conversation after dinner and we want you to know that you are going to have to do whatever it takes to get back on your feet once you get out of prison. Please don't try to place a burden on us. Seriously Russ, we have lives of our own to struggle with, let alone your life.

Dad mentioned that you wished we all could send you a few dollars each month. Well, I see how you are thinking of us. But you've got to understand how hard we must work for our money, and we just cannot keep you supplied with candy bars and coffee. But that's just like you, always so damn self-centered. I am praying for you.

Your brother,

Roy

This next letter was written by Russ's daughter, age thirty-two. Russ and her mother divorced when the daughter was a young child, but Russ did his best as what the world has called a "weekend Dad."

Dear Dad,

I hope you are doing fine in prison. I did get your letter, the one asking me if I could send you some money. I realize its only a few bucks you asked for, but I'm sorry Dad, you must know how hard I work. Besides my car insurance was just due. Please realize that your mistakes in life are not mine. So why would you ask me to sacrifice my hard earned wages? Really Dad!

I hope you are going to church services in prison, and if you're not, then you need to start. By the way, have you ever asked God to forgive you for your drinking problem?

Ya know dad, you were never around when I was growing up, but now you want my help. Please know that I pray for you.

Love,

Erika

This next letter was written by Russ's longtime friend, and showed up on a day when Russ needed it most.

Hey Russ,

I hope you had a pretty good holiday season in the joint! Just joking. I can imagine how tuff it must be. Susan and I went to California and visited the wine country. Man, do I ever say it is simply Heaven! The wine was good—too good. Moderation has got to be our motto at our age, now. Right?

Hey, I'll write later with details of our trip. For today I just wanted to pop a few dollars in the mail to you. Have some coffee on me. Make sure to buy the best they sell.

Please write me a few lines, or even pages if you'd like. I'll be happy to give you both ears. Hang in there buddy!

Your pal,

Bill

A Course in Miracles teaches us: "For the memory of God can dawn only in a mind that chooses to remember, and that has relinquished the insane desire to control reality."

Need we say more about these letters, sent to a man in prison who dwells all day long on the terrible mistake he made, which imprisoned him in more ways than one? Then there is the world we made that cannot control itself, but thinks it can control the universe.

Remember, the real world, our real mind, was given to us by our Creator in loving exchange for the world we made. But we can only become aware of this exchange when we can look at the "pleas for help" as Mother Teresa asked, and as Russ's friend Bill was able to do. He was able to look at the moments Russ was spending in prison, rather than the ego-based errors that placed him in trouble.

As we contemplate the real world, that true reality of who we are, let's begin to look at each moment in this forgiving fashion. Only then can we leave behind the ego and its insane nothingness, which will help us to awaken. Remember, we are all in this together.

Chapter 43

My Dude Ted

Many people think that prison life can be compared to being in the military. As a military veteran myself, I can tell you this is absolutely not so. There are very few similarities, and even those do not accurately match up—although the barracks-style living quarters, the feeling of oppression by authority, and the regimented daily routine might offer a slim comparison.

Prison cells are pretty much a thing of the past, except for maximum security, which is generally for intake and reception, or for solitary confinement. Most prisoners would prefer to have cells for the sense of privacy. But the prison system has discovered in recent years the cost-effectiveness of packing, or I should say *stacking*, more prisoners into these open barracks. As I have described earlier, rows of double-bunked, top and bottom racks are crammed a tight thirty inches apart from one another, with an aisle between the rows of these steel racks called "streets." The two-man racks, top and bottom, are often called the inmate's "house." Worse yet, some prisons are *triple-*bunked.

These streets (aisles), lined with double racks, hold approximately three hundred prisoners to a single room, with bright overhead mercury lights beaming down onto all. The streets are so narrow that two men walking toward one another simply cannot pass by shoulder to shoulder. One of the two men must turn sideways to allow the other to pass. This often leads to a problem, depending on attitudes and unwritten rules governing which man is to turn to allow the other the right of way.

These narrow walkways remind me of the inside of a submarine, as shown in war movies. We are warehoused and stacked like cordwood. The volume of noise is extremely high—ear-shattering and relentless. There is constant bickering and physical violence over inches of living space. Being in someone else's space is almost entirely unavoidable, when one must step over another to get dressed, or simply to climb into his own rack, not to mention the sharing of trough-type sinks and minimal toilets and showers. There is usually a line to use a commode or the shower—another cause for violence.

Today's prison structure is not only overcrowded, but inhumane, and can be considered "cruel and unusual punishment." "How can they get away with this?" is a topic of discussion everywhere among inmates. But nothing is ever done about it. It is evident that the saving of dollars is the number-one cause of the spreading of disease in these germ-infested conditions. At this time I am in a particular area of a prison that houses 214 inmates and only has three commodes. Nobody seems to care enough to help make change, even though countless inmates have written their families about these conditions.

An inmate in prison is treated as the lowest life on Earth. No effort is made to use rehabilitation methods to improve their chances to reenter society. The sole aim in prison is to survive, make time pass, avoid trouble, and of course, get released. Getting out is the most sought-after goal, and any early release is totally up to the efforts of the prisoner himself. Parole and parole boards are being phased out, soon to become a thing of the past, and in some states are already obsolete.

With inconsistent and ridiculous sentencing guidelines, designed only to lure federal money into state prison systems, early releases are limited, but are available, if a prisoner understands what must be done. He must pursue complicated and intellectual avenues on his own or with the help of an attorney. Let's face it: It's no secret that the average felon has no high school diploma; minimal, if any, education; and no money to afford an attorney. The judicial system and the prison system do not inform a convicted felon about his early release options. An inmate who has no lawyer working on his side either researches this on his own or sits in prison for the duration of an unfair and lengthy number of years.

This is where help from family and friends is so desperately needed for an inmate's chances of freedom, as a result of good behavior after a certain amount of time already served. If help cannot be obtained from family or friends, or from another advocate, a prisoner remains a prisoner, regardless of any progress he has made in changing his behavior and his outlook for a better life. The inmate often ends up in some type of trouble just trying to defend himself for mere survival. Just out of cruelty, other inmates can interfere with a man's chances of release by involving him in some type of misconduct to tarnish his record.

Men in the military share a certain trust that can be looked at as a brotherhood. In prison, inmates are in one another's faces. They are enemies, never knowing when someone will strike next. Your own bunkmate can set you up for harm, all to earn a bag of coffee or a pouch of tobacco. In the military we worked closely together and looked out for one another, and in battle were prepared to rescue one another. Staying alive could depend on the soldier next to you, or a para-rescue team dropping into a hostile jungle to save just one man. The common theme in the military is "defending your country," whereas in prison it is defending your own few inches of space in hell.

Inmates seldom relax their guard, and anxiety is always high. We remain skeptical even with the ones we know, our dudes. An inmate cannot get the help or trusted advice necessary for early release from those who must only look out for themselves. Relying on someone from the outside is crucial. There are procedures to follow, motions to file in court, county systems to deal with. What might be required in one county may not be acceptable to the county where your case originated. It is truly an uphill battle, and if an attorney can be sought out to help, it can make a world of difference. But an inmate cannot make the progress necessary from behind bars unless he has help from the outside.

This brings me to my dude Ted, whom I met at Belmont Prison. Ted is forty-eight years old, and he lacks a formal education; he has only completed the fifth grade. Nonetheless, he has been a great teacher, and I am fortunate to have learned much from him about the meaning of friendship. I say that I am fortunate, because in prison a friendship such as I have maintained with this gentleman is virtually unheard of. They just don't exist.

Ted is a sincere, good man who just missed out on opportunity. He had a nasty divorce some years ago, when his two daughters were young and in school. He always worked as an automobile mechanic for a local repair shop in southern Ohio—that is, until the garage went out of business due to the economy, and Ted began having trouble paying his court-ordered child support. When the arrearages on the support obligation became severe, Ted was threatened and warned by a judge that if he did not get his debt in line, the judge would send him to jail.

Panic stricken, Ted began writing bad checks for cash to various grocery stores and drugstores, and then graduated to using stolen checks from a purse-snatching scheme he initiated. His only goal was to pay down his child support arrearages. But he does admit the scheme was too easy, and sooner or later he figured he would get caught. It took the law about a year to track down the scheme to Ted. He had a clean record and never imagined that prison would be the result. Ted was arrested and pled guilty to felony charges of theft, forgery, and a few other lesser charges that dished him out a nine-year prison term.

Needless to say he could not afford an attorney and had to rely on a public defender. Ted had never been in trouble before and had no idea what to expect. He was advised by the public defender to plead guilty and hope for mercy from the court. He was offered no plea deal at all. I later found out for myself that this is common with first-time offenders who are far from being career criminals and are not aware of how the system works. This "no plea deal" is exactly what happened in my own case. I simply did not know that one was available. They certainly do not offer one unless you have an attorney who is truly on your side. This ignorance of how the system works is often used against a naïve defendant, while your own attorney will get a special favor from the prosecutor in another case that is more lucrative. In other words, you are used as an unsuspecting pawn in a tradeoff. This could be compared to a sixteen-year-old who gets his first driver's license and pays sticker price for a new car.

As Ted and I continued to talk about the unfairness of the court system, I began to help him do some research on his options, if any, by using the limited legal materials in the prison library. He was already in his sixth year of prison, and we discovered that Ted was eligible to apply for early release, and had been eligible since his fifth year. No one had ever explained this to him, not even the public defender who had advised him to plead guilty without any plea bargain agreement. Since Ted could not afford an attorney, especially from prison, our plan was to ask his eight siblings to help by performing a small and effortless task with no money involved.

We asked his only brother and seven sisters to give him a hand by sending letters of support to the judge and prosecutor assigned to Ted's case. The plan was to submit their letters of support, along with his application for a "judicial release," which is actually a motion for release to probation. It is often noted that family support can weigh heavily in a prisoner's favor, being that there would be no attorney to sell the issue to the judge. This was Ted's only hope.

Ted wrote a letter to each sibling, asking them to prepare a short letter in their own words showing their support for Ted being released from prison and reentering the community. We also thought it appropriate to include his ex-wife, since his own children needed support. We asked that they all mail their support letters to Ted so we could have the letters attached to the motion for release. Thus we could compile a respectable package for the judge's review. Our goal was to be as orderly as possible, so we also included a self-addressed postage-paid envelope. We would now wait for their return letters, as Ted was certain his brother and sisters, as well as his ex-wife, would be glad to help out.

I am sad to say that of the nine letters with return envelopes that Ted sent out to his family, only his brother replied to his plea for help. Ted's ex-wife had no comment, and his brother spoke for the entire family, saying that they were not willing to help Ted. His brother went on to say that none of them could spare enough time to get involved with Ted's own "self-made problem." The brother added that Ted should stop trying to "play lawyer" and just "grit and bare" the time he had remaining, which was three more years.

Ted's brother also suggested that Ted put more effort into praying, rather than doing his own legal work. He accused Ted of living some kind of fantasy in thinking he could get released early from prison. Ted is still serving the nine-year prison sentence for approximately $6,000 in bad checks, while his own children remain without financial support from Ted.

Chapter 44

There's Only One Response to Reality

A Course in Miracles asks us to contemplate this question: "Can anyone be justified in responding negatively or with attack to a brother's call for help?" The *Course* goes on to teach us that our own willingness *to not* help him, or our willingness *to not* respond at all, shows that what we judge about his reality, and our interpretation of it, is what we see fit for him. In other words, we tell ourselves what is best for him based on our fears of helping him.

But there is huge danger in this to your own mind. If you believe an appeal for help is something else, you will react to something else. Your response will not help such a person's reality as it is, but it will help you to perceive his reality as you think it should be. This unreal perception is your judgment of his reality.

If you continue in this selfish manner, there is nothing to prevent you from recognizing all calls to you for help as occasions for your own imagined need to attack. Think about this. It was this fear and illusory judgment that made Ted's family willing to condemn him, making a reality they wished him to have in order to justify their own fears. They denied their own reality a chance to see truth by making Ted's true reality unreal. In other words, they allowed their egos to make a reality for Ted. Who was truly in denial here, Ted or his family? This is not about who is right or wrong here; no finger pointing intended. My point is this: When we answer a plea for help with the frame of mind, "You made your bed, now sleep in it," what are we really doing to ourselves?

Because of fear of something, for whatever reason, Ted's family had an unwillingness to accept reality as it truly was. They put effort into unwillingness, so that an illusory reality could maintain their comfort level. But is it really comfort if you are a host to fear? Why were they afraid to get involved? Most likely for a number of reasons the world would be proud of—but I'll leave that for you to decipher. The bottom line is, they made their own illusory reality and chose to withhold what is real from themselves.

Anyone can tell us that it's not good to judge a person's situation that you do not understand. However, the truth to us is what we choose it to be, regardless of what rests deep within us. Why? Because somewhere deep down we do know the real truth, and it always tries to surface, but we keep pushing it back down deeper in hopes that it will go away.

I'm sure to this day that Ted's family is still living with their reasoning as to why they refused to help their brother. But they do know the truth. What they most likely don't know is what it is they actually fear. If you are unwilling to give help and also to receive help, it is because of some form of fear that is unreal. To fail to recognize a call for help is to refuse help. Would you maintain that you don't need it?

Let's go a little deeper here, and as we do, please allow yourself to feel a sense of relief, an excitement of sort if you will, that you are seeing Truth. When you refuse a brother's call for help, are you not stating that since no one is helping you, then your help is unavailable? Where is the Truth in this? It is covered up by the illusion of fear. What is it that we are afraid of losing by offering help?

Even if it is control that you feel you may lose, then this is your fear. But if you would only realize that by answering or even acknowledging someone's call as real, you agree that help is needed, and this alone is what will help him. Nothing material or physical is involved. Otherwise you continue to cover yourself deeper and deeper with fear.

Whether you actually get involved firsthand or not, you still have shown the person who asks for help that your heart is open to his situation. But most important, you are showing to yourself your opened heart, or your true essence. It's your *being*. But if you deny him even this, you will not recognize God's answer to you when that time of need comes to you. You must understand that when you answer your brother's call for help, this is one and the same as God answering him. Remember, you are of God, and His Thought is also yours. The Holy Spirit does not need your help in interpreting your brother's situation. But guess what? You, indeed, need His.

Only appreciative responses should be given to a brother in need of help. Your gratitude is due him for thinking of you to help him. Remember, do not try to interpret why he asked you; it is his reality and not yours. Even if his reasons for asking you were out of greed or selfishness, it's his greed and selfishness. It's his reality and not yours. Your concern need only to be about bringing love to him with your response. The Holy Spirit will take your love and use it for his reality of the need for help. Any sense of strain or uneasiness you may feel comes from *not* doing just that.

If you truly cannot help in a physical way, then you can truthfully say to him from your open heart that you do understand help is needed and that you will help in finding someone who *can* perform the task. By answering truthfully in this way, you have answered his call for help.

There is only one response to reality. Does this now make sense, with all that we have discussed so far in this book? This is so, because reality brings on no conflict at all. How can it, when it is One? The Holy Spirit is the only teacher of reality, because true reality does not change. Your own interpretations of reality are meaningless in a separated state of mind, and His remain constantly true. He will give you His interpretations, so be alert, listen, and you will know what to do. If you find yourself stuck, indecisive, or confused on what to do, merely use the meditation I prescribed earlier, and let the "whole" help you.

Do not attempt to help a brother in your own way, based on your reality. The Holy Spirit does not want you to tell your brother he needs to "learn his lesson the hard way," or "he made his bed now sleep in it," or any of the other cruel ways the world has taught us about learning. These are attack thoughts and are not of anyone's true reality. But if these are your types of thoughts initially, that's okay. Simply acknowledge them as ego thoughts, use your spiritual flashlight, and move on to a more right-minded way of thinking. Keep it simple, and certainly do not be hard on yourself. Your errors in thought will be *undone* for you. You will automatically be forgiven.

You will recognize God's answer through the Holy Spirit as you truly want God's answer to be. It will be comfortable and not fearful. It will be of Truth, which is what you are, and it will entail your own capabilities. With every appeal for help you answer, you are bringing yourself closer to your radiant Christ Self. This will enable your brother to see the Christ in you reflecting back to himself like a mirror. And it won't be a scary carnival mirror. So be sure to hear every call for help as the reality it truly is.

When you can more and more consistently use the Holy Spirit's interpretations of the reactions of others, you will gain an increased awareness of His Thought equally focused on you. Have you been able to recognize your own fears, but are not able to escape from them? You are going to need to recognize them in order to start tossing them aside, and leaving it up to the Holy Spirit to translate your fear into truth. Answering a brother's call for help can be the start of the Holy Spirit's translation. It will lead you to Truth.

Fear is a symptom of our own deep sense of loss, and if we can perceive this in others, and learn to offer compassion and love in response, the basic cause of fear is removed. Thereby, we teach ourselves that fear does not exist within us, and we demonstrate this by giving love.

Remember, fear and love are the only emotions we have to choose between. Which one do you choose to live your life by?

Part XI

You'll Find It Once You Know It

Chapter 45

A Tinderbox Ready to Explode

The volumes upon volumes of noise throughout the prison house can be painfully unbearable, only adding to the stress that exists daily, and can bring any individual to his breaking point. On this particular day I had had enough. I felt exhausted, stressed, and plain sick of prison life. Trying to regroup or gather one's self can be a tough task to accomplish when surrounded by a crowd of insane gestures, with lunatic talk, boisterous bellowing, and loud, evil-sounding laughter echoing off the concrete block walls. There's no place you can go to escape it. You either are able to block it out or you snap. The latter choice can be hazardous for your safety.

A black man, Frank, was standing at the three-way intersection with three of his dudes, boisterously "kicking it" at the foot rail of my top bunk. I was trying to rest, with blinders over my eyes to obscure rays from the bright overhead mercury lights. I was wearing my headphones, playing a smooth jazz station on the radio. I could not hear the music on a normal volume setting, due to the roar in the air. One of Frank's dudes decided to get some exercise by performing a few pull-ups on the foot rail of my rack. The house (bunk) was shaking, and my mercury was climbing. These dudes simply would not let up. I gave them a minute or so longer in hopes they would move on, but no such luck. I asked them firmly, but as politely as possible for prison, if they would mind moving on, away from my house. They chose not to hear me. My bunkie was not home, and I was alone.

I took long overdue action by jumping down off my top rack, directly between Frank and his four or five dudes, and put my face within inches of Frank's face. I was ready to blow, a tinderbox ready to explode. They were certainly aware of the steam venting out of me. I was so hot I did not care one bit about the possible consequences. I was completely aware this could mean injury, plus about sixty days in the hole. Frank and his dudes knew things were looking ugly, and since there was a group of them, it would be me looking ugly when this was over. But I really did not care, I was at my limit. Okay, my ego's limit.

Just before I was about to utter some spontaneous prison profanity into Frank's ears, and expecting the worst, Frank spouted out to me some of his own choice prison verbiage; then he, along with his dudes, turned and walked away. Nothing further happened. I found myself with a pounding heart and a huge lump in my throat, and gave a thankful sigh of relief, coupled with disbelief, that I was not lying on the floor, waiting for medics to arrive.

Later that day, still carrying around inside me a bit of steam, or stress, or an unknown ill feeling that prison gives to anyone of us behind bars, I did the right-minded thing and went to the yard for a brisk walk. I needed to calm down. The yard was unusually quiet. Only a few inmates were out, due to some on-and-off rain, so I was enjoying the space and the hint of privacy, which is extremely rare. I almost had the entire huge yard to myself—an unheard-of luxury. The more I walked, the calmer I became. I thought to myself, *This is as good as it gets in prison*, and continued to feel myself coming alive as the blood pumped its way through my heart. This was a feeling I had always enjoyed in my jogging days before prison, so I kept the pace moving along.

As I circled the yard, which was about one quarter of a mile, I approached a set of concrete benches, where I saw Frank sitting alone. Of all the 2,500 inmates in this prison, it certainly was Frank, and I immediately thought to myself that he must be looking for me. I was sure there was going to be trouble, and I instantly tried to prepare myself for defense.

But as I drew closer, I noticed he was sitting with his head down on his lap with arms crossed over his knees. Something told me to just keep my pace, and as I passed him I realized that he was crying, actually sobbing. I kept to my pace and stuck to my own business, which is the prison technique for avoiding trouble. My initial thoughts that poured quickly into my mind were that this had something to do with our episode earlier. But with this type of sobbing, I soon dismissed any like thoughts. Clearly whatever was wrong was something serious.

My next lap around the yard, Frank had raised his head, revealing his teary, swollen eyes and the red, flustered look on his face—and he was staring directly at me. He seemed lost and confused, as if he needed help. I saw no anger, only despair. This time, that "something" in me told me to stop and say a few words. But what would I say?

I calmly said to him something like this: "Hey man, when I got in your face earlier I was filled with stress and anxiety from all this prison crap." He responded in an emotionally drained way. "Hey dude, it ain't no-thing at all to worry about. Okay, okay," he muttered.

Frank harshly added that he had more to worry about now than just this prison thing. He went on to tell me that just about a half hour before, the prison chaplain had informed him that yesterday his sixty-two-year-old mother had been killed in a car accident. It turns out she was taking care of his two teenage daughters while he was serving his ten years in prison. He had already served three years and the remaining seven years were mandatory, with no chance of early release.

It seems the mother of his two daughters was nowhere to be found and had been missing for six years. The family had presumed her deceased. There were no other family members to take in his daughters, who were at the moment staying with members of their church. Frank's own father was also deceased.

Frank accepted my concerned gesture of simply listening for about five minutes, as he gave me a nod of his head. I mumbled lightly to him, "I'm very sorry," and I began to walk off. But when I stopped to look back at him, only a few feet away, he added, "Hey dude, back at your bunk today, when you got mad at me and my dudes, ah, ah, you passed the test." He nodded again, and then said, "You're okay, dude. I mean it, you're a good dude."

I simply nodded back to him and said, "Good luck to you. I wish you the best," and I proceeded with my laps around the yard. There was really nothing else for me to say, nor was I supposed to. But I did understand why he and his dudes felt they needed to test me. I'm not a threat to them any longer. If you have ever been in prison, then you would understand.

Chapter 46

When We Least Expect It

There is a lesson in the *Course* that teaches us, "In every child of God His blessing lies, and in your blessing of the children of God is His blessing."

When we can feel a sense of learning something new about our real self, we are also learning something new about our brothers and sisters. Need I say that prison is certainly teaching me much about my own true self, and the reality of all that exists—which can only be you and me, at-one with each other. We can learn that our minds truly are the one mind of Christ; this lesson in and of itself has been a miracle for me.

The deeper I become involved as a student of *A Course in Miracles,* the more I want to write about what I have learned. I am continuously seeing myself in others. Here in prison I can see the reflection in the eyes of not only other prisoners, but also the guards and other staff members. I am able to see their grandeur—the same as mine—as well as their fears, the same illusory fear that puts its hold on me. These reflections are merely glimpses, but time has a way of lengthening these glimpses into moments, and from moments who knows how far we can go? It's never-ending.

The *Course* tells us that this perception is holy. When this happens we have become whole, however briefly it might be. Yes, that's right; if you can see a part of yourself in another individual, you have experienced the Sonship. These brief moments add up, so to speak, which radiates the Atonement within us to everyone the Holy Spirit sends our blessings to. These brief moments of wholeness, even if for a second or two, bring us a sense of relief from fear. These brief moments are when we tap into our true unseparated, non-dreaming self, held in the arms of God, in Heaven. This is why the relief from fear is briefly felt. The relief part is our realization that we are safe at Home while we dream. The brief part is due to the ego trying to make fantasy out of it, thus ending its reality. When will we learn that fear never wins at anything, and that there is nothing that can feel as good as Truth?

When I gave Frank my acknowledgment of his despair by allowing him to mention his loss, we experienced a connection, though ever so briefly. There was no goal or probability for Frank and me to build a friendship, but we did share a brief sense of oneness—a sameness of understanding that what he was going through was also deeply felt by me. This momentary understanding went beyond the varying degrees of our struggles as prisoners, to encompass our struggles as beings of God.

Since that day we have not formed a special friendship, nor do we hang out together as dudes. We don't have to; it's not in the cards to do so. It's not a part of our true free will. But we have connected as part of the whole, and this is unity.

When I pass Frank in the yard on any given day, or run into him anywhere around the prison, there seems to be an understanding along with a mutual respect that holds. It's not bondage; it is freedom. The understanding came from a perception that has shifted over to the right-mind. This perception is not to be confused with knowledge. But knowledge is, as well, involved here, and it is knowledge that holds the right-minded perception.

Everyone plays their part in wholeness being whole. We don't even realize when it's happening. Take the way Frank and I both not only see each other in a different way now, but also how we view others because of this experience. Once again, here we have "cause and effect." It does not take physical friendships to play their part in Oneness, or the Atonement. In fact, these type of "buddy" relationships are often of the ego. Our part in the

Atonement takes place when we least expect it, and however slight it might be, it is always the effect of the Holy Spirit.

The Holy Spirit is always there, and we learn what He enables us to do as we go along, bit by bit. This is how we move up toward understanding how He works. If I had approached Frank in the yard that day, not seeing my own reflection in his pain, it would have been an ego-based exchange for ego-based gain, and would most likely have led to turmoil. There was no magic spell in our brief connection—only what miracles are created from.

Jesus tells us in the *Course* that, "He in His part of the Christ Mind which we are joined with, is the manifestation of the Holy Spirit, and we will see Him when we invite Him." What does this mean that "We will see him?"

Try to see this picture without thinking too hard; instead, try more to get a sense of it: I recognized my own pain in Frank as I acknowledged his loss, however briefly it may have been. I saw how he was feeling: the anxiety, the despair, the confusion, and the hopelessness, to say the least, that prison lends us, amplified by the loss of his mother and the homeless situation with his daughters.

I was able to see in Frank what I felt in myself, and accept the brief moment of peace we each felt and shared. We were able to achieve this within each other once we realized the unspoken understanding between us. The peace that was felt and shared was also hope. This hope was the face of Christ. The organizing of events and situations were part of the undoing process by the Holy Spirit. What did the Holy Spirit undo, you might be asking? That answer is simple. The Holy Spirit got rid of bundles of ego, making room for hope.

But it doesn't stop there. The *Course* adds, "He will send you His witness if you will but look upon them." Who is His witness in this case? It was that ever-so-slight moment of peace Frank and I shared, otherwise called the "vision of Christ." And it will extend to include the furthering of peace that will result from our experience.

Chapter 47

Seek and You Will Find

I am extremely grateful to my friend of many years, Ron, who makes his way from Florida to visit me regularly here in prison. As I mentioned earlier on, he says that he recognizes the good these visits do for him, as well as for me. I see that these visits, which Ron goes out of his way to make, give him a chance to vent his own frustrations about an uncertain world. We discuss subjects and feelings from our open hearts that as friends we probably would not ordinarily discuss if I were on the outside and not in prison. We have touched a depth that would not have been discovered on the golf course or in a coffee shop on Saturday mornings. He senses the solitude of imprisonment himself when he walks into the prison visiting room. He says, "It's in the air."

Recently at a visit he wanted to openly talk about an important matter that was causing him much anxiety. I was grateful he wanted to confide in me. He was about to ask his lovely friend Karen to marry him, and he was certain it was the thing to do. However, a bit of indecisiveness had haunted him about the timing of the event. He was going back and forth in his mind, wondering if it was too soon for the two of them to take this serious step. Ron also sensed a fear of commitment, and he dwelled on the words, "You know what they say; if there is any doubt at all, don't do it."

I continued that statement as I replied to Ron, "Who are *they*?" I went on to add, "So what you are telling me is to seek but do not find?" He looked at me strangely, unaware that I had pulled that line from *A Course in Miracles*. He had no idea where I was coming from, and I enjoyed it for the moment. At that time I had not yet opened up to him about my involvement in the *Course*.

I wanted to keep it to myself, at least for a while longer, though for how long I did not yet know. *A Course in Miracles* is an extremely personal matter and is not intended to be flaunted. There is a certain "esoteric" quality to its content and within its students. Those who are ready are led to it by the Holy Spirit in a manner that was intended to be. However, I did add to Ron that the world does a good job at helping us to decide when it is the right time to give and to accept love.

I asked Ron to look around out there and see how the world is simply starving for love, and engaged in the endless search to find it—but are afraid of it once they do find it. I went on to share my ideas about the ego, and the wrong kind of perceptions it plants in our minds, without mentioning my involvement in the *Course*. This was not because I wished to withhold the teachings from Ron, but because I was not ready to explain the depth of the *Course* within *me*. I was the one who needed more time, not Ron, or anyone else for that matter. I will be led to the individuals that I can discuss this with when the time is right. This is not my decision alone. The readiness in all individuals to see their true light is in their foundation. This is something that is at different levels in each of us. Your readiness may not be the same as mine. The Holy Spirit deals with everyone based on their own readiness level.

Jesus talked about foundations built from rock or sand, the stability of one versus the shifting nature of the other. But once again, the ego took off with its own interpretation and instituted the fear factor when referring to this adage. As Ron and I talked that day in the visiting room, we both looked closely at the way that the world dictates what is actually rock or sand. What is a solid foundation of love and faith really built on? The dictates of the world, based on the ego's interpretations, have created a breeding ground for hypocrisy. Thus too many people marry for ego-based reasons concerning money, security, flattery, and other illusory rewards that only lead to later heartbreak.

The ego never comes right out and admits to you, or to anyone else, that it is terrified of love. What is it afraid of? It's aware that it can never know love, because love is real and true, and the ego is a phony. The ego cannot win and it knows this, which is why it wants us to see it as our own identity. Therefore, it guides us to go on a journey that in the end is always self-defeating. In Ron's case, there was nothing for him to be afraid of once he ruled out the world's warnings. Ron and Karen are both, in their own way, like Mother Teresa suggested we should be: "givers" and "receivers" of love, who can hear a plea for help. I see this light in Ron as he helps me to remain positive while I endure this prison term. This is not rocket science, but it is the real world, or as Ron would say, "the real deal."

The ego itself cannot love; therefore, it stresses itself out by trying to find a replacement. It is obsessed with the body and the physical realm, where it must constantly battle for material and psychological gain. It's always trying to find something it's severely afraid of, and this makes its searching an effort of constant fear. Fear is its oxygen.

The ego's search continues only while your body exists, as it is part of your mind that is controlled by your body. You made it up. The instant your body dies, the ego will vanish, and it does indeed know this. Because of its source, which is fear, the ego is not wholly split off from your mind in one huge chunk, but rather it has fragmented itself into several splintered beliefs in separation. Just like a fingerprint, no two fragments are alike. Each fragment is constantly fighting the other fragments for control, producing additional fear within you. Does this seem like sanity to you?

With this constant production line of fear being fragmented into more fears, your real mind has the power to deny the ego's existence. Simply shine your *spiritual flashlight* directly onto the fears as they surface, and this will surely give you the strength to *just say no*. There is nothing wrong with being firm, and being firm with yourself, as well as others, with an indication that *no* is your response. There is no anger or hostility involved. Therefore, when you firmly say *no* to what is not of the truth, or right for the real you, this is in no way to be considered as an attack thought. The Holy Spirit, who is also the real you, is behind you when you use a firm *no*. In fact, when a firm *no* is necessary and you use it appropriately, doesn't it make you feel better? Of course, it does. So don't allow the ego to slip in the back door on you and tell you otherwise. Keep your spiritual flashlight ready, and don't be afraid to use it. You will know when the time needs light.

When you have firmly given your response, the ego will see that you are not willing to take the journey it directs you on, but it still will not give up its fight for control. The real you will have the upper hand, however, because you could care less. You may still feel a fraction of fear in the background, but this is nothing but the ego's worry about what to do next.

Can you see now that you do not have to set out on a journey to search for what will ultimately defeat you? Love cannot be searched for, because it simply *is* what you are. But the ego wishes to have your loving help in its search for a love it does not want. It wishes to search for love, but knows it cannot survive in love's presence. So in reality, it is searching for nothing, because nothing is what the ego is.

The ego will tell you that love has no answers, and that love is "not all it's wrapped up to be." By following this insane belief system you will always be searching for "special wrappings" and never find what's inside. Love has no special wrappings, and it is not intended as a surprise. If you seek for a disguise, that is exactly what you'll find.

The Holy Spirit will offer you a better deal, because He is you. It will lead you to joy within an instant. His deal is always to *truly* "seek and you will find." This is not a reward for "working hard enough" or if you "promise to attend church services." But it is a guarantee that under His guidance, regardless of how often you "bow your head," you will not be defeated, and most definitely not self-defeated.

There is no winning or losing with the Holy Spirit because He is in your mind. What He promises you is already what has happened; you simply have not yet projected its image in the dream. It is your free will. Your true free will does not play games with life circumstances. Remember, you are dreaming, and your free will was scripted in timelessness when you were created, regardless of your separated thought system. But your separated thought process cannot play the role. The ego is interfering against your free will and is trying its hardest to be the producer, director, and writer of a different script as it tells you how to act.

The Holy Spirit's journey is one of accomplishment of God's Will, and the goal is for you to achieve what is in your heart. You cannot go wrong. This is why you must *let go*, because He is going to make certain you act out your own part in His Will, which is already written, directed, and produced. This is why you can relax. He will never deceive you with special wrappings, because that would be deceiving everyone else.

By the way, Ron and Karen did get married, and have a great, fun, and loving relationship as husband and wife. I plan to visit them often, hopefully in the not-too-distant future, at their home in Florida, rather than from behind bars.

Chapter 48

Something Always Seems to Be Missing

We seem to always be searching for our life's purpose because we're not at home in this world. We're always sensing that something is missing, so we search continuously to find a place that suits us. If we believe that what we are searching for is outside of us, then the search will be miserable, because we're looking for it where it cannot be found.

The reason we don't know how to look inside is because we don't believe our real Home, Heaven, is in there. We are afraid to see it this way. It is easier for us to believe that one day we will be united with all the physical bodies that ever lived or that we will go to a physical location beyond the sun and stars, with golden gates, and Saint Peter as the gatekeeper. Can we really and truly, seriously believe this? No, we don't, but this is what we were taught out of past confusion, due to a fragmented thought system. It is safer for us to try to believe this. This story is the ego's last-ditch effort to hold onto the body for eternity. But there are those of us who are not afraid to look within, and this is where we come to gain a knowledge of real vision.

The Holy Spirit knows this for us, because He is our real mind. But if you are hoping to view this mind as someplace located "out there," you will get lost *out there*. He cannot, nor is He available to be found *out there*. Even physically, the only method you have for seeing yourself as outside yourself is through reflection, as in a mirror. Even that reflection is judged by the world who taught you to see physically.

The Holy Spirit's mission is to guide you because He is you, and you are Him. This One Mind is the only mind that fulfills the lesson you need to learn, and what you are learning is that your mission is the same as His. So once again, you can relax.

When you help out a friend, as Ron has helped me, you are healing yourself. This is so, because the Mind of the Holy Spirit is also the mind of you and your friend. Are you now starting to feel how all this takes place within your true essence, and not *out there*? When you are able to feel this and not think or analyze it, you will have learned that you are eternal life. This is so, because eternity cannot exist without you and me. If you do begin to analyze this, you need to stop the moment you notice it, and allow your essence and feelings to flow over that thinking. Only the ego will try to analyze this. Any analyzing you do is always of the brain, which is the body. But your mind is your sense of eternity, without need for flesh and bones.

Can you remember where you were when you first noticed a shooting star streak across the sky? Or heard a wood hen echoing in the woods? The awe of that instant was a place within you that was not outside of you. Even as you read my words and searched within yourself for a memory of such an awe, where were you? It was some time in your past when you went there, but as you sense it, somehow you are still there. Even if it is only for an instant, you are there.

Your spirit is of this awe, which is of your mind, and is the essence of who you are that makes you whole. What is your spirit? It is your true free will. The Holy Spirit is the guiding Mind to provide the means necessary to fulfill your free will, in an instant.

Chapter 49

Entering a Holy Instant

Have you ever had an instant when you felt as though you had no cares, no worries, no anxieties, and were perfectly calm and quiet? Or, since your understanding of the ego now, have you ever had an instant, however brief it may have been, when you decided to accept the ego as the illusion it is? These instants are when you are receiving and recognizing a lesson from the Holy Spirit. This is a *holy instant*. But sooner or later the ego sneaks in to grab your attention. The Holy Spirit's goal is to help you be more consistent in these *holy instants* without interruption from the ego. In time, these instants will lengthen. When you are able to learn only from the Holy Spirit, and have been a consistent learner, you will no longer need time in which to learn.

You might be discouraged, thinking that learning to overlook the ego takes time, and the results you might hope for from the Holy Spirit are too far into the future; you may want to give up. This impatient-type thinking is what the ego wants, however. Instead, try to view this in a more right-minded fashion. The Holy Spirit uses time in His own way, based on your needs, your level of readiness, and your ability to shift over to right-minded perception. He uses time as His friend, or as an aid in teaching. Remember, the Holy Spirit will use ego devices and ego-based thoughts when He finds them useful for your benefit. There is no wasting of time; when He uses it, He uses every *nanosecond* in His teaching. Any waste of time you sense is your identification with the ego, which uses time for destruction. The ego will use time to convince you that there is not enough of it and that anything at all you do experience will come to an end.

How many times have we heard it said, "All good things must come to an end?" Songs have been written about this. To the ego, the goal is death, which is its end. It knows that when death arrives, it will no longer have to hide from the truth. The ego eagerly looks forward to your death, but is so afraid of its own. This is why one of its favorite comments is, "I'll take it to my grave," or "Let me die with dignity," and always talks about the "good ole days when things were different."

But the Holy Spirit does not need the past, and His goal has no end in sight. The ego has its strange religion, which believes it can pursue us beyond the grave and that we will either find peace after death or spend immortality in hell. As long as the ego continues tugging away at you, you will continue to fear God.

The ego continues to show you the security of having "this" or "that," but on the flip side will show you the insecurity of giving. It will teach you that it's okay to give as long as there is enough left over to secure your abundance. It religiously makes rules on the proper percentages to give. It loves such rules because they teach you the safety in percentages. It tells you, "For what you give, so shall you receive."

The ego is bleak and despairing in its use of time. It insists that the future must be like the past. It wishes that we learn from the past, but the present is a threat. The ego has its worshipers believe it can offer them escape by looking "out there" to some location for peace and quiet, or for love and forgiveness. The ego teaches us to "Enjoy it now because it won't last." Or to "Get all you can now because you can't take it with you." Or, "If you don't do it now you'll have hell to pay later."

The Holy Spirit teaches this way: There is no hell. Hell is nothing, and so is the ego. The only hell is in not understanding the present because you are afraid of it, and fear is not real. The Holy Spirit leads us steadily to the kingdom, just as the ego drives us to hell, or nothingness. The Holy Spirit, who knows only the present, unless He needs to undo fear, will show us the ego is nothing.

The Holy Spirit gives us glimpses of eternity in a period of physical time called a *holy instant*. Each instant is a clean, untarnished birth, in which the whole Sonship can emerge from the past into the present. The present extends forever. It is as close to eternity as we can comprehend, as long as we have ego interference. The present is as it always is. It is free of guilt, where nothing but true light can be. This would be called "now."

The lesson of using the holy instant takes no time, other than an instant. It has taken much time for the ego to misguide us, but in only an *instant* we can be what we truly are. Try it. Take this very instant right now to experience that it is all there truly is of time. Nothing can reach you while you are inside of this instant. When that instant is gone, you begin another instant, and so on. All the time, you are consistently entering a new instant.

Inside this instant you are completely whole. In an instant you are choosing the Holy Spirit over the ego. Have fun with this. Always keep seeing yourself inside of an instant. Now stop and ask yourself: *How long is an instant?* Never let an instant get by you without the next one taking over. As long as you remain inside a holy instant you are experiencing eternity, where there is no fear.

When you catch yourself angered for any reason, or fearful of something, take an instant and ask the Holy Spirit to release you from whatever it is that is occupying your mind. Then take another instant and say to yourself that "you hear" the Holy Spirit's lesson. Then take another instant to recognize that you are actually inside of a holy instant. When you use your spiritual flashlight, you are operating from a holy instant. Try to always be operating from a holy instant. Will this make you seem like a zombie or seem like you are in a hypnotic state? Only to the ego it would seem that way. These holy instants become more and more automatic as you continue to communicate with the Holy Spirit, who is the natural you. He is the part of you that gives the rest of you true lessons.

Time will certainly change, but holiness will not. You will learn from this *holy instant* that hell does not exist. Let me ask you a quick question. When you experienced that sun setting over the green meadow as a flock of geese flew overhead, did you have any thoughts of hell? The awe you sensed was a holy instant. Within that instant is your kingdom. Your holy instant is your salvation from change. The *Course* teaches us that "change is an illusion, taught by those who cannot see themselves as guiltless." The holy instant is your place of freedom and security where "now" you remember God.

How do you enter a holy instant? If you find yourself needing to get into a holy instant, all this means is that you must have slipped out of one. Just acknowledge to yourself that you are now entering a holy instant. Sooner or later you will get tired of re-acknowledging to yourself to reenter a holy instant, and you will one day realize that you are almost always automatically in a holy instant. It really does become quite simple once you get the hang of it.

Your anger or fear cannot enter you if there is no guilt, and there can only be guilt when you live in the past. So how long is an instant for you? The answer should be, the length of time you are free of guilt. It happens in an instant. When you are in the holy instant, you are sharing it as well with your brother, because you are both of the whole. While inside of a holy instant you are whole.

To try and understand much better how you are sharing this holy instant with your brother, look at this instant as yourself in eternity and eternity as being where we all exist. Dr. Wayne W. Dyer, in his book *Real Magic*, says that your life can be like a phrase in parentheses on an endless sheet of paper. Inside the parentheses is your life in the physical realm. But when you take away the parentheses, you are still a part of the endless sheet of paper. So with this analogy, practice taking the perception of yourself beyond the parentheses, by living inside a holy instant.

Part XII

Being on Your Way

Chapter 50

Naturally Offer a Holy Instant to a Brother

Of the three prisons I've been to, Belmont certainly was the toughest test of a man's will to keep his sanity, let alone safety. We would walk to the chow hall three times a day, which can be compared to a full city block away from the housing unit. Belmont is extremely segregated between blacks and whites, though unofficially and only by the doings of the inmates. This helps keep the gang activity alive.

Walking to chow you will see blacks with blacks and whites walking with whites. There are two sides to the chow hall with separate entrances. One side is usually where blacks sit to eat, while whites sit on the other side. But sometimes, with the overcrowding and time restraints, a guard may direct an inmate to sit on the opposite side of his racial choice. An inmate must take his tray of food and find a seat quickly, with eight minutes to enjoy the lovely slop. Any talking during a meal can mean a trip to the hole for five days or so. In this regard, eating is not a pleasurable event and is seen more as a necessary activity of the day.

One day, when my attitude was already edgy while waiting in line to be handed a tray of food, I was directed by a guard to enter the side of the chow hall where the blacks sat to eat. This was really not a big deal for me, as I had no reason to worry about conflict. As I carried my tray from the food line to the seating area, I came upon two tables for four, each having one available seat. In an instant, without hesitation, I sat at the table on my left. I did not recognize the three black men, all much younger than me, with whom I was seated.

A typical method of eating so that one may comply with the eight-minute rule is to keep your face turned down toward the tray and proceed to shovel it in. While I was minding my own business, the man across from me discretely spoke, saying that he would like to see me outside when finished eating. Without any thought of danger or possible conflict, without hesitation, I looked up from my tray of food and said to him calmly, but with a hint of firmness, "That will be fine." We both left the table at the same time, and as we exited the building with lots of other traffic going to and from the chow hall, I said to him in a quick, straightforward fashion, "You wanted to speak with me?"

He looked straight at me and said that he had not noticed me around and that I carried myself as though I wasn't afraid of anyone or anything. He added that he'd noticed that I seemed to stick to myself and didn't mingle much. Immediately I thought I was being recruited for his gang or for some other kind of problem. Then he asked me a question in a challenging way, as though he were testing me. "What are you about?" I was prepared to tell him he needed to mind his own business, but my poor attitude seemed to have calmed down. I looked straight at him again, and with firm sincerity said, "Look here, this prison thing is a real bitch on all of us, and we all have our own peaceful way of dealing with it. So if you don't mind, my way of dealing with it is simply sticking to myself."

He looked around to make sure nobody was looking, then gave me a quick "thumbs up" with one fist. A "thumbs up" in prison is equivalent to a handshake on the outside. Handshakes are nonexistent in prison. Since then, occasionally we would pass one another in the yard, or somewhere else while on business as usual, and there would be an affirmative nod of a head by either of us as we continued on our way. The "nod" is simply a positive, good-natured acknowledgment.

For me, there was a crystal clarity within me that I had nothing to feel guilty about when he first approached me at the chow hall table. Because I was guiltless I had no fear. Whether he realized it or not, there was a brother-to-brother exchange of releasing each other from fear, and freeing each other from guilt. What guilt, you may ask? The guilt of choosing not to be afraid of the unknown. Do you see what an insane vicious circle the ego creates? At first I did not realize this entire encounter with him was not only a *holy encounter*, but also a *holy instant*. I noticed that the initial confrontation did not shake me a single bit, which built a certain confidence in me when we met outside the chow hall to talk. Even though I had no idea what might transpire, I truly felt no fear. The "no fear" feeling was actually a sensation of relief. But it was not a relief from fear; it was more of a feeling of wholeness, or "Here I am, and I am as I am."

As you offer a holy instant, your brother, with the help of the Holy Spirit, gives it back to you. Time is our friend, if we leave it to the Holy Spirit to use. He needs very little to restore to you the wholeness of what you are. Offer the miracle of the holy instant through the Holy Spirit, *but* leave His giving it to you, up to Him.

Chapter 51

The Holy Instant and Your Relationships

Most of us have had a special relationship some time in our lives, only to be disappointed within time, causing heartbreak, agony, and grief, and possibly courtroom battles over who gets what that put your money into the pockets of lawyers who don't really care. This simply adds to our habit of defense, leading to more attack thoughts, cautioning us for the next time. But we continue the search, thinking that love is waiting "out there" for us to find. We are obsessed with believing that a special relationship is waiting to bring us happiness and peace, while all the while, we remain confused about love.

A special relationship cannot offer us the Heaven we are looking for, however heightened the sex may seem to be. But it can give us companionship that can set us up for false love.

The only true love is that of the changeless love our Creator has for us—the love we *are*. When our companion can understand this together with us, it can lead to a real, true, joyous, loving, and peaceful commitment with each other. But not *to* each other; rather, shared *with* each other, as well as the Oneness of the whole Sonship.

The *Course* asks us, "How can we decide that special aspects of the Sonship can give us more than others?" In other words, how can a single individual give us the love of the whole Sonship, and likewise, how can we give such love back to this individual? We can't—and this is why something, however tiny, always seems to be missing in a so-called love relationship. This incompleteness results in guilt, because it is the ego informing us of lack. But real love does not lack. The Sonship is not lacking. Love is what it is, and can only be whole. It cannot be cut into pieces because this would be separation, which is illusory.

The role-playing of love in the special relationship causes anxiety and doubt, jealousy and fear. This is not love; this is the ego's attachment to the body. Love does not change; it is changeless. Remember, we said earlier that change is the illusion of something better. Isn't this what caused our separated mind? Only by understanding this in an intimate relationship can love be shared—but only shared, and not "given away" to one another. Let me ask you a simple question, and please be honest with yourself. At the height of a love relationship you have had, was it the body of your mate you were in love with?

Most may answer this as the love being something beyond the body, and this is good. But if this is so, why are we so concerned about the body as who we are? And why do we fear death? Try to see the Holy Spirit as the interpreter of the special relationships you make. He uses them as learning experiences that lead to truth. These become the true lessons, if we can listen from our right-mind or see His message.

I once met an extremely attractive woman in an elevator. This meeting eventually turned into a long relationship. If either of us had arrived at the elevator ten seconds sooner or later, the meeting would have been missed. We had many good times, along with some bad times when, over the years of the relationship, neither one of us could end the love-hate struggle. Was it intended that I meet this woman as I did in the elevator at that particular time in both of our lives? Yes, I believe so.

However, it was not necessarily the intention or the direction given by the Holy Spirit for me to continue or for the two of us to make a relationship. The Holy Spirit merely used our ego-based decision making, our wrong-mindedness, to give each of us certain lessons, and to provide lessons for others as well. The Holy Spirit also showed us qualities in each other that brought joy. But with the hold our egos had on us, we could not experience the joy that was there as a whole, let alone love. As long as my ego, along with her ego, needed us to use each other, the Holy Spirit simply used what He could from it.

Let's face it, not feeling whole is a guilty feeling. What I decided to do with the lessons was simply based on my readiness to learn something from the giving and receiving that was involved. There is nothing bad about a relationship coming to an end. It's all in how we view the lesson or if we even see the lesson. In fact, just because the relationship ended doesn't mean that effects from it are not ongoing. There may be some effects that were necessary, in addition to my own learning. It's all in how each party sees his or her purpose.

The Holy Spirit knows no one is special. Yet He also knows that you made the relationship, and He can translate the relationship into holiness by removing as much fear as you will let Him. We all have fear in relationships. You can place any relationship under His care and be sure that it will not result in pain, only if you offer Him your willingness to serve no need but His. Remember, His need is your need minus the ego. All guilt in the relationship comes from your use of it. All the love comes from His use of it. The Holy Spirit is not concerned with the number of years you remain in a relationship, but the ego surely is.

Regardless of the time involved in a relationship, the Holy Spirit will need to use this relationship for the purpose of the whole, which means you. Try to think briefly here, how it is that *you* are *the whole*. When you and your partner understand this, there is no need to be afraid to let go of your imagined needs; ego-based needs will only destroy the relationship anyway. Your only need while you enjoy each other is the Holy Spirit's need of the relationship for His use. In this, all relationships are blessed as one.

If you try to benefit from a relationship at the expense of another, you're going to have guilt. If you condemn a part of a loved one, you are not going to have peace. Each relationship we have must be a total commitment—but the commitment must be to the understanding of the relationship that exists in the Oneness, without guilt. Therefore, there will always be faith. There will be guilt if you think you can make your partner into something he or she is not, just because you want it so. Does this sound familiar? Yet, this is the same thing you do to yourself when you live under the ego's illusory thought system—try to be something you are not.

Chapter 52

The Holy Instant Holds Perfect Love

We have so little faith in ourselves because of the constant fears we face in our lives. We really need to understand the fact that each one of us is perfect love. This is why *you* are the *whole*. But we're always looking for something better that we think we might find "out there," when the best there could ever be is directly within us. It is the understanding of the perfectness in each of us individually that will give us fulfillment in our special relationships. Each of us was created by one Creator, who created us as perfect. We all have our perfect part within the whole, and not without.

If you share a thought of oneness, all separation vanishes in that instant. Life is that instant while you are here on Earth—a holy instant. No matter how long an instant it is, it gains strength by sharing it. When you share love, you are inside a holy instant. But we are taught that "what we gain, he loses." We think that someone must always lose. Why?

If you are living a life of scarcity, then scarcity is what you believe in, and love will have no meaning. You are accepting *gain* or *loss* as a way of life. In the holy instant we must recognize the idea of love in ourselves first, and then we can see love in our brothers and sisters, where gain or loss has no meaning. When we hold onto the idea of love as being within ourselves, only then can we unite this idea of love within us by sharing with the *One Mind That Thought It*. By holding it within as a unified feeling, there is no loss. How do you get this unified feeling? By perceiving the love you feel as the same love in others you see throughout your day. Whether they feel it or not is not important; but what is important is that you quietly perceive it in them. Your grandeur will open your heart to this perception.

This perception of love becomes a holy instant in which you are accepting the laws of God as your own free will. Your free will is not about loss; it is meant to be used for completion of your purpose, as well as for the benefit of your sisters and brothers. The completion can be seen as a blessing for everyone to experience—a gain with no loss.

This makes me think of my love for music, though I never have been a musician myself, other than singing in the shower after a nice round of golf—not profitable, and probably not enjoyable when heard by others. But seriously, I specifically have always loved the piano and dreamed of playing it. Growing up I always had the belief that I could never learn to play the piano because my parents could not afford to purchase one. But I never asked. I gave up on the idea due to the scarcity thoughts that struck me at a young age.

My love for music continued into my adult life, and my favorite musicians are pianists. When I listen to a piano soloist play compositions by Beethoven or Chopin, or when I have attended a concert by my favorite rocker, Billy Joel, I would be in awe over the piano playing. These performances are able to capture me in a realm of pure thoughtlessness. I am filled with peace and joy, with no scarcity thinking during these moments. It's a gift to me.

On the other side of the stage, but within that same loving realm, the pianist himself is in awe as he holds feelings of pure joy while he is "giving" me this gift. His giving, with the sensation of a packed auditorium receiving his offering, as we applaud and plead for encore after encore, is a holy instant where everyone has gained, with no loss whatsoever. This is the "shared One Love" I'm talking about. It is not the music, but rather it's that *essence* beyond the music, that the music itself is able to direct us to. A place where scarcity is nonexistent. That place is your Kingdom of Heaven, and is beyond any thinking the ego could ever muster up. It's a place where the body is incapable of entering.

However, the Holy Spirit has used my ego-based scarcity thinking and my experience of prison to direct me into realizing that I do not need to own a piano in order to learn how to play it. In fact, I am not too old to learn the piano, either—an added scarcity thought as I have aged.

Earlier I talked about the black man I instantaneously sat with in the chow hall that day, who questioned me while we walked back to our separate housing units. It turned out, after several occasions of our nodding to each other, we mutually decided to have a friendly chat and get to learn something of each other.

The nice man's name is Charlie, and he is serving thirteen years in prison for manslaughter. Charlie shot and killed the drug dealer who'd gotten his twelve-year-old daughter strung out on heroin and was abusing her sexually. Charlie is a musician and has played the piano since his childhood, and of course there is no piano in prison. However, there is an electric keyboard that is used for church services, and the chaplain allows Charlie to keep his fingers in shape.

After finding out about my love for the piano, Charlie has explained to me the many avenues I can take when I am released from prison to learn to play piano. In fact, these avenues are how Charlie learned as a child. His parents could not afford a piano, either, but Charlie's desire found a way. Not until he was an adult did he own his own piano.

Needless to say, my meeting with Charlie was a gift, and I truthfully can see myself one day behind the piano, once my "gig" in prison is up. Thanks to my "dude" Charlie, and to our holy encounter, this is a goal in the foreseeable future that offers me peace and joy, and who knows—possibly to others as well.

Can you see the "whole" being played out by this encounter, and beyond? If you can, then you will have no problem yourself offering peace and joy through the holy instant, where the *whole* will come to you.

Chapter 53

A Holy Instant at the Fork in the Road

Since we are enjoined with other minds, *we* are the face of Christ. Try to bring this vision of Christ closer to the surface of your mind. Initially, your body may want to see an image of Jesus, which is okay. Many of us were taught to think of Jesus as Christ, and our thoughts here are not entirely of the ego. In fact, you are heavily weighted with right-mindedness by now. So relax, and simply just notice any ego chatter as background noise. Try to blend the image you now have of yourself into the vision of Christ, along with your elder brother Jesus. Bring this vision from its depths to you through a holy instant. Every time you practice a holy instant your awareness will be brought closer. Try to take time each day for this, and see the wholeness of all that exists. It is really all about you, which is also me, and everyone else you encounter.

Consider at certain times in your day giving a holy instant to an impatient situation you find yourself in, such as waiting in line. For example, the post office always seemed to test my patience, with long lines that never seemed to move and only one attendant working the counter. I always dreaded the thought of having to go to the post office. In a case like this, you are already late in your day, and the person in front of you is loud and obnoxious, and your frustration is mounting; this is a chance for you to enter a holy instant.

Begin by quieting your insides as you feel your body go from rush to calm. You do this by taking a breath in and feeling it go into your lungs, then exhaling slowly. Feel your breath on its intake go through your body's nerve endings. Say to yourself, *I am entering a holy instant.*

Think of all the reasons *why* you were rushed to this point in your day, due to all the concepts the ego-based world has taught you. Then consider all the images you have of yourself. Empty your mind by letting go of all you think to be either true or false. Let go of what you had been thinking about the ridiculous long line, and notice it to be neither good nor bad. It merely is, and anything else was only ego-based thought—a thought you made up, a thought about nothing.

Now simply forget this world, forget the line you are standing in. Feel the wholeness that you are, beyond your body, and your connectedness to the One Thought of God. Feel the stillness as though you can feel the blood pumping through your heart and through your veins. Feel your heart gently beat. Feel your inward self as united with the air you are breathing and the air you are standing in. Repeat to yourself, *I am one with it all*. Now you are at the counter in the post office; just don't forget to pay for your postage.

This type of meditation can be used when you are on the move, and where sitting down or lying on your back is not possible. I will often use this while jogging, walking, or working out. This has especially saved me while waiting on long lines, which is common in prison. Be sure to understand that in all meditation practice, the idea is to let the mind be quiet and still, and be of itself. There is no right or wrong way to achieving this calmness, where you serve as or offer a connection to all that exists. The minutes you give to this sensation of wholeness are multiplied over and over to the awakened awareness of the whole—or, more simply, to those minds on the same page as you are. This awakened awareness of the whole, which includes you, extends into the minds of all humanity, and helps the unawakened to awaken when the time is right for them.

Give these moments to the Holy Spirit and count on Him, who will use time for the purpose of the unawakened, which also includes you. A part of you sleeps, while another part of you knows who and what you are. The Holy Spirit will use His communication powers for every little effort you make in carrying out God's Will, which is your free will.

Remember, the Holy Spirit is of you, and you are of Him. He will also use time to enhance your sisters and brothers. You are the spirit whose mind He uses, where miracles happen. Your holy instants will bring the stillness needed to help you understand that you are the spirit that abides within the Holy Spirit. It is "one" and the same. Through His voice, a call is made to everyone, offering His sight to all who ask and replacing error with simple and natural truth.

The Holy Spirit will take your minutes, or instants, of stillness, and carry them around the world, where pain and confusion appear to be running someone's life. This is evident in the Holy Spirit's manifestation in Mother Teresa, and so many other givers of the real world. Why should this ever exclude you and me? The Holy Spirit will not overlook one open mind that is ready. He will offer healing everywhere He knows it will be accepted. The Holy Spirit's Thoughts will increase in healing power each time someone accepts them and uses them as his own thoughts to heal.

Each minute you turn your right-minded thoughts to the Holy Spirit will be multiplied a thousand-fold more, and will surprise you in strength compared to what you originally gave. Through consistent, effortless practice of this giving, even if you feel yourself being off course, or off your chosen path, you will still be at-one with the whole, which is never-ending. Your feeling of being off course, if this is truly so, is simply the ego making a fuss a bit. Simply use your spiritual flashlight on the fussing face of the ego, and trust that the Holy Spirit will always accept your gifts, increase their power, and give them back to you.

Let's take this a bit further and allow me to share a few words with you from the student workbook of *A Course in Miracles*.

You can use this in the form of a prayer, as I do, whenever you feel off track and need a boost.

> A spirit I am, a holy Son of God, free of all limits, safe and healed and whole, free to forgive and free to save the world.

You may notice that you have been on a particular path for some time, and the ego continues to chirp in your head as you stop at what seems to be a fork in the road. It's evident you cannot go ahead any further. You must decide to turn one way or the other. The direction you were traveling has come to an end and now leads to nowhere. The reason you have traveled this far was to prove to yourself that the path you were on does indeed come to an end. It also served no other purpose than to get you where you are now.

Whichever direction you choose to take now is not a wrong decision; however, if you linger at the fork in the road trying to decide which way to go, you will only become more uncertain, and the ego will try to comfort you with safe, secure, and complacent thoughts. You can delay and live this time recalling your travels along the road you just came off, but you cannot travel back to where you started from.

Once you decide to take one of the forks in the road, your first few steps will seem hard, but will be the right decision. Why? Because *you*, not the ego, chose this direction. But because the first few steps were difficult, you may think you can simply turn back and take the other fork. This is not so. The choice you made was decided for you by the Holy Spirit, and it cannot be undone. You way has been decided before you even began your journey.

If you can acknowledge this and see the truth in your steps on this new path, there will be nothing you will not be told. So be sure to listen, look, and trust as you keep moving along the road taken.

There is a legendary poem written by Robert Frost that I always found meaningful. While I was stationed in Denver with the U.S. Air Force back in 1976, I was fortunate to have been in a volunteer group in my spare time, which was headed up by a few Buddhist nuns. Our work was with the elderly, assisting them to attend attractions in the area, such as a circus that comes to my memory. One of the nuns in particular, named Shanna, took a liking to me and was influential regarding many of my unanswered questions about Divinity in general. At that time I would guess Shanna was aged in her mid-fifties, which is where I am now.

She gave me this poem, which she had hand written, and suggested I keep it for my years ahead. I did exactly that. Eventually I lost the piece of paper with her handwritten version, but I never did lose its meaning. One day in the prison library, as I was paging through a poetry book, I came across it once again. Its meaning for me has changed quite a bit, but every time I think of this wonderful poem I see Shanna's smiling, confident face. I do believe she had some insight that I would cling to its several messages as my journey lengthened. I was able to have a photocopy made and keep it taped to the inside of my footlocker, where I see it daily.

Here it is, and I hope you can see its reflection in the road you and I have traveled so far in this book. The poem is called "The Road Not Taken."

Two roads diverged in a yellow wood,
And sorry I could not travel both
And be one traveler, long I stood
And looked down one as far as I could

To where it bent in the undergrowth;
Then took the other, as just as fair,
And having perhaps the better claim,
Because it was grassy and wanted wear;
Though as for that the passing there
Had worn them really about the same,

And both that morning equally lay
In leaves no step had trodden black.
Oh, I kept the first for another day!
Yet knowing how way leads on to way,
I doubted if I should ever come back

I shall be telling this with a sigh
Somewhere ages and ages hence:
Two roads diverged in a wood, and I—
I took the one less traveled by,
And that has made all the difference.

—Robert Frost (1916)

I certainly see myself in this wood, and in his words as well. The poem is in my mind, and it is in my mind where I sense that I am whole, that I'm part of something. My mind is not split when I read these words by Robert Frost. The ego in me does not understand this poem for what it is. It doesn't even want to try. The poem's grandeur is too grand for grandiosity to understand.

I can hear a voice, which I accept with all certainty, and it is certain that I must go "this way." Because I am aware of an idea that is of my Source, I don't try to understand it; just knowing it is enough for me.

All of my losses are restored and my errors are forgiven. The last line of this poem embodies all that is necessary for me to understand my own strength.

A Course in Miracles says it appropriately here. "Every mistake you and your brother make, the other will have gently corrected for you."

Chapter 54

The Holy Instant Will Show You No Sin

You and I have both come a long way since we began our look at the imprisonment of the world. I hope you have begun to see yourself as the Light for who you truly are. While you are listening, looking, and moving along the road taken, you will automatically penetrate deeper within yourself. You must understand that the Holy Spirit will never teach you that you harbor sin. You are bound to nothing, which is what sin is: nothing. Errors we have all certainly made, which the Holy Spirit will undo. This undoing is His task for you and will never make you fearful. You are either of the Holy Spirit or of the ego. It certainly is not the ego, because that would be nothing. Sadly, thanks to much of the world teaching us we are born with sin, we are afraid to look deep within. We are afraid to see the sin we think is there. We even admit this.

The ego feels comfortable when we accept ourselves as sinners. It comes up with ways for making penance so we may be forgiven. But this is simply another way of giving, or sacrificing, in order to receive. The ego is not concerned if we feel ashamed, because then it thinks we need its help. It is proud of our belief in sin, and it surely encourages us to admit we are sinners. The ego feels this is necessary so we may be forgiven. Our desire for sin is really where the fear begins.

But don't get the ego wrong. It makes no argument that it does not want to look within, because if you do, it expects you will see sin. Then you will go on to think that God will demand penance or that you will burn in hell. This is our choice, the ego tells us. This we believe, because, after all, is this not the way it has always been since the Garden of Eden? It's no surprise that with this belief we decide not to look. This really is not what we fear, but the ego tells us it is. Beneath our fear to look deep within because of sin, there is another fear, and this one worries the ego more than anything.

What if you looked within and saw *no* sin? Your ego at this very moment is probably thinking, "What the hell is he talking about, no sin?" Once you see you hold no sin, your separated thought system will not know how to defend itself. Once you have been able to penetrate into your deepest depth, you will be joined with the whole Sonship.

You may be asking yourself, "How do I actually go this deep within?" It's easy. We have discussed repeatedly your *true essence* as who you are. That place that holds and comforts your right-mindedness sits beyond and simply knows without having to analyze. Merely enter a holy instant and just *be* your true essence and nothing else. Going deep within yourself does not require some type of a sedative state. The easiest and only way to do this is to simply be who you truly are, without an ounce of fantasy and regardless of any outside influence. This is where there is no sin. Errors, yes, but no sin. You only dream of sin. Now that you have acknowledged this, you can detach yourself from the belief that your identity lies in fantasy dreamed up by the separated mind, or ego. This is where I have continued to find an abundance of strength, and so will you.

However, you are not yet fully liberated. There is still some incompleteness that has taught you to buy into the world's view of truth. But you are now willing to look on much of your insanity and recognize its ego-based madness. Your faith is moving inward, past insanity and on to reason. You are beginning to notice the world's great emphasis on the body, even of those who are no longer in a body. Now the Holy Spirit's purpose has been accepted by the part of your mind the ego does not like, because it fears it. Therefore, this free part of your mind, which you can now identify with, is not afraid to look even deeper. You now find that within all this depth you are sinless. This is why you can now see the Holy Spirit's purpose as your own. This is wholeness.

From this point on, what you will start learning from the Holy Spirit will not be inconsistent. This is your sane reasoning. You are no longer afraid of the ego's influence on you. There will be a few times when you will be deceived, but your sane reasoning will keep fear away. When you see deception trying to penetrate you, take a holy instant by shining your spiritual flashlight into the ego's deceiving eyes and expose it for the nothing that it is. Without any emotion whatsoever, you now know that the few senseless gifts the ego offers you, you could care less about. You don't need them. You are now beginning to realize your Kingdom of Heaven and will not "sell it out."

Now you have got the ego in you deathly afraid. Now you can look at all your sisters and brothers, awakened or unawakened, and know when you see the ego's weakness in them and in you. You will be able to spot this automatically. Thus, what the ego has tried to keep apart you have met and joined. Your oneness with the Sonship now looks at the ego unafraid. Remember that when you see the ego in your brother, you are able to look beyond it to the wholeness he is not yet aware of or has momentarily lost touch with. Either way, this is forgiveness.

The ego will not stop, and will persist with all its trickery, but simply follow the Holy Spirit happily. There is no need to question what He knows. Your will is in His hands, while the ego remains an illusion.

Therefore, at least for me, in the real world I have awakened to, the dream of sin and guilt is over. The real world is where I accept God's promise as a gift. *His Will*, which is my own free will, shows me not to worry over time, as the ego would have it. The Holy Spirit has no need of time once He has served His purpose, which is our will. He continues with the use of time while He waits for God to take the final step where time will disappear.

This will be one *holy instant* where all perception will dissolve, leaving only truth, which will eternally be all that is needed. This holy instant yet to arrive has been the goal all along. Throughout our journey, our dream of separation, as we faced struggle upon struggle in this ego-based world, we have been forgiven and never understood so. The Holy Spirit's purpose has been to use time in helping us find our true identity, which is the face of Christ, and the Christ vision is our true sight. Or should we say *insight*?

Christ's second coming is as certain as God, but does not involve the appearance of some man or woman. It will be a return of our sanity. The ego will no longer exist. The Second Coming will be the gathering of all minds, including the mind of our elder brother Jesus, who formed the Sonship and called it Christ. This will be full Atonement and the invitation by God for the split-mind to be completely healed. It will be overtaken by the Sonship. The completed Atonement is the "shield" and the "sword" worn by the Son, which has witnessed all minds being as one. The separated mind will be gone. All that will remain is the whole Christ. This is when we will see the face of Christ in ourselves, and in everyone we encounter. Oneness will be finally recognized, and good is all there will be.

The Second Coming will end the lessons the Holy Spirit teaches, making way for the Last Judgment. This is where learning will end. The lessons and guidance of the Holy Spirit will no longer be needed, as we all will extend inward to God. Everyone whose body ever died, or is yet to come, or who is present at this final tick of time, or the end of the dream, will be equally released from the errors he or she made out of ego-based thought.

For the Second Coming to arrive, it needs our voice and our willingness to help each other recognize God's Will, so we can join together. We will once and for all realize that what is false is false, and what is true has never changed. We will finally see that there has always been plenty of food to feed the hungry, for example, and plenty of housing to shelter the homeless, without making judgments of their capabilities. There will be no winning or losing. These truths, and eternity, are what the Last Judgment will show us; there will be no punishment as the ego has taught us. Rather, we will smile and give a sigh of relief that truth is finally accepted. It will put an end to all this nonsense, and judgments made from perceptions.

We only need to welcome the Last Judgment without fear of condemnation by God. God does not condemn; only egos do. We will see the world as totally forgiven for all its errors, and we will see that sin never existed. Now without cause and without a function, bodies will be useless. We will wake up.

Since the dream of separation began millions of years ago, or an instant ago, the physical universe has been expanding, but now will start to contract. There will be one final contraction that ends the dream. A final heartbeat, and a final breath of air. This is when, within an instant, the physical universe will simply fade away. All material figures will become nothing, just as they always have been. The dream of separation will be no more, as our minds will be at Home with God, just as they have safely been all along.

So for the time being, let's not place fear in God, only love. It is okay to look deep within, and help to heal all the sorrow and pain the ego has made. Looking within will help you to be free and fearless and to become a giver as well as a receiver. It is the Holy Spirit in the mind of both the giver and the receiver where the gift abides. It cannot be lost or taken away. Don't waste it. You have been given His lessons, and they continue, guaranteed by God, who we are of.

The Holy Spirit asks your help, since He is of you. Whenever your thoughts are lured to illusion that still attracts you, enter into a holy instant. It is as simple as just being your true self. From there, let Him release you from illusory thinking. He needs only your willingness to know that your own free will is also God's

Will. That's it! Your willingness does not need to be perfect, because His is perfect.

It is His task to make your willingness, perfect willingness. The Holy Spirit's perfect faith in your true free will becomes your faith in Him. Out of the recognition of your own willingness, His perfect willingness will be given to you.

Once you have this understanding, what concern, then, can the *Voice for God* possibly have about how you use His gifts? He was given to you by your Creator. A holy instant is all it will take, wherein God, the Son, and the Holy Spirit are known by you as One Mind. Therefore, *you* as this Oneness are the Master of Everything.

AFTERWORD

When our body dies, many like to say that the spirit goes somewhere. But isn't "somewhere" a place, though unspecified, which indicates a location? We can contemplate the meaning of spirit till the end of time, always to be led back to spirit as "thought." A thought certainly is of the mind and is no place, but is "everywhere" rather than "somewhere."

A Course in Miracles teaches that the mind "represents the activating agent of spirit," supplying its creativeness. When the term Mind is capitalized, in its most vast sense it means God. Spirit is the Thought of God, which he created like Himself. The unified spirit is God's one child, or Christ. You've learned through this book that because the human mind has split, it can process thought either right- or wrong-mindedly, depending on the voice it listens to: the Holy Spirit of God, or the dreaming ego? It's your choice.

The goal of this book has always been to strike a chord within you and open your right side of the split-mind, to bring it forward in your expressions of life, so you can begin to see what others continue to deny. I want to encourage you to go yet deeper into right-mindedness, where you'll experience the bridge guiding you to the true knowledge of yourself, which is the Universe. I say "Universe" because you are all that exists.

It wasn't till my fifth year of serious, daily involvement in *A Course in Miracles* that I struck a chord within myself. Suddenly, it seemed—although really it was a gradual process, now that I look back—I realized I was actually making decisions and thinking *as* the Holy Spirit in my right-mind. Oh sure, I still hear the ego, but in the background, trying to rush me and fill me with anxiety. But even making its best efforts now, the ego can only "weak-knee" itself forward, and it quickly gets ushered by Truth to a back-row seat in my mind, where it settles down.

The vast percentage of my mind is no longer concerned with outcome. The process itself, in anything I pursue, is what creates the joy in me, which I'm able to extend. I feel completion in this.

One day, while I was writing an outline for my second book of this series, called *Mastering Your Own Spiritual Freedom*, I looked up from my writing tablet and said, "That's it!" All those past years of my life, my separated dreaming mind had been signaling my brain what to see, hear, think, do, and experience, while my real, unseparated, non-dreaming, fully awakened mind continued to shine its light. It was sending messages, if you will.

I did "know" this all along, of course. But now it hit me in a new way, acknowledging that my brain is the programmed hardware that runs and regulates my body. The projected images replay from my innermost thoughts and become my life. For me, this insight was a revelation. Now I can accept the magnitude of my mind.

My fear of death is minimal, and even that is only due to my ego's occasional background chatter, which I recognize as unreal. I know that all decisions that spring from illusions, or wrong-mindedness, are consciously made and then acted upon in the false universe, or the physical world. But the light of the real, unseparated mind shines through to tell me that everything is fine; relax and trust.

I agree whole-mindedly with Marianne Williamson in her book *A Return to Love*, that the *Course* may sound "absolutist or unyielding," but one of its "saving graces" is that it claims to be only one version of a true "universal curriculum." The Course generally endorses the world's other spiritual and psychological paths for their innate wisdom. But what does this really do? It teaches us that where communication exists, so do peace, love, and forgiveness.

In my next book, *Mastering Your Own Spiritual Freedom*, you'll come to form your own understanding as to why Jesus really entered the dream of separation. As we've been projecting it, "He was born" into this world to teach us the true condition of love. This is a good, right-minded projection, teaching us that communication remains unbroken or "unseparated," even if the body is destroyed, provided that you don't see the body as the most necessary means of communication. By grasping this lesson you will realize that to sacrifice the body, or anything material, is really to sacrifice nothing. With this understood you'll have a vision that communication is of the mind, which cannot be sacrificed. It's impossible. *Mastering Your Own Spiritual Freedom* will open you up to real freedom by your own interpretation, not based on rules derived from fear.

In Book 3 of this series, you'll learn that the only way we can give of our mind is to extend it, and this will mean true joining. This is why I've titled the third book *And Then I Knew My True Abundance*. Sacrifice is proven unreal—just another wrong-minded attempt to keep you devoted to the false idea of fear. Instead, *And Then I Knew My True Abundance* invites you to experience the abundance that is the signature of your true free will—the life you deserve.

The Holy Spirit has whispered Truth into your dreaming mind about your next move. I'll end here by asking you to consider one more question: With all this understood, where now will your life take you while on this planet? I hope you'll join me in subsequent books in *The Master of Everything* series. I offer you all I can be, and I have tremendous real faith in the real you.

God bless.

Your brother in Light,
James Nussbaumer

Bibliography

A Course in Miracles. Temecula, CA: Foundation for Inner Peace, 1975.

Campbell, Joseph. The Hero with a Thousand Faces. Princeton, NJ: Princeton University Press, 1968.

Chodran, Pema. Start Where You Are. Boston: Shambhala Publishing Co., 1994.

Coleson, Charles. Born Again. Grand Rapids, MI: Baker Publishing, 1976.

Dyer, Wayne W. Real Magic. New York: HarperCollins, 1992.

Gawain, Shakti. Living in the Light. Novato, CA: New World Library, 1986.

Gawain, Shakti. Creative Visualization. New York: Bantam, 1982.

Hall, Manly P. Lectures on Ancient Philosophy. Los Angeles: Philosophical Research Society, 1942.

Hoeller, Joseph. The Gnostic of Jung and the Seven Sermons to the Dead. Wheaton, IL: Theosophical Publishing Co., 1982.

James, William. The Will to Believe. New York: Dover Publishing, 1956.

Jung, Carl. Memories, Dreams and Reflections. New York: Random House, 1989.

Peck, M. Scott. The Road Less Traveled. New York: Simon and Schuster, 1980.

Perls, Fritz. Ego, Hunger and Aggression. New York: Vintage Books, 1969.

Tolle, Eckhart. A New Earth. New York: Penguin Plume Books, 2005.

Tolle, Eckhart. The Power of Now. Novato, CA: New World Library, 2001.

Viscott, David, M.D. The Language of Feelings. New York: Pocket Books, 1976.

Williamson, Marianne. A Return to Love. New York: Harper Collins, 1994.

Young, Arthur. The Reflexive Universe. Mill Valley, CA: Robert Briggs and Assoc., 1984.

About the Author

James Nussbaumer, a former financial advisor of twenty-five years following service for his country with the U.S. Air Force, was indicted in 2007 and received a comparatively exorbitant sentence of ten years in prison for a foolish securities violation to offset losses he incurred for clients—the entire amount of which has been repaid. The severe sentence was overtly political, meant to "set an example" during a period of panic and abuses in the investment industry. Some months after he found himself in prison at age fifty, a remorseful and shattered man, he was moved to a section housing "old" prisoners: anyone over thirty-five. There, he was stunned when the locker he was assigned contained a worn, yellowed, and dusty book no one would claim—a book he'd been searching for to no avail: *A Course in Miracles.*

Along with frank descriptions of prison life, Nussbaumer shares what he spent every single day studying and writing about: the nature of the prison in which virtually all of us dwell, a world of illusion where fear drives us to make wrong turns and to live in despair. He admits nearly eight years in prison was surely hell, yet also unexpectedly fruitful, resulting in his return to his first love, writing. While surrounded by the chaotic, volatile, and often violent din of the cell block, he writes about redirecting the mental power of our mistakes—before we act them out—into positive results. This book is the first of an ever-developing series. Written from deep within the rabbit hole of the prison system, his voice is so direct and real enough that readers won't realize the pages are turning while on their way through his remarkable and personal story.

Though a free man now, thanks to a forgiving judge, he continues to operate on equal parts of determination, faith, and hope, while guiding his readers to a supreme knowledge of their own. He lives in Massillon, Ohio, and has three lovely adult daughters and four grandchildren. His public speaking is gearing globally with lectures that are instructive, challenging, humorous, and elevating. Nussbaumer's inspirational messages take us on an inner journey to becoming **The Master of Everything.**

Other Books By Ozark Mountain Publishing, Inc.

Dolores Cannon
A Soul Remembers Hiroshima
Between Death and Life
Conversations with Nostradamus,
    Volume I, II, III
The Convoluted Universe -Book One,
    Two, Three, Four
The Custodians
Five Lives Remembered
Jesus and the Essenes
Keepers of the Garden
Legacy from the Stars
The Legend of Starcrash
The Search for Hidden Sacred Knowledge
They Walked with Jesus
The Three Waves of Volunteers and the
    New Earth
Aron Abrahamsen
Holiday in Heaven
Out of the Archives – Earth Changes
Justine Alessi & M. E. McMillan
Rebirth of the Oracle
Kathryn/Patrick Andries
Naked In Public
Kathryn Andries
The Big Desire
Dream Doctor
Soul Choices: Six Paths to Find Your Life
    Purpose
Soul Choices: Six Paths to Fulfilling
    Relationships
Tom Arbino
You Were Destined to be Together
Rev. Keith Bender
The Despiritualized Church
O.T. Bonnett, M.D./Greg Satre
Reincarnation: The View from Eternity
What I Learned After Medical School
Why Healing Happens
Julia Cannon
Soul Speak – The Language of Your Body
Ronald Chapman
Seeing True
Albert Cheung
The Emperor's Stargate
Jack Churchward
Lifting the Veil on the Lost Continent of Mu
The Stone Tablets of Mu
Sherri Cortland
Guide Group Fridays
Raising Our Vibrations for the New Age
Spiritual Tool Box
Windows of Opportunity

Cinnamon Crow
Chakra Zodiac Healing Oracle
Teen Oracle
Michael Dennis
Morning Coffee with God
God's Many Mansions
Claire Doyle Beland
Luck Doesn't Happen by Chance
Jodi Felice
The Enchanted Garden
Max Flindt/Otto Binder
Mankind: Children of the Stars
Arun & Sunanda Gandhi
The Forgotten Woman
Maiya & Geoff Gray-Cobb
Angels -The Guardians of Your Destiny
Seeds of the Soul
Julia Hanson
Awakening To Your Creation
Donald L. Hicks
The Divinity Factor
Anita Holmes
Twidders
Antoinette Lee Howard
Journey Through Fear
Vara Humphreys
The Science of Knowledge
Victoria Hunt
Kiss the Wind
James H. Kent
Past Life Memories As A Confederate
    Soldier
Mandeep Khera
Why?
Dorothy Leon
Is Jehovah An E.T
Mary Letorney
Discover The Universe Within You
Sture Lönnerstrand
I Have Lived Before
Irene Lucas
Thirty Miracles in Thirty Days
Susan Mack & Natalia Krawetz
My Teachers Wear Fur Coats
Patrick McNamara
Beauty and the Priest
Maureen McGill & Nola Davis
Live From the Other Side
Henry Michaelson
And Jesus Said – A Conversation
Dennis Milner
Kosmos

For more information about any of the above titles, soon to be released titles,
or other items in our catalog, write or visit our website:
PO Box 754, Huntsville, AR 72740
www.ozarkmt.com

Other Books By Ozark Mountain Publishing, Inc.

Guy Needler
Avoiding Karma
Beyond the Source – Book 1, Book 2
The History of God
Sherry O'Brian
Peaks and Valleys
Riet Okken
The Liberating Power of Emotions
John Panella
The Gnostic Papers
Victor Parachin
Sit a Bit
Nikki Pattillo
A Spiritual Evolution
Children of the Stars
Rev. Grant H. Pealer
A Funny Thing Happened on the
    Way to Heaven
Worlds Beyond Death
Karen Peebles
The Other Side of Suicide
Victoria Pendragon
Sleep Magic
Walter Pullen
Evolution of the Spirit
Christine Ramos, RN
A Journey Into Being
Debra Rayburn
Let's Get Natural With Herbs
Charmian Redwood
Coming Home to Lemuria
David Rivinus
Always Dreaming
Briceida Ryan
The Ultimate Dictionary of Dream
    Language

M. Don Schorn
Elder Gods of Antiquity
Legacy of the Elder Gods
Gardens of the Elder Gods
Reincarnation...Stepping Stones of Life
Garnet Schulhauser
Dancing Forever with Spirit
Dancing on a Stamp
Annie Stillwater Gray
Education of a Guardian Angel
Blair Styra
Don't Change the Channel
Natalie Sudman
Application of Impossible Things
Dee Wallace/Jarrad Hewett
The Big E
Dee Wallace
Conscious Creation
James Wawro
Ask Your Inner Voice
Janie Wells
Payment for Passage
Dennis Wheatley/ Maria Wheatley
The Essential Dowsing Guide
Jacquelyn Wiersma
The Zodiac Recipe
Sherry Wilde
The Forgotten Promise
Stuart Wilson & Joanna Prentis
Atlantis and the New Consciousness
Beyond Limitations
The Essenes -Children of the Light
The Magdalene Version
Power of the Magdalene
Robert Winterhalter
The Healing Christ

For more information about any of the above titles, soon to be released titles,
or other items in our catalog, write or visit our website:
PO Box 754, Huntsville, AR 72740
www.ozarkmt.com